National Pastime

The American Ways Series

General Editor: John David Smith
Charles H. Stone Distinguished Professor of American History,
University of North Carolina at Charlotte

This series provides concise, accessible treatments of central topics in the American experience. Titles first appear in hardcover and eBook editions for a general audience and subsequently appear in reasonably priced paper editions for classroom use.

Current Titles in the Series

How America Eats: A Social History of U.S. Food and Culture, by Jennifer Jensen Wallach

Popular Justice: A History of Lynching in America, by Manfred Berg

Bounds of their Habitation: Race and Religion in American History, by Paul Harvey

This Green and Growing Land: Environmental Activism in American History, by Kevin C. Armitage

NATIONAL PASTIME

U.S. History Through Baseball

Martin C. Babicz and Thomas W. Zeiler

ROWMAN & LITTLEFIELD
Lanham • Boulder • New York • London

Published by Rowman & Littlefield
A wholly owned subsidary of The Rowman & Littlefield Publishing Group, Inc.
4501 Forbes Boulevard, Suite 200, Lanham, Maryland 20706
www.rowman.com

Unit A, Whitacre Mews, 26-34 Stannary Street, London SE11 4AB

British Library Cataloguing in Publication Information Available

Library of Congress Cataloging-in-Publication Data Is Available

ISBN 978-1-4422-3584-7 (cloth : alk. paper)
ISBN 978-1-4422-3585-4 (electronic)

♾™ The paper used in this publication meets the minimum requirements of
American National Standard for Information Sciences—Permanence of Paper for
Printed Library Materials, ANSI/NISO Z39.48-1992.

Printed in the United States of America

To the memory of my grandfather, the original Martin C. Babicz, who used to make the annual pilgrimage to Cooperstown with me; and to my grandchildren—Hazel, Julian, Alex, Brenda, and Osmara—may they come to love history and baseball as much as their grandfather does.

And to Jules Tygiel, a friend, colleague, and inspirational historian of baseball.

Contents

Acknowledgments

BASEBALL IS A TEAM SPORT, and so is writing a book. *National Pastime: United States History though Baseball* would not have been possible without the assistance of many people who aided in all stages of the research and writing of this book.

We would like to thank Jon Sisk and John David Smith of Rowman & Littlefield, who have shown an enormous amount of faith in this project. We would also like to thank Katelyn Powers of Rowman & Littlefield, who has assisted with the illustrations for this volume.

Dr. Steve Dike-Wilhelm, a historian at the University of Colorado Boulder, read the entire manuscript and offered numerous suggestions to improve it. Other people who read portions of the book and suggested improvements include Dr. Karen Lloyd D'Onofrio, who at the time was a doctoral candidate at the University of Colorado, and Scott Wilson, a history teacher at Omaha Central High School.

Librarians at the University of Colorado Boulder have been of great assistance in searching for and locating resources, especially Brittany Reed, who literally retrieved dozens of volumes necessary for this book's completion, and Michael Harris, who helped with identifying the publishers of baseball songs.

People with firsthand knowledge of various aspects of the game's history were generous in sharing their expertise. A special thank you goes out to Major League Baseball senior vice president Katy Feeney, who provided information about women in baseball, and former professional softball player Mary Lou Pennington, who answered questions about the International Women's Professional Softball Association.

Kelli Bogan and John Horne at the National Baseball Hall of Fame and Museum Library in Cooperstown have been a great help in providing photographs for use as illustrations. Jacob Pomrenke at the Society for American Baseball Research in Tucson has also helped with locating illustrations.

The hundreds of students who have enrolled in our course, America through Baseball, as well as smaller seminars on sports and society, deserve a callout. Many were and are fans who also questioned our analogies, analyses, and, sometimes during our ranting fits, our sanity! All are to be thanked for challenging us to be better teachers as we linked baseball to history.

Finally, we would like to thank our families for their patience and understanding over the past three years. Marty Babicz is especially grateful to his wife, LouAnn; his daughters, Brittany and BreeAnna; his son and daughter-in-law, Benjamin and Lupita; his grandchildren, Hazel, Julian, Alex, Brenda, and Osmara; his mother, Aneita; and his mother-in-law, Mary Lou, for the love and support they provided him while he worked on this project. He would also like to thank his late father, Ronald, who, in the 1960s, introduced him to a band of lovable losers called the New York Mets. Tom Zeiler thanks Rocio, Jackson, and Ella for their long, patient support, and his father, Mike—a Red Sox and Ted Williams fan with the misfortune of growing up in Yankees territory—who instilled a love of the game. This book would not have happened without them.

Foreword

THE POET WALT WHITMAN triumphantly noted baseball's connection to the American democratic experiment. In his collection *Leaves of Grass* in 1855, and a few years later in an editorial to the *New York Times*, he followed the outcome of some games played in Brooklyn. But as the game matured and professionalized (he sniffed at play for pay) over the next three decades, Whitman came to believe that baseball was more than just a sport. Near the end of his life, as he witnessed the two American teams return from a world tour in 1889 led by sports equipment tycoon and baseball owner Albert G. Spalding, Whitman yearned to hear about the players' adventures as young Americans representing their dynamic country. For him, baseball had become "the game of the republic!" It was, simply, "our game: that's the chief fact in connection with it: America's game . . . [was] just as important in the sum total of our historic life." Toning down the hyperbole, we agree with his linkage of baseball and history.

National Pastime shows how baseball is interlinked with the history of the United States, and, to an extent, vice versa. While it would be presumptuous to claim that the sport shaped America, it certainly serves as a window through which we can examine and clarify American history. And at key moments, it actually defined historical and contemporary discourse. For instance, well before the US military was desegregated or Martin Luther King Jr. was a household name, baseball pioneered integration with Jackie Robinson's debut in Brooklyn on April 15, 1947. This is the most famous case in which baseball influenced the course of history, but it should also be acknowledged that the sport led the way in drawing the color line in the first place, a decade before the Supreme Court's *Plessy v. Ferguson* ruling allowed legal segregation in 1896. Our book seeks to trace the history of baseball, but more than that, the history of America *through* baseball. Thus, it aims to point out trends, issues, and change in American society (and, by the concluding chapters, other parts of the world as well).

Other historians have written books about the history of baseball, but few have tied American history and baseball history together in a comprehensive fashion, covering the broad chronological sweep of three

centuries in a relatively short space, and done so with no apologies for
drawing connections many mainstream historians might consider trivial.
We follow in the giant steps of great writers and scholars on baseball—
Jules Tygiel, Charles Alexander, David Voigt, George Vecsey, John
Rossi, and even Albert Spalding—who proved that baseball reveals the
history of the United States. *National Pastime* is indebted to them, but
their audience was different than ours. While we welcome the public as
readers, we target students in the hopes that they will absorb American
history in a new and engaging way. We are academic historians but also
fans of the game, so we have an eye on teaching through the medium of
sports.

And why not? Considering that sports, like food and music, are among
the few universal means of provoking deep, gut-level emotions in people,
a book about the intimate ties of baseball to history seems necessary. After
all, as readers will note in the following pages, baseball paralleled many
of the developments and issues facing society at large (professionalization,
labor/management relations, reform, war, westward expansion, technology, globalization, race, gender, etc.). But it also generated a rising tide of
fortunes—first for owners and then for players, cities, and the media—as
well as persistent excitement that prompts fans today to spend billions of
dollars watching, analyzing, and playing the game. Spectators are pro-
voked into fits of joy and awe, or sadness, disgust, and anger, if their team
wins or loses. That is the immediate draw, but the sheer athleticism of the
sport is not our focus. The profound, long-term effect, we believe, is how
performances on the field shape or reflect on the history off of it.

The book proceeds chronologically through the history of baseball and
America. It is accompanied by charts, tables, and an appendis that chron-
icle important moments in the history of the game. We hope the book's
chapters stand alone as useful tools in investigating individual eras, but
we also project that the entire book can serve as a companion to standard
historical texts and narratives of the United States. And above all, we
seek for students to understand the ability of baseball to reflect history,
whether it is good or bad. Walt Whitman would have approved of that
mission, as he steadfastly believed that because baseball was "our game,
the American game," its legacy needed to be included in the story of the
nation.

1

Baseball in Tocqueville's America (To 1870)

IN 1831 A FRENCH BUREAUCRAT named Alexis de Tocqueville arrived in the United States and became so intrigued with American society that he wrote about it in a two-volume book called Democracy in America. *Tocqueville was impressed with the absence of great wealth and great poverty in the United States. This was very different from the European world Tocqueville knew, where a small group of individuals held a great deal of wealth while a large majority of the population suffered in abject poverty. Tocqueville was sensing America's concept of equality. Not only did the Declaration of Independence state that "[a]ll men are created equal," but, Tocqueville realized, Americans believed that statement to be true, at least for white men. Because the young nation lacked a super-wealthy class to act as community patrons, Tocqueville recognized that average Americans had to form organizations to accomplish common goals. Key among the differences between America and Europe in the 1830s was the availability of land in the former, which allowed almost any white man to become a landowner and have a farm. When Tocqueville came to the United States, two-thirds of Americans lived on farms, while only 10 percent lived in cities or towns with more than twenty-five hundred people. But America was already changing. By the second and third decades of the nineteenth century, strings of factories sprang up along fast-running New England streams. First employing young women and later hiring male immigrants, these factories transformed America in less than a lifetime. Factory owners had to pay their workers in cash. The introduction of money into the American economy, known as the Market Revolution, transformed the US economy from one based on personal favors to one based on monetary exchanges. With the development of an internal market,*

a national economy replaced the dozens of local economies that had character-
ized the United States before the Market Revolution. And the nature of work
changed, as the growing class of factory workers lacked the autonomy of farm-
ers or shop owners and found themselves no longer in control of their time or
of how they did their jobs. It was in the midst of this disappearing preindus-
trial environment that the game of baseball emerged and developed.

Although he is not well-known, few people contributed as much to the
sport of baseball as Alexander Cartwright. He was born in New York
City in 1820, just as America was beginning a significant economic and
social transformation from a primarily rural to a manufacturing and
commercial nation. As a boy, Cartwright loved to play the various ball
games popular among children in New York in the 1820s and 1830s.
When he was sixteen, he took his first job as a clerk for a Wall Street
broker, a position that illustrated the growing importance of business
in early nineteenth-century American society. Thrown out of work by
a fire that destroyed the bank building where he worked—and perhaps
influenced by the entrepreneurial spirit that seemed to be spreading
across the country—Cartwright started a stationery and book store with
his brother, Alfred, in the mid-1840s.

In addition to running a business, Cartwright, like many other young
men in New York at the time, became active in a local volunteer fire company, but he never abandoned the game he played as a child. To relieve
the periods of boredom between stressful bouts of firefighting, Cartwright encouraged fellow members of the Knickerbocker Fire Engine
Company to pass the time playing baseball. In 1842 he organized his col-
leagues into the Knickerbocker Base Ball Club of New York. Soon other
"Base Ball clubs," which had sprung up in Manhattan and Brooklyn in
the 1840s and 1850s (and perhaps even earlier), began to model themselves after Cartwright's team. Cartwright did not stay in New York
long enough to see the impact of his game, however. Enticed by the Gold
Rush, he left for California in 1849, and later settled in Hawaii, where he
made a living shipping food to the miners. Cartwright died in Hawaii in
1892, the year before the United States annexed the island group into its
empire. By the time he died, the United States had become the world's
leading industrial nation, and baseball had become its leading sport.

Alexander Cartwright, the founder of the Knickerbocker Base Ball Club, standardized the rules of "base ball" in 1845. National Baseball Hall of Fame and Museum. Cooperstown, N.Y.

Baseball is a product of the rural society that existed in America before the Market Revolution. Although baseball as we know it emerged in early nineteenth-century America, bat-and-ball games had been around for centuries. Ball sports originated as religious rites in ancient Egypt. Early Christians adopted ball games as ritualistic symbols of Easter and the Resurrection. In England, games with bats and balls were played at least two centuries before Abner Doubleday supposedly invented baseball. The same was true in America: William Bradford, the governor of Plymouth Colony, complained that on Christmas Day 1621, non-Puritans at Plymouth played stoolball, a game that used stools for bases.

Baseball descended from a British game called rounders, which was played by an unspecified number of players divided into equal teams. Also a forerunner of cricket, rounders featured four stones or posts, called goals, arranged in a diamond pattern. A player called a feeder or pecker tossed the ball toward a striker, who tried to hit it with a stick. If the striker hit the ball, he ran to as many goals as he could. The striker was out if he missed three swings, if he hit the ball behind him, if the ball was caught on the fly by a member of the other team, or if he was struck by a thrown ball as he circled the diamond. The other team came to bat after every player on the offensive team had been put out.

The rules for rounders were first published in an 1829 book by William Clarke called *The Boy's Own Book*. Five years later, the same rules

were published in *The Book of Sport* by Robert Carver. Instead of calling the game rounders, however, Carver called it "base or goal ball." In
1835 his book was republished under the title *The Boy's and Girl's Book of
Sport*. This time the book called the game "base ball." Although the rules
of the game are unknown before 1829, the term "base-ball" appeared at
least eighty-five years earlier in a book written by John Newbury called *A
Pretty Little Pocket Book*. Newbury's book, which first appeared in London in 1744 and was republished in America several times between 1762
and 1787, contained an engraving of children playing "base-ball" along
with a poetic description of the game.

Americans continued to use some variation of the term "base ball" after
they declared their independence from Britain. In 1778 the journal of an
American soldier at Valley Forge reported that he had played a game
of "base." A diary written by a student at Princeton in 1786 described a
game of "baste ball" played on campus. In 1791 the town of Pittsfield,
Massachusetts, adopted an ordinance banning "any Game called Wicket,
Cricket, Baseball, Batball, Football, Cat, Fives, or any Game or Games
with Balls within the Distance of Eight Yards from said Meeting House."
In 1823 a New York newspaper called the *National Advocate* printed a
story referring to Saturday "base ball" games being played on the corner
of Broadway and 8th Street in lower Manhattan.

In the early nineteenth century, several different games were played
in North America that could be characterized as "base ball." In New
York, descendants of Dutch settlers continued to play stoolball. In New
England, pairs of children often played barn ball, in which the defensive player first threw a ball against a wall, then the offensive player
attempted to hit the ball on the rebound; if he made contact with the
ball, he would run to the wall and back. The game of old cat could be
modified to fit almost any number of players: from one-old-cat, which
had two bases and one striker, to four-old-cat, which had four bases and
four strikers. Keeping the number of bases at four but employing a single
striker, or batter, produced the direct ancestor of baseball. Children in
New England also played a game known as town ball or the Massachusetts game, which utilized four bases and one batter. In the Massachusetts game, the batter stood midway between home and first base. Farther south, a nearly identical game called the New York game developed;
the only major difference between the two is that the New York game
placed the batter near home.

Americans' habit of forming organizations impressed Tocqueville, and that habit was certainly true in baseball. In the 1870s, New York political boss Thurlow Weed boasted in his autobiography that in 1825 the city of Rochester had a "base-ball club, numbering nearly fifty members" that "met every afternoon during the ball-playing season." Alexander Cartwright's Knickerbocker Base Ball Club, formed in 1842, was primarily a social club dedicated to playing baseball. In many ways, the Knickerbockers were similar to a modern country club: Membership, capped at forty, was limited to the social elite, including professional men, merchants, and white-collar workers. Club members gathered on Mondays and Thursdays, when they divided into teams and played baseball.

The rules of early baseball captured the values of preindustrial America. Early America had an abundance of land; baseball requires an expansive playing field. Before the Market Revolution, the sun, not the clock, marked the workday of farmers and craftsmen; baseball, alone among major American sports, is not governed by a clock. In Tocqueville's time Americans took equality seriously; in baseball every player comes to bat and every player has an opportunity to score a run. In 1845 Cartwright codified the rules, which included the banning of the town ball practice of "soaking" or "plugging" a base runner by hitting him with a thrown ball to put him out. At first, the Knickerbockers played their games in a field on the corner of 27th Street and 4th Avenue in lower Manhattan, but as the Market Revolution transformed New York City, that playing site became unavailable. Across the Hudson River in Hoboken, New Jersey, Cartwright found a playing site used by other clubs called Elysian Fields, which was easily accessible to lower Manhattan by the Barclay Street ferry.

The Knickerbockers were not the only baseball club to form in Manhattan. Other baseball clubs organized in the 1840s and 1850s, usually around a single profession. Members of New York's Mutual Fire Company, a rival of the Knickerbocker Fire Engine Company, organized the Mutual club. Members of New York's police force formed the Manhattan club, while bartenders established the Phantom club. New York's teachers created the Metropolitan Base Ball Club, a name that was revived by New York's current National League entry. Because the growing city quickly gobbled up the few available expansive fields found on Manhattan, New York clubs often resorted to playing their games across the Hudson River in New Jersey or on fields in Long Island, including Brooklyn, which until 1898 was a separate city.

The first *recorded* baseball game between the Knickerbocker club and another club took place on June 19, 1846. The Knickerbockers' opponent that day was an organization called the New York Base Ball Club, often called the New York Nine by modern historians. On that supposedly historic afternoon, New York defeated the Knickerbockers 23–1 in four innings. Some historians have erroneously referred to this event as the first baseball game, but it was not. The Knickerbockers had been playing baseball for more than three years; the New York club might have been playing even longer. The game played in Hoboken on June 19, 1846, was not even the first recorded baseball game. Eight months earlier, on October 23, 1845, the *New York Morning News* ran a newspaper account of a baseball game played the previous day between the New York Base Ball Club and the Brooklyn Base Ball Club. The New Yorkers, showing the same prowess they would display against the Knickerbockers eight months later, won the game by a score of 24–4.

Although the Knickerbockers dominated baseball in the 1840s and 1850s, they were by no means the only powerful baseball club in the New York area at the time. Other significant clubs based in Manhattan included the Mutual club, the Gotham club, the Eagle club, and the Empire club, while across the East River the Excelsior club, the Putnam club, the Eckford club, and the Atlantic club outshined the competition in Brooklyn. In 1858 Henry Chadwick, the pioneer sportswriter of the *New York Clipper* who invented the baseball box score, helped organize a three-game all-star series pitting the best players on clubs based in New York against the best players on clubs based in Brooklyn. The series was played on Long Island at the Fashion Race Course in Corona, which was then a village in Nassau County but today is a neighborhood in Queens near Citi Field. Railroads scheduled special trains, served by ferries from Manhattan, to carry fans to the racetrack. To cover the cost of renting the facility, attendees paid fifty cents admission to watch the games. The Fashion Race Course series proved to be a remarkable success, with up to ten thousand or more people attending the three-game series. The series also proved that fans were willing to pay to see quality baseball. The Fashion Race Course series could be considered baseball's first "subway series," except for the fact that it predated the construction of New York's subway system by forty-six years.

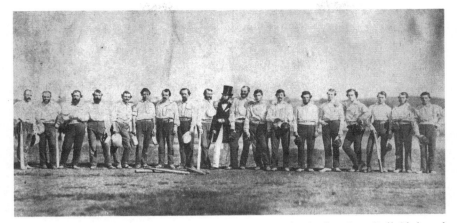

Two important clubs from the amateur era, the Knickerbocker Base Ball Club and the Excelsior Base Ball Club, pose together in 1859. National Baseball Hall of Fame and Museum. Cooperstown, N.Y.

Eighteen months earlier, in January 1857, the popularity of baseball in the New York metropolitan area necessitated a convention of New York–area clubs. More than a dozen teams sent delegates, who officially adopted the Knickerbocker rules for games played between them. In March 1858 the Knickerbocker, Gotham, Eagle, and Empire clubs called another convention. Confirming Tocqueville's observation that America was a nation of joiners, the delegates at the March convention established the National Association of Base Ball Players, baseball's first organized league. Other New York–area clubs responded to the call to join the association, and by 1859 almost fifty teams from New York and Brooklyn were members. The delegates also agreed that at the end of each season, the association would award a whip pennant to the newly crowned baseball champion.

Although baseball first developed and took hold in the New York area, it quickly spread beyond the metropolis. In the early 1850s, clubs were formed in New Jersey and upstate New York, and by the middle of the decade the game was being played as far west as Cleveland, Detroit, and Chicago. In the late 1850s and 1860s, former members of the Knickerbocker and Eagle clubs, who brought the game with them as they pursued their fortunes in the goldfields, formed clubs in California. Government clerks established the Potomac Base Ball Club of Washington, DC, in 1859. A year later an existing organization, the Olympic Town Ball

Club of Philadelphia, abandoned the game it had been playing in favor of the Knickerbocker rules. In 1857, in what was perhaps the most ominous development for Boston-area fans until the Curse of the Bambino, the Tri-Mountain club forsook the Massachusetts game for the New York game. In time, the other Boston-area clubs would follow the Knicker-bocker rules. By 1867, four hundred clubs, including teams as far away as California and Louisiana, were members of the National Association of Base Ball Players.

As baseball grew in popularity, pressure began to mount on high-pro-file clubs to win. The association required that all players on its mem-ber clubs be amateurs, but by the 1860s the more important clubs began to secretly enlist ringers on their teams. Opposing clubs originally lured players from other clubs with promises of jobs, gifts, or clandestine pay-ment. Baseball's first star, and perhaps its first professional, was Jim Creighton, the greatest pitcher of his time and the first pitcher to develop a fastball. In an era when pitchers were required to throw underhand, Creighton added speed to his delivery by flicking his wrist when he released the ball. Creighton pitched baseball's first recorded shutout in 1860. He was also the greatest hitter of his time; he did not strike out at all in 1861. In 1862 Creighton reached base safely every time he came to bat. He jumped from the Star club of Brooklyn to the Excelsiors in 1860 when that team secretly offered to pay him. Sadly, Creighton was also the game's first fatality. According to legend, he hit a home run in a game against the Union club of Morrisania in October 1861, but the power of his swing either aggravated a previous injury or ruptured an internal organ. He collapsed after crossing home plate and died four days later.

Although still officially banned by the association, the practice of clubs paying their star players soon became an open secret. In 1866 the Athletic club of Philadelphia was accused of paying three of its players. The critics were wrong. The Athletics were actually paying four players, the fourth being Al Reach, whom the A's had lured from the Eckford club by secretly agreeing to pay him. To pay these stars, the more popular clubs began requiring fans to pay a fee to attend. In 1864 the prominent clubs in New York and Brooklyn were charging admission, with the winning club keeping the gate money. By 1868 the top seven or eight clubs in the association pulled in a total of $100,000.

As winning baseball clubs brought fame to their host cities of the East, civic boosters in Cincinnati wanted to attract the same glory for their city. In 1867 they established the Cincinnati Base Ball Club, better known as the Red Stockings after the color of their leggings, and entered the team in the association. Civic morale took a beating, however, when the visiting National club of Washington, on a ten-game tour of the Midwest, pounded the Red Stockings by a score of 53–10. The loss to the Nationals was a blow to Cincinnati's pride. Determined not to repeat the embarrassment, in 1868 the Red Stockings followed the lead of the top teams in the East and covertly paid four players. Chief among the ringers was Harry Wright, an English-born cricket player who had already proven his proficiency at baseball in stints with the Knickerbockers, the Gothams, and the two previous seasons in Cincinnati. Wright was secretly paid $1,200 to play center field and manage the team.

The undefeated 1869 Cincinnati Red Stockings, baseball's first openly all-professional team. Standing (left to right): Cal McVey (RF), Charlie Gould (1B), Harry Wright (CF/MGR), George Wright (SS), Fred Waterman (3B). Seated (left to right): Andy Leonard (LF), Doug Allison (C), Asa Brainard (P), Charlie Sweasy (2B). National Baseball Hall of Fame and Museum. Cooperstown, N.Y.

The 1868 Cincinnati season was so successful that when the association lifted its ban on professional players in 1869, the Red Stockings decided to put together a team composed exclusively of professionals. Led by Harry Wright and his younger brother George at shortstop, the 1869 Cincinnati Red Stockings fielded a team of ten professionals (nine starters and a backup) who were each paid between $600 and $1,200 for the season. Boasting some of the best players of the era, the Red Stockings toured the nation and, for a fee, took on all comers. Traveling from city to city, the Red Stockings operated like a circus or a vaudeville show—or, to use a more modern analogy, the Harlem Globetrotters basketball team—as spectators filled the stands to see whether a seemingly invincible team would lose. They never did. Against association foes, the Red Stockings finished the season with fifty-seven wins and one tie. The club also played more than seventy games against nonassociation teams, winning every one of them.

The unbeaten streak continued into the following season, as the Red Stockings won the first twenty-four games on the schedule. Finally, in June Cincinnati fell to the Atlantic club in Brooklyn by a score of 8–7 in an extra-inning affair that lasted eleven innings. Although the team would only lose five more games that year, the loss to the Atlantics marked the death knell of the club. No longer undefeated, their luster was gone. Facing mounting debt, the promoters of the club dissolved the Red Stockings following the 1870 season. The Red Stockings may not have achieved the financial success the team's promoters wanted, but on the field, the club's accomplishments were unparalleled. The Red Stocking's influence was immediate. By 1871 every major baseball team in the country had adopted Cincinnati's all-professional model.

Baseball during the amateur era reflected the America that Tocqueville witnessed in the 1830s. Baseball's need for an expansive playing field characterized the vast amount of land available in the United States in the early nineteenth century, and the game's lack of a clock captured the rhythm of work in preindustrial America. Baseball, however, also embodied something else Tocqueville noticed about America in the 1830s: equality. Preindustrial America prided itself on being a democratic society in which people triumphed on their own merits. The same was true in baseball. Every player got a chance to bat, and therefore every player had an opportunity to score. Baseball, like Tocqueville's America, also celebrated the individual: The batter stood alone as he faced a pitcher and eight other defensive players.

If baseball represented preindustrial America, football, a sport that emerged several decades later, represented industrial America. Football is played on a confined playing space—the gridiron. In contrast to baseball, football is governed by a clock. And, much like workers on an assembly line, football is a game of very specialized playing positions. Football lacks the element of equality found in baseball, as different squads play offense and defense, and not every player can score or even touch the ball.

Well into the twentieth century, however, Americans saw baseball as the sport that best represented their culture. In 1911, sporting goods magnate and former nineteenth-century baseball star Albert G. Spalding wrote a book called *America's National Game*, in which he argued that baseball, like America, is democratic. Pointing out that Americans did not recognize arbitrary class distinctions, Spalding declared that the "son of a President of the United States would as soon play ball with Patsy Flannigan as with Lawrence Lionel Livingstone." It did not matter that Flannigan may have been the son of an immigrant or the Livingstone family may have arrived in America on the *Mayflower*. All that mattered was whether "Patsy could put up the right article."

2

The Industrialization of Leisure (1871 to 1883)

BY THE END OF THE NINETEENTH CENTURY, the America Tocqueville visited, with its lack of great wealth and great poverty and its emphasis on equality, no longer existed. A huge gap separated rich and poor. In 1890 the top 10 percent of the American population owned 73 percent of America's wealth, while 55 percent of all wage earners made less than a living wage, which at the time was $500 a year. America was no longer an agrarian nation; by 1880 a majority of Americans worked in nonagriculture jobs. The United States was quickly becoming the world's leading industrial power. Industrialization brought rapid technological advancement, including the telephone (1876), the phonograph (1877), the incandescent light bulb (1878), and the motion picture camera (1888), as well as the advent of the modern American corporation. With industrialization, however, came economic problems, including two severe depressions, the Panic of 1873 and the Panic of 1893, both of which lasted about four years. Industrialization also brought predatory business practices and bitter labor disputes over dangerous working conditions, bad pay, long hours, and growing inequality. Historians often refer to the period between the Civil War and 1900, when this transformation was at its peak, as the Gilded Age, which suggests that the allure of the United States in the late nineteenth century was a mirage—it looked like a golden age, but it wasn't. It was just gold-plated, with something of lesser value at its core. During the Gilded Age, a tiny elite of monopolists—including Cornelius and William Vanderbilt, Jay Gould, and Jim Fisk in the railroad industry; John D. Rockefeller in the oil industry; Andrew Carnegie in the steel industry; and John Pierpont Morgan in the banking industry—dominated the economy and expanded American economic power, while increasing their own wealth

and exploiting the masses. Critics saw them as robber barons who wielded
power without accountability in an unregulated marketplace. Corporations
sought to maximize their profits by creating monopolies and trusts to reduce or
eliminate competition. These businesses drew on the massive influx of immi-
grants, 14 million of whom arrived in the United States between 1860 and
1900, and rural and small-town Americans who sought factory jobs in cities.
Urban areas became centers of both factories and recreation. Most workers
did not have the time or money to pursue traditional forms of entertainment,
such as the opera or the theater. Instead, they sought out inexpensive diver-
sions, such as imbibing in saloons, the most popular manner of leisure during
the Gilded Age, or hoofing it in a dance hall, a very popular form of amuse-
ment among young couples. Roller-skating rinks and bowling alleys opened in
Gilded Age cities. In 1876 a carousel was installed on Brooklyn's Coney Island;
soon amusement parks and pleasure gardens sprang up all over the country.
Starting in the 1890s, nickelodeons—storefront theaters that exploited the new
moviemaking technology—began appearing in working-class neighborhoods.
In this context, some promoters turned to baseball. The Fashion Race Course
series of 1858 had proved that fans would pay to see quality ball. In the 1860s,
the more prominent clubs charged admission in order to secretly pay their
stars. By the late 1870s and early 1880s, leisure would be industrialized with
the creation of the first professional baseball leagues.

The arrival of professionals in the 1860s transformed the game of baseball. The quality of play improved, games took on greater importance,
and the sport increased in popularity. In the decade after the Civil War,
baseball's first superstar emerged—an infielder from Marshalltown,
Iowa, named Adrian Constantine "Cap" Anson. With six years of professional experience already under his belt, Anson joined the Chicago White
Stockings in 1876. He remained on the White Stockings for twenty-two
years, retiring after the 1897 season. During that stretch, Anson became
the first major leaguer to collect three thousand hits. He led the National
League in batting twice, including in 1881 when he hit .399. In all, Anson
hit over .300 twenty-four times.

In 1879 Anson took over the managerial reins of the White Stockings, earning the nickname "Cap," short for Captain. He guided Chicago to five National League pennants. The White Stockings dominated
baseball in the 1880s, partly because of Anson's skill as a player but also

Adrian "Cap" Anson, baseball's first superstar. National Baseball Hall of Fame and Museum. Cooperstown, N.Y.

because of his brilliance as a skipper. As a manager, he transformed base-ball from a gentlemanly game to one of intense competition, inventing new strategies to give his club the edge. The innovations introduced by Anson include the pitching rotation, the hit-and-run, the hook slide, and hitting the ball to the opposite field. Anson was the first to employ a third base coach to signal to batters and base runners. In 1885 he initiated spring training, taking his ball club south before the start of the season. Sadly, Anson was also a racist who helped institute baseball's color bar-rier. In many ways, the intensely competitive Cap Anson and his innova-tions symbolized America during the forty years between the start of the Civil War and the beginning of the twentieth century.

With the success of the Cincinnati Red Stockings in 1869, openly pro-fessional baseball clubs emerged. Following the completion of the 1870 season, Cincinnati's board of directors announced that it could no lon-ger afford the "enormous" salaries the Red Stockings were paid. The announcement may have been a bluff to encourage players to accept lower salaries, but many players took the announcement at face value and jumped to other teams that would pay them more. Player-manager Harry Wright, along with his brother George and two other stars, Charlie Gould and Cal McVey, joined a newly formed club in Boston. As the four were already famous for playing for Cincinnati, the new Boston club began calling itself the Boston Red Stockings. With the loss of its top players, the directors of the Cincinnati Red Stockings dissolved the club, and baseball's first openly professional team went out of business.

The triumph of the Cincinnati Red Stockings on the field, if not at the ticket office, inspired other clubs to adopt professional rosters. In May 1871, ten professional clubs met in New York and formed baseball's first professional league, the National Association of Professional Base Ball Players, or the National Association. The National Association established the first rules for professional baseball. Teams could join the association for a ten-dollar fee, and each club was expected to play five games against each of the other member clubs. The National Association did not set the schedule; each team was left to arrange its own games. At the end of the season, the association would award a championship of the United States pennant to the club with the most victories. Ten teams joined the National Association in its inaugural season: the Boston Red Stockings; the Chicago White Stockings; the Forest City club of Cleveland; the Kekionga club of Fort Wayne, Indiana; the Mutual club of New York; the Athletics of Philadelphia; the Forest City club of Rockford, Illinois; the Union club of Troy, New York; and the Nationals and the Olympics, both of Washington, DC. When the Kekionga club withdrew due to financial difficulties, the Eckford club of Brooklyn, which in May declined to commit ten dollars to such a risky endeavor, paid the membership fee and replaced the team from Fort Wayne. With a record of twenty-two wins and seven losses, the Philadelphia Athletics won the National Association's first pennant.

The clubs in the National Association were not the only baseball teams in the early 1870s, but they were among the clubs with the best players. Despite attracting many of the stars, however, the association was not without its problems. Membership in the association was fluid, as the ten-dollar fee meant that almost any club could afford to join. In the ensuing years, new members would join the association willy-nilly; for instance, three different clubs represented Philadelphia in 1875. Many teams that joined the association dropped out before completing a single season. Other clubs joined midseason.

Failure to keep commitments was another problem that plagued the National Association. Because of the high cost of travel, some clubs canceled road trips, especially if they were hopelessly out of the pennant race. This left the host club without an opponent, which cost the home team revenue. League discipline was weak. Not only was the National Association virtually powerless to force clubs to complete their schedules, but it also could not prevent players from jumping from one club to another when they received a better offer. The atmosphere at National Association games did little to encourage attendance. Gamblers in the stands openly bet on games, sometimes taking wagers from players in uniform, leading to a suspicion among fans that games were fixed. Clubs sold beer and whiskey at games, and drunkenness and rowdiness were prevalent. The National Association's greatest weakness, however, was the lack of balanced competition. The Philadelphia Athletics won the association's first pennant, but the Boston Red Stockings won the next four championships. In 1875 the Red Stockings dominated the league, winning seventy-one games and losing only eight, for an incredible .899 winning percentage.

Despite its problems, the association showed promise. In May 1875, a crowd of ten thousand "cranks," as baseball fans in the nineteenth century were called, turned up at the Hartford Ball Club Grounds to watch the practically invincible Boston Red Stockings take on the yet to be defeated local club. Among the attendees of the game was novelist Samuel Langhorne Clemens, better known as Mark Twain, who, after a young boy at the "great baseball match" walked off with his imported English umbrella, famously took out a classified ad in the *Hartford Courant* promising a $5 reward for the return of the umbrella and $200 for the remains of the boy.

Given its many difficulties, however, the National Association offered less than ideal circumstances for promoters attempting to make a profit from baseball. Among those disillusioned with the association was William Hulbert, the president of the Chicago White Stockings. Hulbert wanted a more orderly, professional league, but he also wanted his White Stockings to dominate. In 1875, while the baseball season was underway, Hulbert approached four players on the Boston Red Stockings about playing for the White Stockings. Even though he sought their services for the 1876 season, Hulbert's effort was legally dubious because the players were already under contract for the current season. Enticed by Hulbert's offer, the "Big Four" of the Red Stockings—catcher James "Deacon" White, first baseman Cal McVey, second baseman Ross Barnes, and pitcher Albert G. Spalding—agreed to come to Chicago for the next season. At Spalding's suggestion, Hulbert also signed Adrian Anson of the Philadelphia Athletics to a future White Stockings contract. At the time, Spalding, whom Hulbert appointed the player-manager of the White Stockings in 1876, was one of the best players in the game, but he retired just two years later. While Spalding was at the tail end of his career when he joined the White Stockings, Anson's illustrious career was just beginning. In 1879 the White Stockings chose Anson to replace Spalding at the helm of the team, and in 1888 he would become a co-owner of the team.

Anger rose around the association when Hulbert's plan leaked out. Hulbert knew the association could respond by expelling the White Stockings, but he also recognized an opportunity to form a more orderly league. By having the best players in baseball under contract for 1876, Hulbert was holding all the cards. During the winter between the 1875 and 1876 seasons, Hulbert and Spalding sat down to write a constitution and by-laws for a new league. They named it the National League of Professional Base Ball Clubs, or the National League, a circuit that is still in operation today. Hulbert sought to establish an organization in which baseball clubs could earn a profit. In this regard, the National League was a league of "Base Ball Clubs," not "Base Ball Players."

In order to earn a profit, baseball clubs needed to compete in a stable association. Therefore, Hulbert and Spalding set the membership fee at $100, ten times the fee of the National Association. Members of the National League would have territorial control over their local markets, as no more than one team would be admitted from any city. Membership was limited to clubs in cities with a minimum population of seventy-five thousand, but this requirement could be waived with the unanimous approval of the league's other teams. As baseball clubs often supplemented their schedules by staging exhibition games against independent teams, the National League protected its members from outside competition by barring its clubs from playing games against nonleague teams within a five-mile radius of another National League club's home city.

The National League constitution and by-laws included a number of rules to make the environment at ball games more fan friendly. No games were permitted on Sundays. Beer and alcohol were not served at

National League ballparks, and gambling was not allowed. And to keep out the riffraff, admission would be fifty cents, rather than the twenty-five cents that was customary at most ball games at the time. Hulbert and Spalding created a league that could enforce strict discipline, as the National League had the power to expel players, or even clubs, that violated its rules. By 1879 the league would increase its authority over players to bind them to their clubs even after their contracts expired.

In February 1876, Hulbert invited representatives from seven other prominent National Association clubs to a meeting in New York, at which he unveiled his plan for a new league. Recognizing the advantages of the new organization, all seven clubs agreed to unite with the White Stockings in launching the new venture. In its first season, each National League team would play every other team ten times, five at home and five on the road. The National League would award a championship pennant to the team with the most wins at the end of the season. Hulbert did not become the league's first president. Instead the honor went to Morgan G. Bulkeley, the president of the Hartford club and of the Aetna Insurance Company. Hulbert may have secretly arranged for Bulkeley's selection, as the future governor and US senator lent an air of respectability to the new organization. Bulkeley served only one year as league president; Hulbert took over the reins after the 1876 season ended.

The eight charter members of the National League were the Boston Red Stockings, the Chicago White Stockings, the Cincinnati Reds, the Hartford Dark Blues, the Louisville Grays, the Mutual club of New York, the Athletic club of Philadelphia, and the St. Louis Brown Stockings. Chicago, with its five new stars, won the National League pennant in 1876, but the Red Stockings, even without three of the "Big Four" (after one year in Chicago, Deacon White returned to Boston), captured

Table 2.1.   The National League in 1876

Boston Red Stockings
Chicago White Stockings
Cincinnati Reds
Hartford Dark Blues
Louisville Grays
New York Mutuals
Philadelphia Athletics
St. Louis Brown Stockings

the 1877 and 1878 National League flag. By the turn of the decade, however, Cap Anson had come of age, and he led the White Stockings to five National League championships in the 1880s.

Although more organized than its predecessor, the National League still encountered challenges. Unlike the National Association, however, Hulbert's National League had the tools to confront many of the problems it faced. In 1876, for example, the New York Mutuals and Philadelphia Athletics, both hopelessly out of the pennant race, did not take their final road trip of the season. Although this practice was common in the National Association, Hulbert realized that the failure of clubs to complete their schedule cost their opponents money. Therefore, even though New York and Philadelphia were the two largest cities in the country, Hulbert expelled both clubs from the league. The National League soldiered on with only six clubs in 1877. To fill the void in the New York metropolitan area, Hartford transferred most of its home games to Brooklyn. The influence of gamblers on the outcome of games overshadowed the National League's second season. In 1877 the Louisville Grays had been cruising in first place all summer. In August, the Grays suddenly dropped out of the top spot after losing seven games in a row. Rumors began swirling that gamblers were paying four Louisville players to lose. Hulbert was furious. He permanently banned the four players implicated in the scandal, and when the season was over, Hulbert revoked the Louisville franchise and replaced it with a club in Rhode Island called the Providence Grays. The Cincinnati Reds presented more headaches for Hulbert. In direct violation of National League rules, the Reds had been selling beer—a beverage in high demand among the city's large German immigrant population—at the ballpark. The Reds also allowed other clubs to rent the ballpark on Sunday, a practice the National League frowned upon. Tired of Cincinnati's unorthodox practices, Hulbert kicked the Reds out of the National League following the 1880 season.

Even with the ability to strictly enforce its rules, the National League got off to a slow start. The Cincinnati club folded in July 1877, only to have new investors step forward to take over the team a few days later. The Reds limped through the rest of the season. When the season ended, the National League debated whether Cincinnati's record should count in the league's final standings. The Reds felt the worst financial hardship of 1877, but all six National League teams, including the champion Boston Red Stockings, lost money that year.

National League membership was unstable during the 1870s and early 1880s. Teams dropped out due to financial hardship. Hartford and St. Louis resigned from the league after only two seasons. They were replaced in 1878 by clubs in Milwaukee and Indianapolis, both of which lasted only one year. In 1879 the National League again fielded eight teams, adding clubs from Buffalo, Cleveland, Syracuse, and Troy, New York. The Syracuse club survived for less than a season, folding in September with fewer than fifteen games left to play. A team from Worcester, Massachusetts, filled the void in 1880. In 1881 the Detroit Wolverines replaced the expelled Cincinnati Reds.

In 1882 the National League finally achieved a sense of equilibrium, operating with the same eight clubs that had constituted the league in the previous season. The National League brought stability to baseball, but at a cost. It had abandoned major population centers like New York, Philadelphia, Cincinnati, and St. Louis, in favor of smaller cities like Providence, Worcester, and Troy. League rules stifled revenue by prohibiting beer sales and Sunday games, and the fifty-cent admission fee limited the number of fans would could afford to attend a game.

Still, others saw opportunity in stable professional baseball leagues. The expulsion of the Cincinnati Reds proved to be the catalyst for establishing a rival to the National League. Undeterred by the actions of the National League, baseball-crazy Cincinnatians established an independent team in 1881, to which they gave the time-honored name Reds. In St. Louis, another city rebuffed by the National League, baseball enthusiasts established an independent club with the traditional name Browns. The new Reds challenged the new Browns to a series of games in 1881. The success of the series convinced baseball promoters in nonleague cities that there was room for a second major league.

In 1882 the Cincinnati Reds, the St. Louis Browns, and clubs from four other cities without National League teams formed the American Association of Professional Base Ball Clubs, or the American Association. The American Association offered a rowdier version of baseball than that of the National League. Because the American Association allowed the sale of alcohol at its games, National Leaguers derisively referred to it as the "Beer and Whiskey League." Clubs in the American Association were

Table 2.2. The Major Leagues in 1882

American Association	National League
Baltimore Orioles	Boston Red Stockings
Cincinnati Reds	Buffalo Bisons
Louisville Colonels	Chicago White Stockings
Philadelphia Athletics	Cleveland Blues
Pittsburgh Alleghenys	Detroit Wolverines
St. Louis Browns	Providence Grays
	Troy Trojans
	Worcester Ruby Legs

also permitted to play games on Sunday, and admission to American Association games was only twenty-five cents, half the cost of attending a National League game.

While the National League found itself in smaller cities, the American Association moved into six large cities: Baltimore, Cincinnati, Louisville, Philadelphia, Pittsburgh, and St. Louis. Even though the American Association had two fewer clubs than the National League, the combined population of the six association cities outnumbered the total population of the eight league cities by a half million people. In 1882 the American Association's St. Louis Browns outdrew every club in the National League, while all six teams in the association drew more fans than the National League clubs in Cleveland, Buffalo, Troy, and Worcester. The Cincinnati Reds won the first American Association pennant, but the St. Louis Browns would dominate the association, winning four straight pennants beginning in 1885.

With the establishment of the American Association, the National League no longer held a monopoly in baseball. A trade war, which cut into both circuits' profits, immediately broke out between the American Association and the National League. The fact that the association and the league originally operated in different cities meant that—at least at first—there was no competition for paying customers. But with a 75 percent increase in the number of major league teams, competition for players increased. Although National League and American Association rules prohibited players from jumping from one team in the league to another when their contracts expired, neither circuit could prevent players from joining teams in the other league. Players' salaries skyrocketed as major league teams were forced to raise the pay of ballplayers to discourage them from jumping to the rival league.

Competition between the two circuits intensified in 1883, when the American Association expanded to eight clubs by adding two new teams, the Columbus Buckeyes and the New York Metropolitans. The addition of the two new teams increased the pressure on players' salaries, but the struggle between the two circuits grew for another reason. In 1883 the National League decided to return to the nation's two largest cities. The Worcester club relocated to Philadelphia, renaming itself the Philadelphia Quakers. Almost immediately, however, fans and sportswriters alike started calling the team the Phillies. At the same time, the team in Troy moved down the Hudson River to New York City. Originally, the club was known as the New York Gothams, but by 1885 it had become the New York Giants. With the addition of a New York club in the American Association and National League teams in New York and Philadelphia, the two circuits began competing for fans in the country's two largest cities.

The creation of the Northwestern League in 1883, a new league in the Midwest, added to the National League's headaches. Because it did not consider itself a major league, the Northwestern League did not compete head-to-head in any National League city, but its demand for players drove up already increasing player salaries. When John D. Rockefeller or Andrew Carnegie faced competition, they sought to reduce or eliminate it with the creation of trusts. Faced with new competition from the Northwestern League, the National League attempted to work out an agreement with the minor circuit regarding control of players. As the negotiations proceeded, the American Association joined the talks. The discussions between the three circuits produced the Tripartite Agreement, or the National Agreement. Under the National Agreement, the three leagues agreed to respect player contracts, including the right of baseball clubs to "reserve," or hold on to, players whose contracts had expired. The three leagues also agreed to respect the markets where the other leagues already had teams. With the exception of the nation's two largest cities, New York and Philadelphia, where both the National League and American Association already operated, the three circuits agreed not to place a team in a city already represented in one of the other leagues. Essentially, the National Agreement created a "baseball trust" comprised of the National League, the American Association, and the Northwestern League.

The collusion orchestrated by the National Agreement fostered a more favorable business environment for baseball club operators. National League and American Association clubs no longer competed for players, which helped rein in players' salaries. And with the reduction of hard feelings, the National League and American Association pennant winners could meet in an annual postseason series. Baseball's first World's Championship Series took place in 1884. In that series, the Providence Grays of the National League swept the American Association's New York Mets three games to none. Champions from the two rival leagues would continue to meet in an annual World Series through the 1890 season.

Baseball in the 1870s and 1880s imitated other sectors of American society. The creation of professional teams and leagues marked the industrialization of leisure. Baseball promoters, like other business leaders, sought to make a profit. Seeing a need for low-cost entertainment, they stepped in to exploit that niche. William Hulbert formed the National League to create a more favorable business environment for his Chicago White Stockings. He and others worked to limit costs and maximize profits. When competition threatened those profits, operators of baseball clubs, like the operators of other businesses during the Gilded Age, colluded to curtail competition. By forming a baseball trust, they kept business costs, as reflected in baseball salaries, down, and by keeping rival clubs out of cities that already had teams, they divided up the market to reduce competition.

3

Color and Global Barriers (1865 to 1918)

THE CIVIL WAR CHANGED RACE *relations in America. In 1862,
in order to help the North win that conflict, Abraham Lincoln announced the
Emancipation Proclamation, which freed slaves in areas still under rebellion.
Following the end of the war, a period known as Reconstruction because it
was during this time that the Union was put back together, the United States
added the Thirteenth, Fourteenth, and Fifteenth Amendments to the Constitution, which ended slavery, promised citizenship and equality, and guaran-
teed voting rights to former slaves, respectively. Reconstruction enjoyed some
success, but many white southerners resented its effects and began to resist the
reforms. Terrorist organizations such as the Ku Klux Klan emerged to keep
African Americans in their place. But even in the North, a growing number
of people also were tiring of Reconstruction. Reconstruction officially came to
an end by 1877, replaced by an economic system that made former slaves little
more than debt peons to their former plantation owners, and a political system
that found other excuses to deny the vote to most blacks. Continued threats and
violence also suppressed African Americans. The law offered no protection;
it allowed the segregation and inequality of African Americans under Jim
Crow laws and practices when, in 1896, the Supreme Court ruled in* Plessy
v. Ferguson *that segregation was legal as long as the facilities were "separate
but equal." Of course, the facilities were never equal. Shut out of the white
world, African Americans had no recourse but to endure the pain of segregation. Baseball was not immune from this development.*

*But racism did not end at the water's edge. In the second half of the nine-
teenth century, many European powers carved out colonies in Africa and Asia
to exploit the local resources and people. They were motivated by industrialization, as the colonies provided raw materials for European factories, new
markets for European goods, and harbors and refueling stops for European*

*steamships; by racism, as Europeans felt they had a duty to "civilize" and
Christianize the rest of the world; and by nationalism, as Europeans believed
building large empires would increase their countries' power in the great
game of imperialism between rival nations. Americans—especially Christian
missionaries interested in proselytizing in China, businessmen in search of raw
materials and markets, and diplomatic and military leaders eager to defend
US commercial interests and enhance American power before the Europeans
took everything—also became interested in extending their country's influence abroad. By the late 1880s and early 1890s, imperialists began to direct US
policy in the Pacific as America came to dominate Samoa and Hawaii. Closer
to home, Cuba entered American calculations as a weakened Spain could not
control its island colony. After Spain suppressed a rebellion of Cuban nation-
alists, the United States declared war on the former world power in 1898. The
Spanish-American War lasted only four months, but it launched more outposts
into America's orbit, including Cuba and Puerto Rico in the Caribbean, and
the Philippines and Guam in the Pacific. Although Cuba nominally received
its independence, it, like the other spoils of the Spanish-American War, came
under the control of US law and power. The United States controlled an
empire, and took baseball with it abroad.*

On August 10, 1883, Cap Anson's Chicago White Stockings, the defend-
ing National League Champions, arrived in Toledo, Ohio, to play an
exhibition game against a minor league team, the Toledo Blue Stockings of the Northwestern League. Shortly before the game, Anson
noticed Moses Fleetwood Walker, Toledo's regular catcher and one of
the few African Americans playing minor league baseball. Toledo manager Charlie Morton had no intention of playing Walker that day, as the
catcher was nursing a sore hand, but Anson nonetheless ardently refused
to play against a black man. Ironically, that outburst led Morton to insert
Walker into the lineup as an outfielder. When the White Stockings
threatened to cancel the game, Morton pointed out to Anson that a forfeit
meant Chicago would lose its share of the gate receipts. Realizing that
skipping the game would cost the club money, Anson reluctantly agreed
to play. The White Stockings defeated Toledo by a score of 7–6 in ten
innings. The game should have been a triumph for African Americans in
baseball, but instead it represented the high-water mark for black baseball players for the next half century.

In 1884 the American Association expanded to twelve clubs, taking in the Blue Stockings as a member of the circuit. With that action, Walker became the first black major leaguer who did not try to hide his race; his brother, Weldy, who played five games for Toledo that year, became the second. Walker was unusual for a ballplayer in that he was college educated; he graduated from Oberlin College in 1883. After his collegiate baseball career ended, Walker signed a contract to play for the Toledo Blue Stockings. Most of the other teams in the American Association did not object to playing against Walker, and many of their fans viewed him as a curiosity. The two teams that did object, the Louisville Colonels and the Richmond Virginians, were located south of the Potomac and Ohio Rivers. In early September, Morton received a letter warning that an angry mob was determined to attack Walker if the Blue Stockings used him in an upcoming game in Richmond. The letter had no effect, however, as Walker had suffered a broken rib in July that ended his season. Following the injury, the Toledo club released him from the team. For the next five years, Walker bounced around the minor leagues. Cap Anson crossed paths with Walker again in 1887, when the Chicago manager refused to play an exhibition game against Newark if Walker and African American pitcher George Stovey played. This time it was

Moses Fleetwood Walker, a catcher for the 1884 Toledo Blue Stockings, was the first African American baseball player in the major leagues. National Baseball Hall of Fame and Museum. Cooperstown, N.Y.

Walker's team that backed down, as neither black player entered the game. By 1890, Walker and other African American players were no longer playing on white baseball teams. Fleetwood Walker's experience was not unique to baseball, as by the last decade of the nineteenth century, African Americans no longer enjoyed access to many amenities available to white Americans.

After the Civil War, many African Americans—baseball players included—tasted the promise of equality before the forces of racism returned them to an inferior social position. In baseball, some doors were closed to black ballplayers almost from the beginning. The National Association of Base Ball Players, the amateur league of the 1860s, adopted a by-law in 1867, two years after slavery was abolished, that banned African Americans from the league. Baseball's first professional league, the National Association, excluded black ballplayers by gentleman's agreement when it was established in 1871. But, as Walker demonstrated, there were still limited opportunities for African Americans to play baseball in the nineteenth century.

The first African American to play baseball in a professional capacity was probably Bud Fowler, who played for an independent team in New Castle, Pennsylvania, in 1872. William Edward White, who played one game at first base for the National League's Providence Grays in 1879, was probably the first black ballplayer in the major leagues, but few people realized the light-skinned White was African American. Fleetwood Walker was arguably the best black player of the nineteenth century. Fleetwood Walker, Weldy Walker, and William Edward White were unusual in that they competed in major league games, but other African Americans also played baseball at a high-caliber professional level. Frank Grant played second base for the Buffalo Bisons of the International League from 1886 through 1888. In 1887 George Stovey, perhaps the greatest African American player to take the mound in the nineteenth century, pitched for the Newark Little Giants, also of the International League.

In 1881 Tennessee adopted a law requiring railroads to provide separate cars for white and black passengers. By the end of the decade, Florida, Mississippi, and Texas had passed similar laws, and by 1900, when Virginia banned African Americans from riding in the same railroad cars as white travelers, every state in the old Confederacy had instituted segregated train service. At the same time that Jim Crow was spreading through the South, it was also taking hold in baseball. Faced with opposition from Anson and others, minor league baseball teams quietly released the few African Americans left in the game. By 1890 American racism had driven black ballplayers from white baseball as the color barrier, an unwritten agreement among major and minor league baseball teams to not employ African American ballplayers, took effect.

Shut out of major and minor league clubs, African American athletes found a place on the growing number of black baseball teams springing up in the 1880s and 1890s. As early as 1869 the Mutual club of Washington, DC, an African American team that included Frederick Douglass's son, Charles, and was commonly referred to as the Colored Mutes, toured upstate New York. The Philadelphia Orions, an independent amateur club that formed in 1882, was probably the first well-known all-black baseball team. By 1884 several amateur African American teams played baseball, including the St. Louis Black Stockings, the Baltimore Athletics, and the Philadelphia Mutuals. The Argyle Hotel, an elite resort on New York's Long Island, established the first professional African American baseball team in 1885. Created to entertain guests from New York City, the hotel christened the team the Cuban Giants to make it sound exotic to hotel patrons. Resort guests could take in a ball game between trips to the beach. The Cuban Giants were good enough to compete against white teams in white minor leagues. In 1889 the Cuban Giants represented Trenton, New Jersey, in the Middle States League, an otherwise white minor league. The team moved to Pennsylvania in 1890 and played in the Eastern Interstate League as the York Cuban Giants. In 1891, with stars like George Stovey, Frank Grant, and Sol White, the team competed as the Ansonia Cuban Giants in the Connecticut State League. The Cuban Giants left a major influence on African American baseball; over the next six decades, countless Negro league teams incorporated "Giants" or "Cubans" into their names.

The color barrier remained in place until 1946. Black ballplayers, like other African Americans after the Civil War, briefly enjoyed the promise of equality. But following the end of Reconstruction, African Americans were pushed out of many mainstream institutions, including white baseball. As they did in many other fields, African American ballplayers responded by creating their own institutions made up exclusively of black baseball players.

Meanwhile, the rest of the world did not seem receptive to baseball. Although he stopped playing baseball in 1877, Albert Spalding never completely left the game, as he continued to be a fan, promoter, and part-time historian of the sport. He eventually became a co-owner of the White Stockings. He also was a businessman. In 1876, the same year the National League was established, Spalding founded Spalding & Brothers, a sporting goods company. Spalding established his company during the Gilded Age, when industrialization was transforming America. Spalding, like his contemporaries John D. Rockefeller and Andrew Carnegie, sought to promote his business by seeking out new customers. And like his contemporaries, Spalding was unwilling to limit his vision to customers in the United States. With the goal of creating foreign markets for his sports equipment, in 1888 Spalding took the White Stockings and a team of baseball's all-stars on a world tour. While the tour did little to spread baseball to the rest of the world, it did demonstrate the influence of industrialization, nationalism, and racism on American foreign policy in late nineteenth-century America.

Nationalism and imperialism helped spread the sport of baseball. During the nineteenth century, baseball spread across the North American continent. It evolved in the New York City area, and at midcentury, most

National League co-founder and sporting goods mogul, Albert Goodwill Spalding organized the 1888-1889 World Baseball Tour. The Library of Congress Online Photo Archive

baseball clubs were located in New York or Brooklyn. By 1860, however, the game had quickly spread to upstate New York, New Jersey, Pennsylvania, and New England. Like Manifest Destiny, baseball spread west across North America. Drawn by the Gold Rush, James and William Shepard, former members of the Knickerbocker club, moved to California and brought the game with them. By 1859 several members of New York's Eagles club had moved to the West Coast, establishing a club in San Francisco also called the Eagles. In 1849 Alexander Cartwright, the man who codified baseball's rules, began teaching Hawaiians to play baseball. American missionaries also helped spread baseball, teaching it to schoolchildren in Japan and Korea.

Baseball had international roots, as it derived from the British games rounders and cricket. Like baseball, cricket is played with a bat and a ball; cricket differs from baseball, however, in that it takes much longer to play. Still, some of baseball's earliest names had a background in cricket. For instance, Harry Wright, the player-manager of the Cincinnati Red Stockings, baseball's first professional team, excelled at both baseball and cricket. Wright was born in England in 1835, and his father was a famous English cricket player. When Wright was three years old, his family moved to the United States, where he grew up playing both cricket and baseball.

Sportswriter Henry Chadwick also bridged the gulf between baseball and cricket. As a boy, Chadwick played cricket in England, where he was born in 1824. Chadwick's family moved to the United States when he was twelve. In the 1850s, Chadwick covered cricket for the *Long Island Star*. At the time, there were at least as many cricket clubs as baseball clubs in the United States. While making his way to a cricket match, Chadwick encountered a baseball game between the Eagle and Gotham clubs. He became fascinated with the sport. Chadwick eventually gave up cricket to cover baseball for the *New York Clipper*, one of the first newspapers to regularly cover the game. As perhaps the first sportswriter to cover baseball on a regular basis, Chadwick helped to popularize it. He invented the box score and helped to standardize the rules.

Because cricket still had many supporters in the United States, British cricket teams often visited the United States in the 1860s. In the early 1870s, Spalding and Chadwick decided that baseball should return the favor. They organized a baseball tour of England in 1874. Two professional teams from the National Association traveled to Britain, the Boston Red Stockings, which featured Harry Wright and Spalding, and the Philadelphia Athletics, boasting a young Adrian Anson. Chadwick accompanied the two teams on the tour. The trip lasted from mid-July to mid-September, which meant that both the Red Stockings and the Athletics missed two months in the middle of the season. In addition to baseball games between Boston and Philadelphia, players from each team also played cricket against British cricket clubs. Even though most American baseball players had never seen a cricket match, Wright had informed the British clubs that Americans were good at cricket. The poor quality of play of the Americans at cricket quickly exposed Wright's lie. Even with extra outs and more players on the field, the Americans could not hold their own against British cricket clubs.

The trip disappointed the ballplayers. The baseball games did not draw the large crowds that were expected. Spalding and Cartwright were especially pained to read the British press's dismissal of baseball as a primitive child's game. Back home, the trip also hurt the National Association, as attendance suffered with the league's two most powerful teams missing the middle of the season. The British reaction hurt Spalding's pride. He believed baseball was superior to cricket, and he could not understand how people in Britain disagreed.

Spalding had another opportunity to take baseball overseas when he scheduled the 1888–1889 World Baseball Tour. On this tour, Spalding's team, the Chicago White Stockings, traveled around the world with a group of all-stars dubbed the All-America team. In order to avoid disrupting the season the way the 1874 tour of England did, the tour began after the 1888 baseball season ended, and the players returned six months later, before the new season was scheduled to start. The two teams had originally planned to travel to Hawaii, then to New Zealand and Australia, before returning home. The ballplayers left Chicago in October, heading for San Francisco and stopping to play baseball games along the way. In San Francisco the ballplayers boarded a ship for Hawaii, where because of a ban on Sunday amusements, no game could be played. From Hawaii the teams sailed to New Zealand and Australia, stopping to refuel along the way in Samoa, which in a few months would become the United States' first colony. In Australia the players learned the tour had been extended to an around-the-world trip, with stops (and ball games) scheduled in Ceylon (Sri Lanka), Egypt, Italy, France, England, Scotland, and Ireland before the ballplayers sailed for New York.

Much of the trip took place within the British Empire. Although an American empire had not yet been established, the tour would come to represent the ideology behind American imperialism. Imperialists sought to spread Western culture to the rest of the world; Spalding and the ballplayers were bringing an important symbol of American culture—baseball—to the places they traveled. American businessmen saw foreign countries as markets to exploit, while Spalding hoped baseball would take hold in the places he visited so he could sell his sports equipment in those countries. And just as imperialists believed Westerners were racially superior to nonwhite people, the ballplayers believed they were racially superior to the people of Hawaii, Ceylon, and Egypt.

Spalding and the players did not receive the reaction they wanted or expected. When baseball failed to excite spectators in Ceylon and Egypt, the touring teams attributed the lack of interest to the racial inferiority of the audience. In Britain polite audiences attended the games out of curiosity, but they did not embrace the sport. To Spalding and his players, this proved that Americans were also culturally superior to the rest of the world. The fact that others could not see baseball's superiority only seemed to demonstrate their inferiority to Americans. But then again, Americans also believed other people could not see the advantage of democracy over monarchy.

Despite the failure of the 1888–1889 world tour, baseball executives organized other tours. Chicago White Sox owner Charles Comiskey and New York Giants manager John McGraw took their players on a world tour following the 1913 baseball season. Like the tour organized by Spalding, the Comiskey-McGraw tour began in mid-November, after the American baseball season ended, and continued until early March, ending in time for the start of the next season. The 1913–1914 tour started in Chicago, continuing to San Francisco and then to Japan, where American missionaries had brought the game in the 1860s. After playing games in Japan, China, Hong Kong, and the Philippines, the tour picked up Spalding's trail in Australia and followed his route the rest of the way. But any impact that Comiskey and McGraw's players may have had on the rest of the world was lost, as five months after the tour ended, World War I broke out in Europe.

In 1934, an American all-star baseball team featuring Babe Ruth visited Japan. The tour of Japan had a larger impact than the around-the-
world trips because American missionaries had already taught baseball
to Japanese students in the nineteenth century, and many people in Japan
looked at baseball as a spiritual exercise akin to the martial arts. Japanese
baseball fans became fascinated with Ruth, and two years later, as a result
of the tour, Japanese entrepreneurs established the country's first professional baseball league.

Just as political leaders used imperialism to promote nationalism,
Spalding, Comiskey, and McGraw used the world tours to promote baseball. As politicians believed imperialism made their nations stronger,
baseball leaders believed world tours made baseball stronger. During this
time, Americans began to recognize baseball as the "National Pastime."
Baseball represented two important characteristics of the national identity: democracy, in which every player comes to bat and has the opportunity to score, and individualism, in which the batter stands alone against
an entire team of his opponents. As baseball represented the American
character, Americans developed a need to prove that baseball was an
American institution. Therefore, Americans believed the national game
must have begun in the United States; it could not have foreign roots.

In the first decade of the twentieth century, several individuals associated with nineteenth-century baseball organized a commission to determine the origins of the game. The Mills Commission, established in
1905, included Arthur P. Gorman, a former US senator from Maryland;
former National League presidents Morgan G. Bulkeley and Nicholas
Young; Alfred J. Reach, a former baseball player from the 1860s and
1870s whose sporting goods company, A.J. Reach, rivaled Spalding's
company in size; George Wright, the star shortstop of the Cincinnati
Red Stockings in 1869; and James Edward Sullivan, the president of the
Amateur Athletic Union. Abraham Mills, who was the third president
of the National League from 1883 to 1884, chaired the commission. The
Mills Commission, which heard from witnesses from all over the country, issued its findings at the end of 1907. It ruled that baseball did not
evolve from rounders, but that it had its origins in the United States. The
commission further stated that, according to the best evidence available,
the game of baseball was devised by Abner Doubleday at Cooperstown,
New York, in 1839.

This conclusion was based on the written testimony of an elderly man named Abner Graves, who claimed that he was there, at Elihu Phinney's cow pasture in Cooperstown sixty-eight years earlier, and witnessed Doubleday invent the rules for a game between boys from the Otsego Academy and Green's Select School of Cooperstown. Graves, a Denver mining engineer, was five years old in 1839. Abner Doubleday, the man the Mills Commission credited with inventing baseball, served as a Union general during the Civil War. He later invented a cable car that is still used in San Francisco. But his connection to baseball is tenuous at best.[1] Doubleday could not have been in Cooperstown in 1839; he was a cadet at West Point that year. Doubleday, who died in 1893, lived long enough to see professional baseball thrive, but he never took credit for inventing the game. Doubleday was a longtime friend of Abraham Mills, yet he never told Mills that he invented baseball. Doubleday did not even reminisce about playing it as a child. In remembering his childhood, he listed his interests as reading, studying, and mapmaking.

Still, the Doubleday myth took hold. In 1934 a farmer discovered a trunk once belonging to Abner Graves in the attic of an old farmhouse three miles from Cooperstown. Among other things, the trunk contained an old, beat-up, homemade baseball. The townspeople of Cooperstown quickly reached the conclusion that the baseball found in Graves's trunk must have been the very same baseball Abner Doubleday used in the very first baseball game. With the "centennial" of baseball only five years away, Cooperstown residents decided to promote tourism by building a museum to showcase the "Doubleday Baseball." Sportswriters and officials from Major League Baseball quickly jumped on the bandwagon. In 1939 the National Baseball Hall of Fame and Museum opened in Cooperstown to mark the centennial of an event that never took place. Two blocks down the street, on the former site of Elihu Phinney's cow pasture—a site where nothing happened a hundred years earlier—the government constructed a grandstand for a ballpark called Abner Doubleday Field. Every year from 1940 to 2008, two major league baseball teams trudged to remote Cooperstown to play a game at Doubleday Field to commemorate the first baseball game at the place where it never happened. The Doubleday Baseball is still on display at the Baseball Hall of Fame, but today it is overshadowed by a great deal of real baseball memorabilia.

Others have continued to promote the Doubleday myth. In 1911 Albert Spalding wrote *America's National Game*, a history of the sport. Spalding's book endorsed the Doubleday myth. In it, he argued that baseball was a purely American game that "conforms in every way to the American temperament." In 1986 a state senator from Brooklyn introduced a bill in the New York legislature to have the phrase "Birthplace of Baseball" added to New York State license plates. The myth did serve some purpose. In the aftermath of the Civil War, it helped unite a divided country, a country that shared a common pastime. And with the emergence of the United States as a world power, it helped establish a unique American identity.

In the early twentieth century, just two years after the Mills Commission issued its findings, baseball received presidential approval. President William Howard Taft, who served from 1909 to 1913, was an avid baseball fan who went to every game he could. In 1910 Taft attended the Washington Senators' home opener, at which he threw out the ceremonial first pitch. Since then, every president has followed that tradition. The practice became a little irregular between 1972, when the Washington Senators moved to Dallas–Fort Worth, and 2005, when the Montreal Expos became the Washington Nationals. Without a team in Washington, presidents had to travel to Baltimore or some other city to participate in the tradition.

The year after the Mills Commission concluded that Doubleday had invented baseball, vaudeville star Jack Norworth and composer Albert Von Tilzer wrote "Take Me Out to the Ball Game." The song, whose lesser-known verses are about a female baseball fan who loves the game more than she loves her beau, reflected the growing suffrage movement that would win women the right to vote twelve years later. In the years since its publication, the song has become baseball's anthem. Like the national anthem itself, which is also song at ball games, "Take Me Out to the Ball Game" is sung standing up, making its appearance during the seventh-inning stretch, the break between the top and bottom of the seventh inning.

Although there is evidence that the seventh-inning stretch began in the nineteenth century to give fans an opportunity to stretch their legs and perhaps seek refreshment from a vendor, another widely circulated baseball myth gives it presidential origins. According to legend, the seventh-inning stretch started when Taft, who weighed more than three hundred pounds, attended a ball game in 1910. During the course of the game, his muscles began to tire and, according to the story, he rose from his seat after the top of the seventh inning in order to stretch his legs. The rest of the crowd, wrongly believing the president was about to leave the ballpark, stood up out of respect. When the refreshed Taft sat back down, the crowd sat down with him. It is now common practice for fans to stand up and stretch during the middle of the seventh inning.

Presidential influence on the game has continued through the years. With the arrival of the Nationals in Washington, DC, in 2005, a new baseball tradition emerged. In the middle of the fourth inning at every game at the Nationals' stadium, four actors dressed in giant masks depicting the four American presidents enshrined at Mount Rushmore—George Washington, Thomas Jefferson, Abraham Lincoln, and Theodore Roosevelt—race around the base paths. In 2013 a fifth competitor joined the Presidents' Race—William Howard Taft, a chief executive known for his strong connection to baseball.

A second song associated with baseball made its appearance during World War I. Many people questioned the practice of playing baseball while the country was at war. To counter critics who argued that baseball should be shut down for the duration of the conflict, the Chicago Cubs hired a band to perform "The Star-Spangled Banner" during the seventh-inning stretch in the first two games of the 1918 World Series against the Boston Red Sox. When the series returned to Boston for Game 3, the Red Sox moved the performance of "The Star-Spangled Banner" to the start of the game. Since then, no professional baseball game has begun without a performance of the national anthem, a tradition that leagues in other professional sports have since adopted.

The message in the Doubleday myth, the presidential first pitch, the singing of "Take Me Out to the Ball Game," and the playing of the national anthem is the same: Baseball and America are intertwined. During World War II, baseball players promoted the message by wearing patriotic patches on their uniforms. During the Gulf War of the early 1990s, baseball players wore small American flags on the back of their caps; after September 11, 2001, players wore uniforms with small American flags on their sleeves. It is a message that serves the United States: If you love baseball, it must also be true that you love the United States. It is also a message that serves baseball: If you love America, you will also love baseball. Baseball is not just the American game, it is America.

4

The American Labor Movement and the Players' League (1884 to 1891)

AS THE UNITED STATES BECAME an industrial nation during the Gilded Age, a wide gap emerged between rich and poor. Businesses did all they could to maximize profits, including increasing income and decreasing costs. Labor became a commodity that workers sold for wages, thereby losing their independence. Along with low pay and long hours, they encountered dangerous working conditions. In response, many states began adopting laws protecting workers by mandating safe working conditions and limiting the number of hours an employee could work. Businesses often used the courts to strike down these laws. Unable to gain protection through the government, many workers concluded they could not accomplish their goals if they did not unite. In 1866, workers in Philadelphia formed the National Labor Union, and in 1869 a more powerful union, named the Knights of Labor, emerged. The Knights wanted higher wages, shorter hours (including an eight-hour workday), and better conditions. Believing that workers, not company owners, should enjoy the benefits of the wealth their labor created, the Knights of Labor also opposed the wage system. As a result, the Knights supported the creation of cooperatives in which the workers owned the company for which they worked. Labor squared off against employers over the next few decades, sometimes violently. Such riots discredited the Knights of Labor, and in 1886, members turned instead to the American Federation of Labor, a more conservative union that accepted the wage system and protested in moderation. Still, labor tension persisted, and whenever a major labor dispute broke out, such as the Homestead Steel Strike of 1892 or the Pullman Strike of 1894, the government stood with the companies and against the workers. Baseball was by no means immune to the fights between workers and owners.

On June 17, 1880, twenty-year-old John Montgomery Ward took the mound at Providence's Messer Street Grounds for a game against the Buffalo Bisons. Although he only had two years of major league experience, Monte Ward had already established himself as the premier pitcher in baseball. The previous year, Ward's league-leading forty-seven victories helped the Providence Grays secure the 1879 National League pennant. That Thursday afternoon in June, he achieved his greatest feat as a pitcher: He did not allow a single Bisons player to reach base. Ward's accomplishment was largely overlooked at the time, however, as only five days earlier J. Lee Richmond of the Worcester Ruby Legs shut out the Cleveland Blues in the National League's first perfect game. Four years later, Ward's promising pitching career came to a disappointing end when, as a member of the New York Gothams (soon to be called the New York Giants), he injured his arm in a baserunning accident. Unwill-

New York Giants' shortstop John Montgomery Ward formed the first union for professional athletes, the Brotherhood of Professional Base Ball Players, in 1885. National Baseball Hall of Fame and Museum. Cooperstown, N.Y.

ing to give up baseball, Ward became a star shortstop for the Giants. He retired following the 1894 season. In his seventeen-year career, Ward played in 1,825 games, amassing 2,104 hits and compiling a .275 batting average. The only player to collect more than 2,000 hits as a batter and tally more than 100 wins as a pitcher, Ward was elected to the Baseball Hall of Fame in 1964. Yet his greatest contribution to baseball occurred off the field, when he formed baseball's—indeed, professional sports'—first labor union.

As a teenager, Ward briefly attended Penn State until he was expelled following a fight with a fellow student. While playing baseball for the Giants, Ward began to take evening classes at Columbia Law School, from which he graduated in 1885. That same year, a Philadelphia sportswriter named William Voltz attempted to establish a protective association for ballplayers. Voltz was primarily concerned with creating a benevolent fund for retired players, but because he never played the game, most baseball players were suspicious of his motives. When Voltz brought his idea to Ward, the Giants' shortstop realized that such an organization could address the many grievances baseball players had with the clubs that employed them.

Gilded Age unions struggled against low pay, long hours, and dangerous working conditions, often unsuccessfully, because the government usually took the side of the companies and opposed the workers. Despite much violence, death, and destruction caused by nineteenth-century strikes, workers in the Gilded Age saw few gains from their actions. Neither did most major league players. Although they worked in a glamorous profession, they, too, felt squeezed by team owners. Denied even the basic right to negotiate with their employers, ballplayers were at the mercy of the teams that employed them. Like workers in other industries, baseball players in the late nineteenth century formed a union and even took part in a labor action.

Like successful industrialists of the Gilded Age, baseball team owners sought to increase their profits. The most obvious way to do this was to enhance their revenue streams. The creation of professional leagues and the establishment of monopolies generated steady revenue for the moguls who operated baseball clubs. Enterprising club owners also found novel ways to increase their income. One strategy employed by team owners was the construction of new ballparks. The novelty of a new park always drew extra customers. New ballparks also generally had greater seating capacities than the facilities they replaced, and often featured premium seating, such as seating under a covered grandstand, for which clubs could charge extra. A number of teams opened new ballparks in the 1880s, including the Brooklyn Trolley Dodgers, who christened Washington Park in 1883, and the Boston Beaneaters, formerly the Red Stockings, who moved into the South End Grounds in 1888.

By the 1880s, baseball clubs discovered that offering food, drink, and other concessions at the ballpark brought in more revenue. As early as 1882, the clubs in the American Association were selling beer and whiskey at baseball games. In the early 1880s, a man named Harry M. Stevens attended a baseball game in Columbus, Ohio, and, disappointed in the quality of the scorecards offered at the stadium, convinced the club to let him have a contract to produce an improved version. Stevens soon obtained contracts to sell scorecards, and eventually food, at many other major league ballparks. In 1893 Chris von der Ahe, the owner of the St. Louis Browns, began selling German sausages at his ballpark. Like von der Ahe, many of the fans in St. Louis were German immigrants who enjoyed the sausage from their homeland. Thus began the long link between baseball and hot dogs.

In order to increase attendance, baseball clubs began to stage promotions. Clubs added doubleheaders to the schedule, which brought in more spectators. In 1883 the New York Gothams held the first Ladies' Day, at which women were admitted to the game free of charge if they attended with a man who paid for his admission. In 1891 the Chicago White Stockings started to hold a Baseball Day, in which boys on amateur teams who showed up in their baseball uniforms were admitted for free. The White Stockings ownership believed that if young people could be lured to the ballpark, they would continue that habit as they grew older. In the 1880s, Chris von der Ahe built an amusement park next to Sportsmen's Park. Fans who saved their ticket stub from the afternoon's game would be admitted to the amusement park for only a quarter. In order to cash in on the bicycle craze of the 1890s, many clubs constructed bicycle tracks along the ballpark's warning track for pregame bicycle races.

In an attempt to make the game more exciting, the major leagues continued to tinker with the rules, still looking for the perfect formula to balance the confrontation between pitcher and batter. In 1876, the first year of the National League, the umpire warned the batter before calling the first strike, essentially giving the batter four strikes, and the pitcher needed to throw nine balls before a batter was awarded first base. That number was reduced to eight in 1879; the rules dropped the number of balls to seven, six, and five before finally settling on four balls for a walk in 1889. Until 1887 a batter could call for a high or low pitch, but beginning in 1887 the batter no longer had a choice. Starting in 1884, pitchers could throw overhand, which meant they could pitch with more speed and power. Baseball also adjusted the distance between home plate and the pitcher's rubber. To encourage more hitting and scoring, the rules set the distance at forty-five feet in 1876, moved it to fifty feet in 1881, and ultimately set it at sixty feet six inches in 1893.

Other rules tried to make the game more interesting, all with the intention of drawing more fans to make the owners more money. In 1882 baseball adopted a rule mandating color-coded uniforms by position, with each player wearing a different color cap and jersey. For instance, first basemen throughout the major leagues wore red-and-white striped shirts and caps, second basemen wore orange-and-black striped shirts and caps, and shortstops wore maroon shirts and caps. A player's team was not identified by the color of his cap or jersey, but by the color of his stockings. The players hated the 1882 uniforms, derisively referring to them as "clown costumes." The major leagues quietly abandoned the uniforms when the season ended.

Baseball club owners not only tried to maximize their income by building new ballparks and adopting gimmicks to attract crowds, but also sought to reduce their costs. Player salaries were—and remain—the largest expense encountered by baseball clubs. Club owners understood that they faced a problem unique to their business: They needed the players, as the ball game was their product, but as the clubs competed with each other for players, they were driving up player salaries. At the 1879 owners' meeting in Buffalo, New York, the National League came up with a solution: the reserve clause, which allowed a club to reserve (or retain) a player after his contract expired. Once a player's contract expired, no other National League team could sign him to a contract; the player had the choice of either re-signing with his existing team or not signing a contract at all. At first each team could reserve only five players. The number of players on the reserve list was expanded to eleven in 1886 and to fourteen in 1887, which, with the small rosters of the nineteenth century, meant virtually everyone on the team was reserved. Eventually, the reserve list was expanded to include the entire team. With the reserve clause in place, major league teams did not need to sign a player to anything longer than a one-year contract. A one-year contract protected the club if the player became injured or lost his skill, because the team would only have to pay the player for that one season.

The reserve clause put baseball players at a severe disadvantage. Once a player signed his first contract, he lost all negotiating leverage for the remainder of his career. Because he could not sign with another team once his major league club reserved him, that player had little choice but to re-sign at whatever terms the club offered. Occasionally, a big star would threaten to sit out the season, assuming that if the team wanted him badly enough, it would give in to his demands. But few players were important enough to have that effect on a club. The reserve clause could even prevent players from playing at all. If a team had no current need for a player but did not want another club to sign him, that team could keep the player on the reserve list without signing him. Because the player had been reserved, that player was not free to sign with another team.

When the American Association was founded in 1882, it announced that it would not recognize the National League's reserve clause. As National League players were no longer under contract when the season ended, American Association teams could legally sign them. The competition for players raised salaries in both leagues. But after the American Association and the National League began to collude in 1883, each league recognized the other's reserve clause. Players again lost their leverage, and salaries tumbled downward.

Having agreed to end competition between the two existing leagues, club owners encountered new competition in 1884. A Missouri millionaire named Henry V. Lucas, having inherited an enormous sum of money from his wealthy father, wanted to own a baseball team in St. Louis. Denied a club by both the National League and the American Association, Lucas created a new team called the St. Louis Maroons and established a new baseball league, the Union Association, in which the Maroons would compete. The UA created problems for the existing major leagues. Lucas announced that the new league would not honor either league's reserve clause. As a result, players' salaries increased as all three leagues competed for the same players. Even without the new league, baseball teams would have experienced increased competition for players, as in 1884 the American Association expanded from eight teams to twelve teams. Competing for players and vying for fans in many of the same cities, teams in all three leagues lost money in 1884. In the middle of the season, the American Association's Washington Statesmen went out of business. A minor league team from Richmond, Virginia, joined the association in August to complete the Statesmen's schedule. When the season ended, the American Association, facing heavy financial losses, contracted to eight teams.

The Union Association suffered the greatest losses. Of the eight clubs that formed the Union Association in April, only five completed the season. As Union Association teams went under, minor league clubs joined to take their place. As a result, even though there were only eight franchises in the Union Association, thirteen teams competed in that circuit in 1884. With only three clubs willing to continue, the Union Association disbanded after a single season. Lucas's St. Louis Maroons moved to the National League in 1885. Chris von der Ahe's St. Louis Browns of the American Association objected, but with both the American Association and the National League suffering heavy losses, neither circuit could afford to fight.

Table 4.1. The Major Leagues at the Start of the 1884 Season

NL Clubs	AA Clubs	UA Clubs
Boston Red Stockings	Baltimore Orioles	Altoona Mountain Citys[2]
Buffalo Bisons	Brooklyn Trolley Dodgers	Baltimore Monumentals
Chicago White Stockings	Cincinnati Reds	Boston Reds
Cleveland Blues	Columbus Buckeyes	Chicago Browns[3]
Detroit Wolverines	Indianapolis Hoosiers	Cincinnati Outlaw Reds
New York Gothams	Louisville Colonels	Philadelphia Keystones[4]
Philadelphia Phillies	New York Metropolitans	St. Louis Maroons
Providence Grays	Philadelphia Athletics	Washington Nationals
	Pittsburgh Alleghenys	
	St. Louis Browns	
	Toledo Blue Stockings	
	Washington Statesmen[1]	

[1] Replaced by Richmond Virginians in August.
[2] Replaced by Kansas City Cowboys in May.
[3] Replaced by Pittsburgh Stogies in August and St. Paul Saints in September.
[4] Replaced by Wilmingon Quicksteps in August and Milwaukee Brewers in September.

The collapse of the Union Association not only meant the major leagues could enforce low salaries through the reserve clause, but it also cut—by more than a third—the number of jobs for big-league ballplayers. When Philadelphia sportswriter William Voltz, the year after the Union Association's demise, proposed a benevolent association to assist ill and needy ballplayers, most players distrusted his intention. Monte Ward, the star shortstop for the New York Giants, however, saw an opportunity, and in October 1885 he established the Brotherhood of Professional Base Ball Players, the first labor union of professional athletes. Ward secretly organized his teammates on the New York Giants, then quietly created locals in the other seven National League cities. In 1886, after the entire league had been unionized, the Brotherhood announced its existence. At first, club owners welcomed the development of the Brotherhood. They believed the organization would help discipline ballplayers by promoting a professional attitude. They also expected the Brotherhood to help establish funds to take care of sick, injured, and retired ballplayers. But the Brotherhood was primarily concerned with the way major league teams controlled players' salaries, and its primary goal was the abolition of the main restriction on players' salaries—the reserve clause.

At the National League owners' meeting in 1888, John T. Brush, owner of the Indianapolis Hoosiers, proposed a new system to determine players' salaries. The Brush Classification Plan assigned all major league ballplayers to one of five classifications, based on skill and character, which he defined as "habits, earnestness, and special qualifications." Players assigned to Class A, the highest level, would be paid $2,500 a year. Players assigned to the lowest level, Class E, would be paid $1,500. Players in between would be paid $2,250, $2,000, or $1,750, depending upon the class to which they were assigned. The Brush Classification Plan eliminated competition for pay. All stars would receive the same salary; all journeymen would receive the same salary.

Ward heard about the proposal while on Albert G. Spalding's World Baseball Tour. He immediately wanted to return home to deal with the issue, but Spalding convinced him to honor his commitment. By the time the ballplayers returned to the United States, the Brush Classification Plan was already in place for the 1889 season. Ward, however, began plotting his strategy for 1890.

Following the conclusion of the 1889 baseball season, the Brotherhood of Professional Base Ball Players announced a work action that essentially amounted to a strike of National League and American Association baseball teams. The Brotherhood established a new league, with John Montgomery Ward as the league president. With the Players' League, which began operation in 1890, the Brotherhood established the type of organization the Knights of Labor had advocated: a cooperative owned by players and investors in which the workers would share in the wealth they created. In this case, it was the players themselves who were the product the customers were paying to see. The Players' League did not have a reserve clause; instead, to provide job security for players and to protect the assets of investors, each player was signed to a three-year contract.

The Players' League began the 1890 season with eight teams, seven of which competed head-to-head against National League teams. Two Players' League teams, Brooklyn and Philadelphia, competed head-to-head against National League and American Association teams. Only the Players' League team in Buffalo escaped major league competition.

Attracted by higher salaries and the opportunity to attack the reserve clause, many stars jumped to the Players' League. By December 1889, Players' League clubs had signed seventy-one players from the National League, sixteen players from the American Association, and four minor leaguers. By one count, when the National League opened its 1890 season, only thirty-eight players on its rosters had played in the league the year before. All major league teams were hit hard, but some were devastated. In the nineteenth century, team nicknames were unofficial; they were

Table 4.2. The Major Leagues at the Start of the 1890 Season

PL Clubs	NL Clubs	AA Clubs
Boston Red Stockings	Boston Beaneaters	Brooklyn Gladiators[1]
Brooklyn Wonders	Brooklyn Bridegrooms	Columbus Solons
Buffalo Bisons	Chicago White Stockings	Louisville Colonels
Chicago Pirates	Cincinnati Reds	Philadelphia Athletics
Cleveland Infants	Cleveland Spiders	Rochester Hop Bitters
New York Giants	New York Mules	St. Louis Browns
Philadelphia Quakers	Philadelphia Phillies	Syracuse Stars
Pittsburgh Burghers	Pittsburgh Alleghenys	Toledo Maumees

[1] Replaced by Baltimore Orioles in August.

usually given by sportswriters and often referred to team colors or a star player. In 1890 so many members of New York's National League club jumped to that city's Players' League entry that sportswriters referred to the Players' League team in New York as the New York Giants. The press called that city's National League team, which was managed by a man named Jim Mutrie, Mutrie's Mules.

The Players' League not only drove up salaries, but, as many Players' League teams sought to rent ballparks that had been the home of National League or American Association clubs, it also drove up rents. Attendance for all three leagues combined in 1890 was probably less than what the two leagues drew together in 1889, and all three leagues lost money. The Players' League had the best attendance—it had clubs in more major cities, and it had attracted the most popular stars. Still, the Players' League drew fewer spectators than the National League had drawn the year before. With the loss of most of its stars, and with a Players' League competitor in every city but Cincinnati, the National League found it difficult to appeal to fans.

The American Association's attendance suffered the most. By the end of the 1880s the National League, with its higher admission price and more respectable reputation, had become the more desirable circuit. Thus, whenever the opportunity presented itself, American Association clubs switched leagues. The Pittsburgh Alleghenys jumped to the older circuit in 1887, while the Cincinnati Reds and the Brooklyn Trolley Dodgers (now called the Brooklyn Bridegrooms because a number of players on the club were recently married in quick succession) joined the National League in 1890. The American Association had to replace deserting clubs with teams in smaller cities like Columbus and Toledo, Ohio, and Rochester and Syracuse, New York. When the Brooklyn Bridegrooms transferred to the National League for the 1890 season, the American Association replaced it with a new club, the Brooklyn Gladiators. Faced with competition from a National League and a Players' League team, however, the Gladiators could not afford to remain in Brooklyn. The team moved to Baltimore in August, replacing the original Baltimore Orioles, which had dropped out of the American Association the year before. The Brotherhood, however, lacked the financial resources of the other major league team owners. Even though the Players' League had the best attendance in baseball in 1890, when the season ended, the circuit went out of business.

The collapse of the Players' League damaged the alliance between the National League and the American Association. After the season ended, the National League angered some American Association clubs by allowing Players' League investors to buy into National League clubs in New York, Brooklyn, Chicago, and Pittsburgh. And although individuals on Players' League clubs were expected to return to their 1889 teams, not all of them did. The best example was Louis Bierbauer, who played second base for the American Association's Philadelphia Athletics in 1889. Bierbauer jumped to the Brooklyn Wonders of the Players' League in 1890. After the Players' League folded, however, Bierbauer did not return to Philadelphia. The Athletics neglected to place his name on the reserve list, and the Pittsburgh Alleghenys of the National League signed him to a contract for the 1891 season. The Athletics accused the Alleghenys of pirating Bierbauer, and almost immediately the team became known as the Pittsburgh Pirates.

Suffering from the financial losses of the 1890 season, stuck in smaller cities, and losing players to the National League, the American Association took steps in 1891 that put it in an even weaker position. Seeking to move out of smaller cities, the American Association replaced its teams in Rochester, Syracuse, and Toledo with clubs in Boston, Cincinnati, and Washington. The move, however, meant that in addition to competing with the National League's Philadelphia Phillies, the American Association was now challenging the Boston Beaneaters and Cincinnati Reds for fans. The Cincinnati Killers could not compete against the more established Reds, and went out of business in August. The American Association convinced the minor league Milwaukee Brewers to join the association to complete Cincinnati's schedule, but the association's days were numbered. Following the conclusion of the 1891 season, Chris von der Ahe's St. Louis Browns applied to join the National League. When word of the Browns' application leaked out, other association teams also applied.

The National League and American Association reached an agreement allowing the association's four strongest teams—the Baltimore Orioles, the Louisville Colonels, the St. Louis Browns, and the Washington Senators—to join the National League. Starting in 1892 and continuing for the rest of the decade, the National League operated as a twelve-team circuit. The remaining four American Association clubs—the Boston

Table 4.3.   The Major Leagues in 1892

The National League

Baltimore Orioles*
Boston Beaneaters
Brooklyn Bridegrooms
Chicago White Stockings
Cincinnati Reds
Cleveland Spiders
Louisville Colonels*
New York Giants
Philadelphia Phillies
Pittsburgh Pirates
St. Louis Browns*
Washington Senators*

* Played in the American Association in 1891.

Red Stockings, the Columbus Solons, the Milwaukee Brewers, and the Philadelphia Athletics—split a $130,000 settlement between them and went out of business. For the remainder of the 1890s, the National League would monopolize the major leagues.

Major league baseball players, like striking workers in society at large, failed to achieve the goals of their 1890 labor action. Although the Brush Classification Plan was abandoned, the reserve clause would remain in effect, in its nineteenth-century form, for another eighty-five years. And with the death of the American Association, the National League would enjoy a monopoly that allowed it to engage in further abuses for the remainder of the century. Gilded Age greed and executive domination would contaminate baseball as it did other segments of American society.

5

Progressivism and the American League (1892 to 1903)

WHILE WORKERS RESPONDED TO Gilded Age abuses by form-ing unions and going on strike, farmers and ranchers fought higher costs, declines in income, and more debt after the Civil War by adopting populism, a grassroots reform movement designed to restore power to the individual by taking on the political and corporate power centers. In 1892, farmers, ranch-ers, and miners in the West and South formed the People's Party, or Populist Party, which attacked the political system formed by the elite Eastern Estab-lishment of corrupt politicians and powerful corporate leaders. In the cities of the Northeast, Midwest, and West Coast, a middle-class reform effort, called the Progressive movement, sought to improve the lot of workers, immigrants, and the urban poor. They targeted corporations, which had increased their wealth through monopolistic business practices and operated under condi-tions that were unsafe for consumers and workers, as well as targeting their government allies. Progressives believed that science, knowledge, and con-scious human effort could create order out of chaos, making the future better than the present. Progressives in both the Republican and Democratic parties set out to seize city councils, state legislatures, and the three branches of the national government to adopt antimonopoly laws, economic regulation, con-sumer protection, and environmental and conservation legislation. Some of their transformative reforms—which crossed into every corner of the Ameri-can economy, society, and political system—included a graduated income tax, direct election of US senators, and woman suffrage. Starting in 1901, Progres-sives had a champion in Theodore Roosevelt, who as president promoted a vig-orous agenda that cracked down on monopolies and robber barons, cleaned up industry, sided with labor in key disputes, regulated the railroads, and turned

over vast areas of wilderness that had been the domain of corporate exploita-
tion to the government under the National Park System. Many special inter-
ests opposed him, but his successors, Republican William Howard Taft and
Democrat Woodrow Wilson, followed his lead with their own reforms. This
wave of Progressivism also swept through baseball and its monopolistic orga-
nization and practices.

Just after he graduated from Marietta College in Ohio, Byron Bancroft
"Ban" Johnson took a job as a sportswriter for the *Cincinnati Commer-*
cial Gazette in 1887. As a reporter who covered the local nine, Johnson
established friendships with many important baseball figures, including
Charles Comiskey, the manager of the Cincinnati Reds. When a midwestern minor league called the Western League went out of business
in 1893, Comiskey suggested that the league reorganize with Johnson as
its head, and Johnson soon restored stability to the circuit. He ended the
rowdy atmosphere at Western League ballparks that kept women and

American League founder Byron
Bancroft "Ban" Johnson broke
the National League's monopoly
in 1901. National Baseball
Hall of Fame and Museum.
Cooperstown, N.Y.

children away. He established order by standing behind umpires and fining or suspending players who challenged them. Most importantly, he created an environment in which all eight clubs in the Western League operated at a profit.

Johnson continued to strengthen the Western League, and began to target the National League monopoly. In 1894 he enticed Comiskey, who recently had been fired by the Reds, to buy into the Western League as a club owner. As late as 1900, Johnson's league still operated as a minor league, but Johnson had prepared it to challenge the National League's monopoly. By taking on the National League, Johnson helped bring order and stability to big league baseball, an institution that had been besieged with problems since the demise of the American Association almost a decade earlier. Order and stability, as well as reforms that allowed more competition in businesses—including baseball—lay at the heart of the Progressive movement at the turn of the twentieth century.

Baseball in the 1890s, like America during the same decade, struggled with severe challenges. For most of the decade, the National League enjoyed a monopoly on the major leagues, but without competition the National League suffered from major problems. With four former American Association clubs joining the National League in 1892, the circuit became an unwieldy organization. Due to the collapse of the American Association following the 1891 season, no World Series was played that year. The following year, the National League's monopoly did not offer a natural postseason formula. Twelve teams in a single, undivided league also meant that too many clubs finished in the second division. As teams fell out of the running in the twelve-team league, fan interest dwindled. League stability was in question.

In an attempt to rectify both of these problems, in 1892 the National League experimented with a split season. The season began in April, and on July 13 the first half of the baseball season ended. The team in first place at that time earned a playoff berth. After a one-day break, the season resumed on July 15, and each club started fresh with a clean record. When the season ended in October, the club that compiled the best record in the second half also earned a playoff spot. Because the season was divided into two halves, starting anew in the second half, clubs that were hopelessly out of the pennant race in June found themselves back in the running in July.

The Boston Beaneaters, who also compiled the best combined record in 1892, finished in first place during the first half of the season, while the Cleveland Spiders finished in first in the second half. The two met in a best-of-nine championship series at the end of the season. After eleven innings, the first game ended in a scoreless tie. Boston, however, swept Cleveland in the next five games, giving the Beaneaters the league championship.

Because the 1892 split season seemed unsatisfying, the following year the twelve clubs in the National League played an uninterrupted schedule. Boston won the 1893 National League pennant, compiling the league's best record—with eighty-six wins and forty-three losses—and finishing a full five games ahead of the Pittsburgh Pirates. In 1894 the National League adopted a new postseason playoff format in which the first-place and second-place clubs played a seven-game series for a trophy called the Temple Cup. The cup was the gift of William Chase Temple, a co-owner of the Pirates.

The Temple Cup series did not prove to be very popular. For pennant-winning clubs, playing the runner-up in a postseason series was a letdown, and the fact that three of the four winners of the cup were second-place teams seemed to devalue the regular season. Every series was also a blowout, with the losing team winning no more than one game. After 1897 the National League discontinued the Temple Cup series. In 1900 the Pittsburgh Pirates, which never had the opportunity to compete for William Chase Temple's cup, finished the season in second place, and Pittsburghers, anxious to see their club in postseason play, sought to revive the series. The *Pittsburgh Chronicle-Telegraph* newspaper donated a new trophy, the *Chronicle-Telegraph* Cup, and invited the National League pennant-winning Brooklyn club to play the Pirates in a best-of-five game series. Brooklyn accepted, and went on to defeat Pittsburgh three games to one. Few baseball fans outside of Pittsburgh or Brooklyn seemed to care. The series was never played again.

Cheating was another problem that plagued baseball in the 1890s, and the National League's Baltimore Orioles were especially notorious. In the 1890s the Orioles, managed by future Hall of Fame manager Ned Hanlon, were a very good team. In addition to Hanlon, Baltimore boasted six regular players who would eventually be inducted into the National Baseball Hall of Fame: catcher Wilbert Robinson, first baseman Dan Brouthers, shortstop Hughie Jennings, third baseman John McGraw, right fielder William "Wee Willie" Keeler, and left fielder Joe Kelley. The Orioles, however, relied on more than just skill. Exploiting the fact that the National League used only one umpire in the 1890s, Orioles base runners often skipped second base and ran directly from first to third. Third baseman John McGraw developed a unique way to prevent opposing base runners from tagging up and scoring: If a runner was on third with fewer than two outs and the batter hit a fly ball to the outfield, McGraw would stick his finger in the base runner's belt; the snag produced a momentary delay that prevented the runner from beating the throw home. One day in 1893, in a game against Baltimore, Louisville Colonels' outfielder Pete Browning reached third base. A victim of McGraw's finger in the past, Browning was prepared. Upon arriving at third, Browning discreetly unbuckled his belt. With the next fly ball, McGraw was left standing at third with Browning's belt in his hand, while the Louisville slugger raced home holding up his trousers.

Despite the humor in the Browning episode, such cheating spoke to a need for reform through an established set of rules and practices. That the Baltimore grounds crew also helped give the Orioles an advantage showed another reason for fairness and standardization, a hallmark of progressivism. The grounds crew mixed the dirt around home plate with clay, making it as hard as concrete. Orioles players would swing down at the ball, causing it to strike the ground in front of home. Because the dirt was hard, the ball would bounce high into the air, and by the time the ball came down, the batter was well on his way to first base. (Today, a batted ball that takes a high bounce in front of home plate is known as a "Baltimore chop.") As the Orioles often relied on bunts to reach base and advance runners, the grounds crew tilted the foul lines so that a bunted ball rolled fair. The grounds crew also allowed the grass in the Baltimore outfield to grow unusually high so Orioles players could hide extra baseballs. When a batter hit a fly ball over an outfielder's head, the lone umpire would watch the base runners. With the umpire looking elsewhere, an outfielder could retrieve one of the hidden balls and throw it into the infield before the base runners advanced too far.

The biggest problem facing baseball in the 1890s, however, was "syndicate baseball," a situation in which the same owner (or group of owners) possessed more than one baseball team. This problem, which lay at the heart of monopoly practices, emerged as early as the 1880s, when John B. Day owned both the New York Giants of the National League and the New York Metropolitans of the American Association. Day discovered that the Giants were more popular than the Mets in New York, so he began transferring his best players to the National League team, which had a higher ticket price. But at least the Giants and the Metropolitans were in different leagues.

With the Giants facing a financial drain created by competition with the Players' League, Cincinnati Reds owner John Brush, Chicago White Stockings owner Albert Spalding, and Boston Beaneaters owner Arthur Soden helped Day's club remain solvent by purchasing shares of the Giants. By the end of the decade, syndicate baseball became a serious problem within the National League. Baltimore Orioles owner Harry Von der Horst also owned a piece of the Brooklyn Bridegrooms. Barney Dreyfuss, the owner of the Louisville Colonels, took over control of the Pittsburgh Pirates. Before the start of the 1899 season, Cleveland Spiders owner Frank Robison purchased the St. Louis Browns from Chris von der Ahe and renamed the team the St. Louis Perfectos. These owners practiced a form of interlocking directorates that typified monopolies in other industries to preserve their domination and profits.

As had happened with the Giants and Mets in the 1880s, these owners transferred their best players to their more popular team. In 1899 Orioles manager Ned Hanlon took over as the skipper of the Brooklyn club. With the arrival of Hanlon, the Bridegrooms became known as the Brooklyn Superbas, after a popular vaudeville acrobatic troupe called Hanlon's Superbas. In addition to Hanlon, the Orioles also transferred several key players to Brooklyn, including future Hall of Famers Wee Willie Keeler, Joe Kelley, and Hughie Jennings. In 1899 the Cleveland Spiders sent almost their entire roster, including ace pitcher Cy Young, to the Perfectos. Left with major league rejects and career minor leaguers, the 1899 Cleveland Spiders became the worst major league team in history, winning only 20 contests in a 154-game season. At the conclusion of the 1899 season, the Louisville Colonels transferred shortstop Honus Wagner and future Hall of Fame pitchers Jack Chesbro and Rube Waddell to its sister team, the Pittsburgh Pirates.

After the 1899 season, the National League, recognizing that twelve teams were too many, decided to contract to eight clubs. A year earlier, Brooklyn, along with the boroughs of the Bronx, Queens, and Staten Island, had become a part of New York City; as New York already had the Giants, which played in Manhattan, some Superbas fans feared that Brooklyn would be one of the four clubs dropped from the league. But Brooklyn fans need not have worried. If it had not merged with New York, Brooklyn would still have been the fourth-largest city in the country. The National League chose to keep the team that would eventually be known as the Dodgers. Instead the National League dropped three of the clubs that were owned by multiteam syndicates: the Baltimore Orioles, the Cleveland Spiders, and the Louisville Colonels. The National League also dropped the Washington Senators, a team that had never finished higher than sixth place during its eight years in the league.

The contraction of the National League left four large population centers without a major league team, while many former major league players were suddenly out of work. Western League president Ban Johnson recognized the opportunity to create a second major league. Johnson was "Baseball's Teddy Roosevelt"; not only did he break the National League's monopoly, but, like Roosevelt, he had a strong personality. Johnson was vain, arrogant, and humorless, and he constantly sought publicity. He reacted to the changes in baseball by immediately transferring the Western League's Grand Rapids team to Cleveland, one of the cities abandoned by the National League. He also allowed his friend Charles Comiskey to move the St. Paul Saints to Chicago. In Chicago, Comiskey's White Sox competed directly against the Chicago Orphans, which is what the city's National League team was called after Cap Anson retired in 1897. Prior to the start of the 1900 season, Johnson renamed his organization the American League. Although the league featured teams in Buffalo, Chicago, Cleveland, Detroit, Indianapolis, Kansas City, Milwaukee, and Minneapolis, Johnson's league was technically still a minor league. It honored the National Agreement and continued to recognize the National League's reserve list, but, having dropped its regional name and operating in eight major cities, the American League looked and felt like a major league in 1900.

On January 28, 1901, Johnson announced that the American League would operate as a major league in the upcoming season. Johnson pulled

the American League out of the National Agreement and stopped recognizing the National League's reserve clause. Johnson also strengthened
the American League's image by placing four franchises in East Coast
cities, replacing the American League clubs in Buffalo, Indianapolis,
Kansas City, and Minneapolis with teams in Boston, Philadelphia, Baltimore, and Washington. In addition to Charles Comiskey in Chicago,
Johnson brought in veteran baseball mind Cornelius McGillicuddy, better known as Connie Mack, to operate the franchise in Philadelphia. As
he had in the Western League, Johnson kept the American League on a
tight leash, imposing strict discipline and backing up umpires when they
were challenged by players or managers.

The two leagues competed for fans in three cities—Boston, Chicago,
and Philadelphia—and they competed for players all over the country.
The American League not only recruited former major league players
who were out of work because of the National League's contraction, but,
because it did not recognize the National League's reserve clause, it also
sought stars from the senior circuit. When the American League opened
in 1901, 111 of the 182 players on American League rosters were former
National Leaguers.

Attracting established players to the American League was easy
because of the National League's $2,400 salary cap. When the Ameri-
can League's Philadelphia Athletics lured second baseman Napoleon
Lajoie away from the Phillies, the National League team sued. Johnson,
not wanting to lose Lajoie, arranged for the A's to trade the second baseman to Cleveland, out of the jurisdiction of the Pennsylvania courts. Cy

Table 5.1. The Evolution from the Western League into the American League, 1899–1901

Western League 1899 (minor league)	American League 1900 (minor league)	American League 1901 (major league)
Buffalo Bisons	Buffalo Bisons	Boston Invaders
Detroit Tigers	Detroit Tigers	Detroit Tigers
Grand Rapids Rustlers	Cleveland Bluebirds	Cleveland Blues
Indianapolis Indians	Indianapolis Hoosiers	Philadelphia Athletics
Kansas City Blues	Kansas City Blues	Washington Senators
Milwaukee Brewers	Milwaukee Brewers	Milwaukee Brewers
Minneapolis Millers	Minneapolis Millers	Baltimore Orioles
St. Paul Saints	Chicago White Stockings	Chicago White Sox

Young jumped from the National League's St. Louis team, now called the Cardinals after the scarlet caps and stockings the club adopted in 1900, to the American League's Boston club. John McGraw, who was also with the Cardinals in 1900, signed on to become the manager of the American League's new entry in Baltimore, where McGraw had flourished playing third base during the previous decade. In 1901 the American League attracted more fans than the National League, and in each of the three cities that had teams in each league—Boston, Chicago, and Philadelphia—the American League club outdrew its National League rival.

Despite its success, the American League suffered from growing pains. After the 1901 season, the last-place Milwaukee Brewers, which had attracted fewer than two thousand fans per game, moved to St. Louis and adopted that city's traditional baseball name, the St. Louis Browns. John McGraw's quick temper created a thornier problem in Baltimore. In 1902, after disciplining the Orioles' manager several times for conflicts with umpires, Johnson suspended McGraw indefinitely. While on suspension, McGraw, livid at not being able to work, secretly signed on to become the manager of the National League's New York Giants, a position he would hold until 1932. Before leaving the Orioles, McGraw released many of the Baltimore players from their contracts, and when McGraw left for New York, he took many of his players with him. With McGraw and many other players gone, Baltimore did not have enough players for its July 17 game against the St. Louis Browns. Johnson revoked the franchise and assigned the ownership of the club to the American League. He arranged for the other seven American League clubs to send enough players to Baltimore to allow the Orioles to limp through the rest of the season. But he also saw an opportunity for his circuit to establish a team in the baseball hotbed of New York City. When the 1902 season ended, Johnson sold the Orioles to a pair of New Yorkers, who transferred the club to upper Manhattan and renamed it the New York Highlanders. By 1913 the team would be known as the New York Yankees.

By 1903 many National League club owners began to realize that they could not afford to continue the hostile relationship between the two leagues. Reform was in order. The National League had lost many players to its rival circuit, and attendance across the league was down.

And now, with the arrival of the New York Highlanders, the National League faced competition in the United States' largest city. The two leagues agreed to negotiate. The National League proposed the same deal it had made with the American Association eleven years earlier: It would expand back to twelve teams by admitting four American League franchises, while the rest of the American League dissolved. Johnson, who was not about to oversee the dismantling of his league, rejected that offer. Instead, the two leagues agreed to coexist. They reached a new National Agreement, similar to the one created by the National League and American Association in 1883. Both leagues agreed to respect each other's reserve clause, ending the competition for players. The American League would be allowed to keep its new franchise in New York but would not be allowed to place a future franchise in Pittsburgh. And Major League Baseball would be governed by a three-person body known as the National Commission. The National Commission—typical of progressivism, which preferred governments managed by apolitical bureaucracies rather than corrupt politicians—comprised the presidents of both leagues and one of the club owners, who would serve as the commission's chairperson. Ban Johnson of the American League and Nicholas Young of the National League joined Garry Hermann, the owner of the Cincinnati Reds, on the commission. Herman remained on the commission until it was dismantled in 1920.

With two major leagues that were no longer hostile to each other, Major League Baseball, as the big leagues would come to be called, could resume postseason play. At the end of the 1903 season, the National League pennant-winning Pittsburgh Pirates met the American League champion Boston club (then known as the Pilgrims or Americans, but now called the Red Sox) in the first modern World Series. The 1903 event was a best-of-nine championship series in which the upstart American League club defeated the National League champion five games to three. Boston repeated as American League champs in 1904, but the World Series did not take place that year. Still angry that the American League had placed a competitor in New York, Giants' manager John McGraw refused to allow his pennant-winning Giants to play Boston. The following year, however, after again leading the Giants to the pennant, McGraw had a change of heart; he not only agreed to play the Phil-

Table 5.2.   The Major Leagues, 1903–1952

American League	National League
Boston Red Sox	Boston Braves
Chicago White Sox	Brooklyn Dodgers
Cleveland Indians	Chicago Cubs
Detroit Tigers	Cincinnati Reds
New York Yankees	New York Giants
Philadelphia Athletics	Philadelphia Phillies
St. Louis Browns	Pittsburgh Pirates
Washington Senators	St. Louis Cardinals

Note: Most team nicknames were not official in 1903. See appendix 6 for the dates when each team's nickname was adopted.

adelphia Athletics in the World Series, but also drafted rules making a best-of-seven World Series an annual event.

Not only did the end of hostilities between the National League and the American League break the National League's monopoly on professional baseball, it also brought the order and stability Progressives so desperately craved to Major League Baseball. Starting in 1903, the pennant winner from each league would play in an annual World Series, and Major League Baseball would remain unchanged for the next half century. While it took a few more years for some major league teams to adopt permanent nicknames, from 1903 to 1952 the same sixteen teams, located in the same ten cities in the northeastern quadrant of the United States, constituted the major leagues.

6

Normalcy and the Black Sox Scandal (1904 to 1922)

PROGRESSIVISM PERSISTED UNTIL 1920, but President Wood-row Wilson's reform agenda at home was interrupted by the outbreak of World War I. In April 1917, less than a month after he began his second term, Wilson asked Congress to declare war on Germany, and he used Progressive methods to manage the war. To convert the peacetime economy to one pro-ducing supplies for the war, Wilson created the War Industries Board. He also imposed travel restrictions to prevent precious resources from being wasted on unessential movement, and signed laws that made it illegal to write or utter statements denigrating the flag, the Constitution, or the military. Thousands of pacifists, socialists, and union members were arrested for opposing the war. By the time the war ended in November 1918, the carnage was horrific. The United States lost 110,000 soldiers in battle and another half million to the Spanish influenza. Wilson traveled to France when the war ended to promote his Progressive solution for keeping peace: a list of fourteen demands for the postwar world that included a provision for a League of Nations, an organiza-tion to prevent future wars. At home, though, many Americans—believing it violated the United States' traditional role of neutrality, national sovereignty, and Congress's authority over foreign policy—opposed the League. The Sen-ate refused to ratify the treaty. Wilson took to the road to promote the treaty, but while in Pueblo, Colorado, the president suffered an incapacitating stroke. In 1919 the country suffered a series of crises that rocked the nation. Labor unrest increased as 20 percent of workers went on strike to protest wages that had stagnated due to wartime controls. Racial tensions escalated. Four hun-dred thousand African Americans fought in World War I, and many of them expected improved race relations when they returned home. Instead the num-

ber of lynchings increased in the South. In Chicago a five-day riot broke out in July when African American teenagers in Lake Michigan swam too close to a white-only beach. When the violence ended, twenty-three African Americans and fifteen whites were dead. Americans also experienced an upswing in anticommunist anxiety with the outbreak of the Red Scare, which was fueled by fear over the 1917 Russian Revolution. Racism also drove the Red Scare, as many white Americans accused Communists of stirring up racial unrest in the country. Thirty states and Congress passed laws that either made it a crime to criticize the government or to promote "radical" movements such as communism, socialism, and anarchism. Under the direction of Attorney General A. Mitchell Palmer, the Justice Department arrested more than four thousand people who were accused of being revolutionaries, holding many of them in jail for weeks without charging them with a crime. More than five hundred leftists who were not citizens were deported. Progressivism had ended, and by 1920 Americans sought a "Return to Normalcy" under President Warren Harding, a Republican. Instead he ushered in an era of corruption and troubled morals. In 1920, Prohibition banned the sale and manufacture of alcohol in the United States, which gave rise to bootleggers and organized crime. Scandals also rocked the highest levels of government. A poor judge of character, Harding often appointed associates who sought to personally benefit from their position. One swindled the nation's Veterans' Bureau, while another sold off the country's oil reserves, held for national security purposes, in the infamous Teapot Dome affair. As punishment for this notorious crime, Secretary of the Interior Albert Fall became the first cabinet officer in American history to go to jail. In this tense atmosphere, baseball faced its own scandal—one that nearly destroyed the sport.

On a hot afternoon in Anderson, South Carolina, in 1908, the local minor league baseball team, the Anderson Electricians of the Class-D Carolina Association, hosted a doubleheader against the Greenville Spinners. During the first game, Spinners center fielder Joe Jackson, a twenty-year-old country boy from Pickens County, South Carolina, complained that his brand-new spikes, which he had not yet broken in, were causing blisters to form on his feet. Between games Jackson discarded the shoes and played the second half of the doubleheader in his stocking feet. In the seventh inning of the nightcap, Jackson walloped a triple. As he was pulling into third, an Anderson fan noticed Jackson's feet and shouted out,

"You shoeless sonofagun!" A reporter for the *Greenville News* overheard the comment and immortalized it in his newspaper story. Although he never again played baseball in his socks, the young man forever became known as Shoeless Joe Jackson.

Jackson, who put together a .346 batting average with Greenville, quickly developed into the top player in the Carolina Association. By midsummer he had caught the attention of Connie Mack, the owner and manager of the Philadelphia Athletics, and on August 24 Jackson played his first game for the A's. An unsophisticated and illiterate country boy from rural South Carolina, Jackson had trouble adjusting to cosmopolitan Philadelphia. Twice before the end of the season, he abandoned the team and headed home. For the next two years Jackson bounced back and forth between Philadelphia and the minor leagues. At the end of the 1910 season, the Athletics sold him to Cleveland, and Jackson blossomed in the more tranquil midwestern environment. He hit .387 in 1910, .408 in 1911, and .395 in 1912. Both the Washington Senators and the Chicago White Sox wanted Jackson, and in 1915 Charles Comiskey convinced Cleveland to trade him to the White Sox for three journeymen players and $31,000 in cash. Jackson thrived in Chicago. He led the White Sox to a World Series championship in 1917 and to another American League pennant in 1919, and he put together a .356 lifetime batting average, an accomplishment surpassed only by Ty Cobb and Rogers Hornsby. In 1919, however, Jackson and six of his teammates threw everything away, agreeing to take money from gamblers in exchange for losing the World Series. The episode was the biggest scandal ever to rock baseball, and it instigated major reforms in the game.

The order Ban Johnson had brought to baseball in the first decade of the twentieth century began to unravel in the 1910s and, with the disclosure that the 1919 World Series had been fixed, collapsed completely by 1920. Progressivism also broke down in that decade. With the outbreak of World War I, the United States entered a period of uncertainty in the mid-1910s, which devolved into turmoil when the war ended. The Black Sox Scandal, as the 1919 World Series fix was called, occurred at that low point.

With the stability brought by the establishment of the National Commission, the game had grown in popularity in the first two decades of the twentieth century. The annual World Series captured the public's attention. During the early years of the century, baseball was played during the day, and without radio or television to relay the news of the game, baseball fans would gather in public places, usually outside of newspaper offices, to follow the World Series. Newspapers set up large boards, visible from the street, that featured pictures of baseball diamonds and images of base runners. As the out-of-town results were telegraphed to the newspaper, the images of base runners were advanced or removed from the diamond to indicate what was happening in the game hundreds of miles away.

Baseball players enjoyed unparalleled popularity in the early twentieth century. Stars like Detroit Tigers center fielder Ty Cobb, Boston Red Sox center fielder Tris Speaker, Pittsburgh Pirates shortstop Honus Wagner, and New York Giants starting pitcher Christy Mathewson became household names.

The Chicago Cubs, as the National League entry in America's second-largest city was now called, dominated the first decade of the twentieth century. Led by its star-studded infield—which featured Frank Chance at first base, Johnny Evers at second base, Joe Tinker at shortstop, and Harry Steinfeldt at third—the Cubs won four pennants between 1906 and 1910. The most exciting pennant race of the era took place in 1908. On September 23, with about two weeks left in the season and the Cubs and Giants locked in a virtual tie for first place, Chicago and New York convened at the Polo Grounds for the third game of a four-game series. With the game tied 1–1 with two outs in the bottom of the ninth inning, the Giants had runners on the corners: Moose McCormick at third and Fred Merkle at first. Giants shortstop Al Bridwell hit a single to center field, which scored McCormick. Merkle, who was running from first to second, saw McCormick cross the plate and assumed the game was over. Before arriving at second, Merkle turned and ran for the dugout, which was common practice at the time when the winning run scored in the bottom of the ninth inning. Recognizing that the game was not yet over, Cubs second baseman Johnny Evers, who spent his spare time reading and rereading the baseball rule book, called for the ball. After a delay of several minutes, Evers received the ball and stepped on second. Then Evers pointed out to umpire Hank O'Day that McCormick's run did not count because the third out of the inning had been a force out. After some thought, O'Day acknowledged that Evers's understanding of the rules was correct. He declared the inning over and the score still tied at one run apiece. Because it was getting dark—and because the New York faithful, believing the Giants had won, had stormed the field—O'Day called the game a one-run, nine-inning tie. If necessary, the game would have to be replayed at the end of the season.

The season ended on October 7, with New York and Chicago possessing identical 98–55 records. The two teams again took the field at the Polo Grounds on October 8 for what was essentially baseball's first tie-breaking play-in game, but in reality was a regular season makeup game. This time the Cubs won, 4–2. Chicago went on to defeat the Detroit Tigers, four games to one, in the 1908 World Series. It would be 108 years before the Cubs would win another World Series.

The Cubs won the National League pennant again in 1910, only to lose the World Series to Connie Mack's Philadelphia Athletics. Mack, who would own the A's during the team's entire fifty-four-year tenure in Philadelphia and would manage the team during its first fifty years, was establishing a new dynasty in Philadelphia. Between 1910 and 1914, the Athletics won four American League pennants and three World Series championships. The Athletics lost the 1914 World Series to the Boston Braves. Boston had been in last place in the National League on July 4, but in the second half of the season, the "Miracle Braves" got hot. Boston leapfrogged the rest of the National League, finishing the season in first place. In the World Series that fall, Boston defeated Philadelphia in four games, becoming the first team ever to sweep a World Series. After its 1914 World Championship, the Braves returned to mediocrity. New England fans, however, still had a reason to cheer, as the Boston Red Sox dominated baseball during the rest of the decade, winning the 1915, 1916, and 1918 World Series.

As the popularity of baseball soared, the first real stadiums appeared. In the nineteenth century, ballparks made with wooden grandstands were always in danger of being destroyed by fire. The new twentieth-century stadiums, made of steel and concrete, were fireproof. Starting with Forbes Field in Pittsburgh, twelve major league clubs constructed new stadiums between 1909 and 1915.

Baseball was so lucrative in the early twentieth century that its success undermined its stability. In 1913 a new six-team minor league, called the Federal League, emerged. Following the end of the season, a wealthy Chicago coal dealer named James A. Gilmore took control of the league

Table 6.1.   Major League Stadiums Built between 1909 and 1915

Stadium	City	Team	Year Built
Forbes Field	Pittsburgh	Pirates	1909
Shibe Park	Philadelphia	Athletics	1909
Sportsman's Park	St. Louis	Browns	1909
White Sox Park (Comiskey Park)	Chicago	White Sox	1910
National Park (Griffith Stadium)	Washington	Senators	1911
Polo Grounds	New York	Giants	1911
Redland Field (Crosley Field)	Cincinnati	Reds	1912
Fenway Park	Boston	Red Sox	1912
Navin Field (Tiger Stadium)	Detroit	Tigers	1912
Ebbets Field	Brooklyn	Dodgers	1913
Weeghman Park (Wrigley Field)*	Chicago	Whales (FL)	1914
Braves Field	Boston	Braves	1915

* The Chicago Cubs moved into Weeghman Park in 1916.

and attempted to turn it into a major league. Gilmore recruited wealthy businessmen to own Federal League clubs. Ignoring the reserve clause, the Federal League attempted to sign major league players. The existing major league teams retained most of their players, but had to offer generous salary increases to do so. Still, the Federal League managed to lure a few major leaguers, including Joe Tinker, who became the player-manager of the Chicago club, and Mordecai Brown, who became the player-manager of the St. Louis club. As a self-proclaimed major league circuit, the Federal League operated in 1914 with eight clubs: four in cities that had American or National League teams—Brooklyn, Chicago, Pittsburgh, and St. Louis—and four in top-level minor league cities—Baltimore, Buffalo, Indianapolis, and Kansas City. Competition was especially stiff in Chicago and St. Louis, which boasted clubs in all three leagues.

Unlike the Union Association of 1884 or the Players' League of 1890, the Federal League did not disband at the end of the season. Instead the league entered the 1915 season with one change. Although Indianapolis had won the 1914 Federal League pennant, Harry Sinclair, an Oklahoma oilman later implicated in the Teapot Dome scandal, moved the team to Newark, New Jersey, in order to tap into the lucrative Manhattan market on the other side of the Hudson. Suffering financial losses, clubs in all three leagues cut ticket prices; a few Federal League teams admitted fans for as little as a dime. In January 1915 the Federal League filed a lawsuit accusing the major leagues of violating the Sherman Antitrust Act. The judge in charge of the case, Kenesaw Mountain Landis, had a history of ruling against monopolies. But Landis, an avid baseball fan and supporter of the Chicago Cubs, allowed the case to languish on the docket while the Federal League slowly bled to death. When the 1915 season ended, the Kansas City club, unable to pay its debts, went out of business. The rest of the Federal League entered negotiations with the major leagues. The American League allowed Phil Ball, the owner of the Federal League's St. Louis team, to purchase the Browns, while the National League allowed Chicago Whales owner Charles Weeghman to buy the Cubs. Weeghman moved the Cubs into Weeghman Park, the ballpark he built for the Chi-Feds. Renamed Wrigley Field in 1927, it remains one of the oldest major league ballparks; the Cubs still play there today. Major League Baseball offered a $600,000 settlement to the other Federal League clubs. Angry at being denied the opportunity to purchase the St. Louis Cardinals and move them to Maryland, the owners of the Federal League's Baltimore Terrapins rejected the offer. Instead they filed their own antitrust lawsuit, which would eventually reach the Supreme Court in 1922.

The Federal League's corpse was hardly cold when baseball encountered a new challenge. In April 1917 America had been drawn into World War I. Major league owners recognized their dilemma: The entire country had been put on wartime footing, and baseball seemed frivolous. Major League Baseball attempted to gain goodwill in wartime by selling war bonds. It also staged exhibition games, with the money going to the war effort. Such games were often played on Sundays. Although many

Table 6.2.   The Federal League, 1914–1915

Federal League in 1914	Federal League in 1915
Baltimore Terrapins	Baltimore Terrapins
Brooklyn Tip-Tops	Brooklyn Tip-Tops
Buffalo Blues	Buffalo Blues
Chicago Whales	Chicago Whales
Indianapolis Hoosiers	Newark Peppers
Kansas City Packers	Kansas City Packers
Pittsburgh Rebels	Pittsburgh Rebels
St. Louis Terriers	St. Louis Terriers

states prohibited professional baseball games on the Sabbath, benefit games were exempt from the restriction. Major League Baseball hoped that if fans became accustomed to attending ball games on Sundays, the restriction might be lifted when the war was over. To boost morale, many baseball clubs had their players conduct military drills before games, but the ballplayers looked silly marching in baseball uniforms and carrying their bats as if they were guns. The Brooklyn Dodgers, realizing how ridiculous this looked, refused to do it.

Many major leaguers served in the war. In October 1918, former Giants' third baseman Eddie Grant became the first major league player to die in the war; he was killed in the Argonne Forest in France. In 1921 the Giants erected a monument in Grant's honor in deep center field at the Polo Grounds. Giants pitcher Christy Mathewson, a member of the army's Chemical Warfare Service, also became a casualty of the war. During training, Mathewson became exposed to poison gas and, with his respiratory system weakened, developed a fatal case of tuberculosis.

Pressure mounted on baseball to shut down. In May 1918 General Enoch Crowder, the head of the Selective Service System, issued a "work or fight" order, which required men not serving in the military to work in the defense industry. Following the edict, club owners decided to end the season on September 1, a month early. The World Series opened on September 5 in Chicago, with the Cubs hosting the Red Sox. When Boston won the series six days later, no one knew if baseball would return the following year.

The war ended in November, and as the 1919 season approached, club owners expected good things. Baseball again had the full attention of the country, and club owners intended to milk it for all it was worth. On September 2, with a month left in the season, the National Commission decided to extend the World Series to a best-of-nine format. Few thought the Cincinnati Reds, who had won their first National League pennant, had a chance in the Fall Classic. The Reds appeared to be over-matched by the American League pennant–winning Chicago White Sox. The White Sox included two future Hall of Famers on their roster: third baseman Eddie Collins and catcher Ray Schalk. The team also boasted Shoeless Joe Jackson, the player with the third-highest lifetime batting average, and the Sox's pitching staff featured two twenty-game winners: Eddie Cicotte, who won twenty-nine games while only losing seven, and

Lefty Williams, who finished the season with twenty-three wins and eleven losses.

Although they were a very good team, however, the White Sox had a very tightfisted owner. Charles Comiskey paid his ballplayers less than the players on other teams: For instance, the Reds' leading hitter, Edd Roush, made $10,000, compared to Jackson's $6,000, even though the Chicago right fielder's batting average was consistently 30 to 40 points higher. Comiskey also skimped on meal money—giving his players a $3-per-day meal allotment when most clubs allowed $4—and on laundry bills. Some historians have even speculated that infrequent washing of the team's uniforms led to the moniker Black Sox being attached to the club.

Fed up with the substandard pay, late in the summer of 1919, first baseman Chick Gandil devised a plan to make extra money from gamblers. As the White Sox would be a heavy favorite to win the World Series, Gandil realized the players could make a considerable amount of money if gamblers paid them to lose; he wanted gamblers to pay $10,000 per participating player. In order for Gandil's plan to work, he needed the team's two best starting pitchers, Cicotte and Williams, to go along with the scheme. He also needed to recruit Jackson, Chicago's best hitter. Gandil also persuaded center fielder Happy Felsch and shortstop Swede Risberg to participate. One other player, a utility infielder named Fred McMullin, who was unlikely to even play in the series, was cut into the deal because he learned of the conspiracy and threatened to expose the plan if he was not included. An eighth player, third baseman Buck Weaver, was not among the players in on the scam, but he was a close friend to many of them and was in the room when the deal was being made.

Gandil made contact with gamblers while the White Sox were in New York to play the Yankees. A major New York gambler named Arnold Rothstein agreed to fund the fix, but he remained in the background to avoid being traced to the scandal. All communication and money was handled by small-time gamblers from New York, Boston, Philadelphia, and Texas. The gamblers gave the players $10,000 before the first game. The money went to Cicotte, who would pitch Game 1. Before the series even started, rumors circulated that the games were fixed. No one wanted to believe the gossip, especially Comiskey, and the gamblers involved were especially upset by the rumors, because the buzz lowered the odds.

The White Sox lost the first two games of the series, but rather than pass the rest of the money along to the team, the small-time gamblers used it to make their own bets on Cincinnati. As Cicotte was the only player to be paid, the other White Sox players in on the fix felt betrayed. Not surprisingly, Chicago won Game 3, angering the small-time gamblers who had bet on the Reds. Fearing he might have a rebellion on his hands, one of the gamblers behind the fix raised an additional $20,000 for the players, and when Cincinnati won the fourth game, the money was given to Gandil, who gave $5,000 a piece to Jackson, Risberg, Felsch, and Williams.

Williams started—and lost—Game 5, putting the Reds one win away from the World Championship. With their backs to the wall, however, the White Sox won Games 6 and 7, pulling within one game of Cincin-

The 1919 Chicago White Stockings. The "Black Sox"—Top Row: Shoeless Joe Jackson (far left), Chick Gandil (second from left), Fred McMullin (third from left). Middle Row: Happy Felsch (third from left), Buck Weaver (far right). Bottom Row: Swede Risberg (second from left), Lefty Williams (second from right), Eddie Cicotte (far right). National Baseball Hall of Fame and Museum. Cooperstown, N.Y.

nati. Chicago manager Kid Gleason tapped Williams to start the eighth game. After the scandal broke, reports would circulate that gamblers, fearing a Chicago comeback, sent a thug to threaten Williams at his home the evening before Game 8. These reports, however, were apparently false. Nonetheless, Williams was ineffective, giving up four runs in just the first inning. Cincinnati won the game 10–5, and with it, the World Series.

Rumors swirled all winter long that the World Series had been fixed, and accusations continued during the 1920 season. In September, while the White Sox were locked in a pennant race with the Cleveland Indians, a grand jury convened to look into the allegations. On September 28, Cicotte admitted to the grand jury that he took money to lose the series. Jackson offered a similar confession. Baseball lore maintains that as Jackson was leaving the courthouse, a heartbroken young boy begged the right fielder, "Say it ain't so, Joe," to which Jackson replied, "I'm afraid it is, kid." Although the exchange appeared in newspaper reports, the story is probably apocryphal, made up by a reporter for dramatic effect. The grand jury indicted the seven ballplayers involved, plus Buck Weaver, but when the case went to trial, their signed confessions—the only evidence against the Black Sox—turned up missing. Without the evidence, all eight players were acquitted of the charges.

The Black Sox Scandal generated tremendous fallout. Baseball had encountered allegations of fixed games in the past, but this was the World Series, the nation's most prestigious sporting event. Major League Baseball's reputation had been tainted. The scandal also ended the often rocky, nearly thirty-year-long friendship between Charles Comiskey and Ban Johnson who blamed each other for how the scandal was handled.

With the aftermath of the scandal threatening to destroy baseball, Albert Lasker, a co-owner of the Chicago Cubs, proposed the creation of a Commissioner of Baseball, a position that would be given sweeping powers over the leagues, to be held by someone who did not have a financial interest in any club. Lasker believed the public would view the commissioner as impartial; therefore, he believed, a commissioner could restore the public's faith in the game. Ban Johnson opposed the idea because the establishment of a commissioner would take power from the American League president. Besides, Johnson would have preferred to see Comiskey take the fall for the scandal. Five American League clubs—Cleveland, Detroit, Philadelphia, St. Louis, and Washington—supported

Johnson's position. The National League, not wanting to see its reputation destroyed because of Johnson's stubbornness, threatened to invite the Boston Red Sox, Chicago White Sox, and New York Yankees into its circuit, and to create its own commissioner for the expanded league. Faced with the possibility of abandonment by the National League, Johnson relented and accepted the establishment of a commissioner.

To fill the position, Major League Baseball selected federal judge Kenesaw Mountain Landis, who, not uncoincidentally, had earlier let the Federal League's antitrust lawsuit linger on his docket until the league, drained of its resources, collapsed. Because club owners were desperate to restore the public's confidence, they gave Landis unlimited power to act "in the best interest of baseball." Baseball's move was quickly copied by Hollywood. In the wake of the 1921–1922 Roscoe "Fatty" Arbuckle scandal, in which the silent film star was accused of raping and murdering starlet Virginia Rappe, the motion picture industry installed former postmaster general William H. Hays as the president of the newly cre-

Judge Kenesaw Mountain
Landis, the first
Commissioner of Baseball.
The Library of Congress
Online Photo Archive

ated Motion Picture Producers and Distributors of America and gave him broad powers to censor Hollywood's films in order to improve the industry's image.

Landis, a tyrant at heart who ranked as one of the most arbitrary judges ever to sit on the federal bench, responded quickly to the Black Sox Scandal. Because the players implicated in the scandal were found not guilty, they all expected to return to baseball in 1921. Landis, however, issued lifetime bans on the seven players implicated in the scandal; he also banned Buck Weaver for not reporting the conspiracy. Landis extended his ban to any other baseball player who might play in a game with any of the Black Sox; thus, the banned players would never find a spot on a minor league team, a semipro team, or even an amateur team, as their presence in a game would immediately disqualify all the other participants from ever playing in Major League Baseball.

The Federal League and the First World War undermined baseball's stability. As with other members of society, greed tempted ballplayers. In the post–World War I era, the same forces that touched off corruption in barrooms, Hollywood, and Washington, DC, caused baseball to sink into scandal. Kenesaw Mountain Landis was given enormous power to restore the public's trust in his industry. His power grew further in 1922, when the antitrust lawsuit filed by the Baltimore Terrapins following the collapse of the Federal League finally reached the Supreme Court. In the case of *Federal Baseball Club v. National League*, the court, in a decision written by Justice Oliver Wendell Holmes, ruled that baseball was not interstate commerce and was therefore not subject to the Sherman Antitrust Act. Essentially, the court held that baseball was a sport, not a business, a ruling that broadly expanded Landis's power. Even today, Major League Baseball is the only sports league exempt from antitrust laws; the National Football League, National Basketball Association, and National Hockey League do not enjoy the same privilege. And, largely as a result of its harrowing experience in the Black Sox Scandal, baseball continues to fixate on gambling: In 1989 Major League Baseball imposed a lifetime ban on Pete Rose, the sport's all-time hits leader, for gambling on the sport.

7

Babe Ruth and the Roaring Twenties (1920 to 1929)

THE 1920 CENSUS WAS THE FIRST that indicated a majority of Americans were living in urban areas. Americans began to believe that they were living in a new era that was different from the Gilded Age of their parents or grandparents—they believed that they were living in "modern times." Capitalizing on this sense of progress, America entered nearly a decade of prosperity. Calvin Coolidge, who became president when Warren Harding died in 1923, summed up the decade by proclaiming that "the business of America is business." Coolidge's statement described the policy of his administration. Unlike the Progressives, who attempted to regulate society, the Coolidge administration tried to stay out of the way of business. The prosperity enjoyed by Americans in the 1920s created a consumer society, as innovative products—such as the radio, new automobile models like the Ford Model A, and new forms of financing such as the installment plan—appeared. Out of the prosperity of the decade, an entirely new culture emerged and flourished. The twenties were a period of indulgence. Americans still drank in spite of Prohibition, and many people abandoned Victorian sexual mores. The twenties also saw the emergence of jazz music, a fusion of two different genres of African American music: soulful blues and rhythmic ragtime. At parties, dancing replaced card games and charades. The 1920s were also the Golden Age of Hollywood, as movies became a very popular and influential form of entertainment. Celebrities captured the public's attention. The best known was Charles Lindbergh, who in 1927 became the first person to fly alone from New York to Paris, but movie stars and sports heroes also became a national obsession. American women also took on new roles. In 1920 the Nineteenth Amendment, granting woman suffrage, became a part of the Constitution.

Emboldened, many women adopted new, modern lifestyles and fashions. For some people, however, the transformation caused tremendous anxiety. They were worried that urbanization was destroying small-town values and that immigration and the changing role of women were threatening the domination of white Protestant males. As a result, the Ku Klux Klan, which targeted blacks, Jews, Catholics, foreigners, and women who refused to be bound by traditional roles, grew to three million members during the 1920s. Evangelicals, who opposed the social liberalism of the era as well as the teaching of evolution, tried to stem the tide of modernity and excess. In baseball, one player came to symbolize the impact of modernism on America.

In October 1926 an eleven-year-old New Jersey boy named Johnny Sylvester was recovering at home from osteomyelitis, a bone infection he contracted after being kicked in the head by a horse. His father sent a telegram to New York Yankees star Babe Ruth, who was in St. Louis for the World Series between the Yankees and the Cardinals. Sylvester's father was hoping that Ruth might lift his son's spirits by sending him an autographed baseball. A few days later, an airmail package arrived containing two baseballs—one autographed by the members of the Cardinals and the other signed by the Yankees. The package also contained a note from Ruth that said, "I'll knock a homer for you on Wednesday." Keeping his promise, Ruth hit three home runs in Game 4, which was played on Wednesday, October 6. The press learned about the incident and quickly reported it—except the newspapers included all sorts of fictional details. According to the papers, Sylvester was bedridden in a hospital and dying from a variety of diseases, including blood poisoning, a spinal infection, and a sinus condition. One report stated that his doctor gave him only thirty minutes to live. In every account, Ruth's home run miraculously saved little Johnny's life. The nation's fascination with Sylvester's recovery demonstrated the power of Ruth's reputation in the mid-1920s.

Baseball rebounded from the Black Sox Scandal and became more popular than ever, but not just because a commissioner restored the public's faith in the game. Baseball also revived because of a player named George Herman "Babe" Ruth. In the 1920s, Ruth, sometimes called the "Bambino" or the "Sultan of Swat," was more than a baseball star; he was an icon. And the celebrity-obsessed press of the twenties, in which

In the wake of the Black Sox Scandal, Yankees' slugger Babe Ruth restored the public's confidence in baseball. The Library of Congress Online Photo Archive

the media sought out heroes in sports as in other walks of life, followed everything he did. Brash, bold, and confident, Babe Ruth personified the decade Americans called the Roaring Twenties.

Baseball also entered modern times in the 1920s. Baseball writers have labeled the first two decades of the twentieth century the dead-ball era because baseball games played during that period were often low-scoring affairs that relied on speed and defense. Stars like Ty Cobb—who, with a .367 career batting average, still holds the highest lifetime batting average in history—bunted to get on base and then exploited the sacrifice, the stolen base, and the hit-and-run to advance around the bases. In the 1920s the larger-than-life Babe Ruth, with his powerful home runs, changed the game, and the excitement generated by Ruth's home runs lured back disaffected fans who had become disillusioned with baseball in the wake of the Black Sox Scandal.

Ruth was born in Baltimore in 1895. His mother died when he was young, and when he was seven, his father sent him to live in an orphanage called St. Mary's Industrial School for Boys. It was at St. Mary's that Ruth learned to play baseball. He was good enough to play for the Baltimore Orioles of the International League in 1914. Because of competition from the Federal League's Baltimore Terrapins, the minor league Orioles were losing money. In July, desperate for cash, Orioles owner Jack Dunn sold Ruth to the Boston Red Sox for $25,000. Ruth broke into the Red Sox starting rotation during spring training in 1915. He quickly proved himself to be one of the best pitchers on the team, which won the World Series in 1915, 1916, and 1918. As a pitcher, Ruth compiled a lifetime record of ninety-four wins and forty-six losses, for a remarkable .671 winning percentage. Ruth won eighteen games in 1915, twenty-three games in 1916, twenty-four games in 1917, and thirteen games in the war-shortened 1918 season. In 1916 Ruth led the American League with a 1.75 earned run average.

When Ruth played for Boston, the Red Sox discovered he could also swing the bat. Boston manager Ed Barrow started playing Ruth in the outfield on days he was not scheduled to pitch, and by 1918 the Red Sox were using Ruth more as an outfielder than as a pitcher. The following season, Ruth hit twenty-nine home runs, breaking the old major league record set by Ned Williamson of the Chicago White Stockings in 1884. Williamson had hit twenty-five of his twenty-seven homers in Chicago's tiny Lakeside Park. In 1919 Ruth knocked the ball over the wall in every ballpark in the American League.

Harry Frazee, the owner of the Red Sox, often found himself in financial trouble. In addition to owning a baseball team, Frazee was also a Broadway producer, and his plays almost always lost money. Whenever he found himself in a financial jam, he would extricate himself by selling a member of the Red Sox to another team. In 1920, again facing financial difficulty, Frazee sold Ruth to the New York Yankees for $200,000. Yankees owner Jacob Ruppert agreed to buy the star for $125,000 in cash, with an additional $75,000, plus interest, to be paid in three increments spread over nine years. Frazee used the money to finance his latest Broadway production, a play written by Frank Mandel called *My Lady Friends*, which would by 1925 evolve into *No, No, Nanette*. For Frazee and for Yankee fans, the deal was a win-win situation: The Yankees acquired the best player in baseball, while Frazee finally had his hit. For Red Sox fans, however, the trade marked the beginning of the Curse of the Bambino, an eighty-six-year drought during which the Red Sox failed to win a single World Series.

As a Yankee, Babe Ruth became an immediate sensation. He hit fifty-four home runs for New York in 1920. That year, the Yankees set a new major league attendance record, drawing 1,289,422 paying customers and becoming the first major league team to draw more than a million fans in a single season. Starting in 1921, Ruth would lead the Yankees to three straight American League pennants. The Yankees would win a total of seven pennants and four World Series championships before Ruth was sold to the Boston Braves in 1935.

Ruth dominated baseball. In 1921 he set another major league record, hitting 59 home runs. Ruth would go on to hit a total of 714 regular season home runs in his career, a record that would stand until Hank Aaron of the Atlanta Braves hit his 715th home run in 1974. Under modern rules, Ruth may have had even more home runs. When Ruth played, a ball that hit the foul pole was a ground rule double, one that curved foul after clearing the outfield fence was considered foul, and the game ended the moment a walk-off run was scored; as a result, walk-off home runs did not count as home runs unless the run scored by the batter was needed to win the game.

Ruth not only hit for power, he consistently hit for average. In 1924 Ruth led the American League with a .378 batting average. The previous

year, Ruth hit .393, just four hits shy of batting .400. Ruth's lifetime batting average is .342, only two points below the lifetime batting average
of Ted Williams, considered one of the best natural hitters of all time.
Today, players who win a league batting championship often do not
compile a batting average for the season that is as high as Ruth's career
batting average.

    With Ruth playing right field, the Yankees were so popular that Jacob
Ruppert decided to build the team a new stadium. His team had been
sharing the Polo Grounds with the Giants since 1913. In 1923 Ruppert's
club opened Yankee Stadium in the Bronx, directly across the Harlem River from the Polo Grounds. Unlike facilities labeled "parks" or
"grounds," the very name "stadium" evinced a modernist outlook. Often
called "The House that Ruth Built" because it was paid for with money
earned from Ruth's popularity, Yankee Stadium held eighty-two thousand fans when it first opened, making it the largest stadium of its era.
The ballpark was specially designed to take advantage of Ruth's swing.
As a left-handed batter, Ruth naturally hit the ball to right field, so the
stadium was built with a right field wall only forty-three inches high,
placed only 296 feet down the line from home plate. Ruth's salary climbed
during the decade. In 1919, his last year with the Red Sox, Boston paid
him $10,000. The Yankees doubled his salary when the club obtained
him in 1920, and in 1921 the Yankees gave Ruth a $10,000 raise. The
following year his salary rose to $52,000, and by 1927, Ruth was earning
$70,000 a year. Ruth was obviously worth the cost to the Yankees, as they
insured him for $300,000.

    Just as America seemed to be entering modern times in the 1920s, with
Ruth's home runs, so did baseball. Ruth transformed the game. In the
nineteenth century and the first two decades of the twentieth century,
baseball was a scrappy, low-scoring game that centered on speed and
pitching , while baserunners got on base any way they could and then
attempted to advance around the diamond. Ty Cobb, who is arguably
the greatest hitter of all time, excelled at this style of play. With a single swing, a home run could score a run or more if runners are on base.
With the effectiveness of the long ball, however, baseball teams began to
rely on the "big inning," using homers to score runs in bunches. Ever the
traditionalist, Cobb—whose career was ending as Ruth's was peaking—
hated how Ruth and the sluggers who imitated him were changing the

game. Believing there was little challenge in hitting home runs, one day in 1925 Cobb remarked to a reporter, "I'll show you something today. I'm going for home runs for the first time in my career." That afternoon, Cobb hit three homers against the Browns. After making his point, Cobb returned to his old style of play. And although Cobb is still considered one of the greatest players ever to play baseball—he was the highest vote-getter in the first class elected to baseball's Hall of Fame in 1936—the game passed him by.

Babe Ruth's style of play was the most obvious example, but baseball was changing in other ways in the 1920s. Historically, major league batting averages have tended to hover around .260, but from 1920 to 1940, batting averages rose to between .270 and .280. In addition to the strategy adopted by Ruth and others, a couple of other factors contributed to the demise of the dead-ball era. First of all, the baseball itself changed in the twenties. In 1920 the Spalding Sporting Goods Company started using Australian wool, a higher quality yarn, in the manufacture of baseballs. Around the same time, Spalding, like many American companies of the time, adopted automation, using machines to wind the yarn around the baseball's cork center. Baseballs wound by machine were much tighter than baseballs made by hand. Hitters received another break in 1920 when Major League Baseball banned the spitball. The application of saliva, grease, or some other foreign substance to a portion of the ball's surface created wind resistance that altered the ball's flight path. Facing a ball that did not travel smoothly through the air, batters found it hard to predict where the ball would cross the plate. Baseball, however, did not uniformly ban the spitball overnight; pitchers who were already throwing it were allowed to continue to do so until they retired. Burleigh Grimes, who finished his career with the Pittsburgh Pirates in 1934, was the last major league pitcher to legally throw a spitball.

The death of Cleveland Indians shortstop Ray Chapman in 1920 led to changes that further enhanced offensive production. At the Polo Grounds in August, pitcher Carl Mays of the Yankees threw a pitch that struck him in the head. Witness reports that Chapman failed to move out of the way as the pitch sped toward him indicate that he may not have seen the ball coming. Seconds later, with blood pouring out of his ears, Chapman collapsed. He died the following day in a New York hospital; he remains Major League Baseball's only fatality. Following Chapman's death, Major League Baseball adopted a rule requiring umpires to replace the baseball if it becomes dirty or scuffed. Like a spitball, a scuffed ball is susceptible to wind resistance that alters its flight path, and a bright, clean baseball is much easier for a batter to see coming.

With pitches that followed smoother arcs and baseballs that were easier to see, batters found it much easier to make contact with the ball. The machine-made balls also traveled faster and farther when struck by a bat. Major League Baseball embraced these changes, as increased offense made the game more exciting, and a more exciting game attracted more fans to the ballpark. Fans turned out to see the home run hitters. Babe Ruth was the premier slugger of his time, but he was not the only one. In 1930 Hack Wilson of the Chicago Cubs hit fifty-four home runs, while Jimmie Foxx of the Philadelphia Athletics smashed fifty-eight home runs in 1932.

Due in part to the prosperity of the decade and in part to the excitement increased offense generated, attendance at major league games climbed to 9.5 million in 1924, and all sixteen major league teams made money between 1920 and 1930. Major League Baseball was still confined to ten cities in the northeastern quadrant of the United States in the 1920s, but the innovations of the twenties helped bring the game to more people. At first, major league owners feared the new technology available in the twenties would hurt attendance. For instance, in the 1920s the popularity of the automobile, which was now affordable for most middle-class Americans, soared. It made Americans more mobile and, by severing the restrictions imposed by the trolley map or the railroad timetable, gave them considerably more freedom. The car also gave fans access to other entertainment opportunities, such as a Sunday drive in the country. Still, the automobile made it possible for baseball fans who lived outside the city to attend games. The automobile, however, illustrated a problem many baseball teams overlooked when building new stadiums—where to park cars in urban neighborhoods. Lack of parking would be one of the reasons the Dodgers would leave Brooklyn in the late 1950s, and even today, parking is scarce near some major league stadiums.

Many club owners also worried about the effects of radio. Fearing fans would stay home and listen to ball games—and other programs—rather than attend games at the ballpark, St. Louis Browns owner Phil Ball attempted to ban the broadcasting of baseball games. Newspaper publishers also feared that if baseball fans listened to games transmitted over the air, they would no longer buy newspapers to read about them. But others saw value in broadcasting ball games. In 1921 a radio station in Newark, New Jersey, aired the World Series between the Yankees and the Giants. Sportswriter Sandy Hunt of the *Newark Call* attended the games at the Polo Grounds, phoning in the descriptions to the station, while in the studio, broadcaster Tommy Cowan relayed the details over the airwaves. In 1925, Chicago Cubs owner William Wrigley allowed all Cubs games to be broadcast on the radio; instead of keeping fans away, the broadcasts built interest in the Cubs. People who could not attend the game listened to it on the radio, and as fans became more excited about the Cubs, they were more likely to attend on days they could make it to the ballpark. The radio also brought the game to people who lived far away from a major league team: People in cities hundreds—or even thousands—of miles away could still follow the game.

If it was not possible to broadcast the game live, radio stations, especially in minor league markets, often re-created ball games. Announcers in radio studios, working from a written description of a game that had taken place hours earlier, gave a play-by-play account of the game, augmenting the narrative with sound effects that gave the impression of a live broadcast. One of future president Ronald Reagan's first jobs in broadcasting was re-creating Chicago Cubs games on a small radio station in Des Moines, Iowa, in the early 1930s.

Like other businesses in the twenties, baseball turned to scientific management to produce a better, cheaper, more efficient, and more profitable product. One of the challenges faced by major league teams was finding quality players. Branch Rickey, the general manager of the St. Louis Cardinals, knew he could not compete with wealthy clubs like the Yankees for new players. Even if he could discover future stars, rich teams would outbid him for their services. Instead Rickey invented another system to supply the Cardinals with ballplayers: He began buying up minor league teams, starting with the Houston Buffaloes of the Texas League and the Fort Smith Twins of the Western Association in 1920, and the Syracuse Stars of the International League in 1921. At the time, minor leagues were separated into five categories—Class AA, Class A, Class B, Class C, and Class D. Class AA was the category with the highest skill level and had teams in the largest minor league cities, while Class D was the lowest skill category and had teams in small cities and towns. Once he took over control of minor league teams, Rickey could sign unproven ballplayers for very little money and assign them to his Class D teams. With proper coaching and experience, some of the players improved. As they did, Rickey promoted them up his farm system. In time, the Cardinals not only had a readily available supply of quality players, but often had a surplus at many positions. Rickey was able to use that surplus to supplement the club's profit. He could sell minor leaguers he did not need to other clubs. And if the Cardinals had a future star waiting in the wings, Rickey could sell an established player he no longer wanted, as other teams were often willing to pay premium prices for famous names.

By 1928 the Cardinals owned five minor league clubs and had a working agreement with several other minor league teams. For a period in the 1930s, St. Louis owned more than three dozen minor league clubs. With a cheap source of quality ballplayers, the Cardinals became very profitable and successful, winning five National League pennants between 1926 and 1934. Cognizant of the Cardinals success, other major league teams began to imitate the St. Louis farm system.

Not only did improvements in technology and changes in business practices impact baseball, but so did changes taking place in American

Branch Rickey revolutionized baseball twice—as the general manager of the St. Louis Cardinals in the 1920s when he invented the farm system and as the president and general manager of the Brooklyn Dodgers two decades later when he engineered the dismantling of the color barrier. National Baseball Hall of Fame and Museum. Cooperstown, N.Y.

society. Having won the right to vote with the Nineteenth Amendment, American women became more assertive in society and adopted new lifestyles and fashions. Young women called flappers acted differently in public than their mothers or grandmothers had in the Gilded Age. Flappers bobbed their hair and wore tight, short dresses and excessive makeup. They also flouted social and sexual norms, drinking and smoking in public and regarding sex in a more casual manner. Flappers even left their mark on baseball, as some determined women formed their own teams, most notably the New York Bloomer Girls and the Philadelphia Bobbies, which were named after their hairstyles. The Bobbies even toured Japan in 1925, playing games against male college teams. At first the women from Philadelphia were warmly received in Japan, but as word spread that they could not hold their own against the men, the crowds at their games started to dwindle. Attendance became so low that the team did not earn enough money to get home. After receiving a $6,000 donation from a British-Indian benefactor living in Japan, nine members of the twelve-woman team headed back to the United States in November. The other three women were not able to secure passage until January 1926. Sadly, their ship encountered a storm in the Pacific, and when the sky finally cleared up to allow passengers back on deck, the first baseman, seventeen-year-old Leona Kearns, was washed overboard by a giant wave and never seen again.

Although most Americans welcomed the arrival of modern times, some traditionalists opposed the changes taking place in society. Not only did the Ku Klux Klan grow in membership, but a number of states passed laws banning the teaching of evolution in public schools. When a Dayton, Tennessee, science teacher named John Scopes taught science in his classroom in 1925, he was arrested and put on trial. The nation became obsessed with the Scopes Trial, which seemed to symbolize the struggle between modernists and traditionalists that characterized the decade. The conflict even spread to baseball in the 1920s as traditionalists fought to protect something they held dear: the Sabbath. Baseball teams had long recognized the advantage of playing games on Sundays. In the days before night games, many working people could not attend weekday games. The American Association permitted Sunday games in the 1880s, but Cincinnati and St. Louis were the only cities whose laws allowed it. World War I offered baseball owners an opportunity to experiment with scheduling games on Sundays, as major league teams played benefit games as fundraisers for the war effort, and by the end of the war, six major league cities—Chicago, Cincinnati, Cleveland, Detroit, St. Louis, and Washington, DC—allowed games on Sundays. But Sunday baseball was still illegal in the states of New York, Massachusetts, and Pennsylvania.

The question of Sunday baseball divided public opinion in the same way the Scopes Trial split the country. Most Catholic priests and modernist ministers, who saw baseball as a wholesome activity the whole family could enjoy, did not oppose Sunday games. Fundamentalist ministers, however, rallied against Sunday games. When a team scheduled a game on Sunday, evangelicals would contact the local police to break up the game, and the players and managers involved were often fined. Clubs looked for ways around the ban. Some teams played games on Sunday without charging admission, but once fans entered the park, they were required to buy a scorecard at the normal cost of a ticket. Other teams scheduled Sunday games outside the jurisdiction of the city government. Both the Yankees and Dodgers played Sunday games on Long Island, where they knew local authorities would not enforce the Sunday ban. The Phillies and Athletics scheduled Sunday games across the Delaware River in Camden, New Jersey. The Boston Braves played some Sunday games in northern New Jersey until the Giants, claiming the Braves were invading their territory, put a stop to it. Sometimes major league teams would ignore the law and play anyway, considering the fine a part of the cost of doing business.

Gradually, the last states to prohibit Sunday baseball removed the ban. New York State legalized Sunday baseball in 1924. The Brooklyn Robins, as the Dodgers were called in the twenties, did not win any friends among the evangelical crowd, however, when the club scheduled its 1924 home opener against the Philadelphia Phillies on Easter Sunday. A state budget shortfall forced Massachusetts to legalize Sunday baseball in 1929, when it created a license fee that allowed the Red Sox and Braves to play on the Sabbath. Pennsylvania, the last holdout against Sunday baseball, finally relented in 1934 when the Phillies and Athletics threatened to permanently move to Camden. Fearful of losing its two Philadelphia teams, the state legislature repealed the ban.

Baseball players, like Hollywood movie stars, were popular—and marketable—figures in the 1920s. Every day, newspapers across the country printed a box called "What Babe Ruth Did Today," which summed up the slugger's accomplishments in the day's game. Ruth, however, did more than play baseball. He starred in ten movies, starting with the silent picture *Headin' Home* in 1921. Ruth hired Christy Walsh, one of the first sports agents, and, with Walsh's help, secured numerous endorsement deals on consumer products ranging from automobiles to tobacco. Some companies used Ruth's star power without his permission. In 1921 the Curtis Candy Company of Chicago introduced the Baby Ruth bar. Even though Ruth was a national sensation in 1921, Curtis claimed that its candy bar was not named after the ballplayer, maintaining instead that the candy was named after the daughter of former president Grover Cleveland, who had left office in 1897. Cleveland's daughter, "Baby Ruth" Cleveland, had died in 1904 at age twelve. In 1995 the Nestle Company, which now manufactures the candy bar, finally reached an agreement with Babe Ruth's estate to continue to use the name, and even to use Ruth's likeness in advertisements for the candy.

Babe Ruth was big, loud, and rambunctious, like the decade itself. He personified the permissiveness of the twenties. He drank to excess, he partied, and he slept around. His Yankee roommate, outfielder Ping Bodie, once joked, "I don't room with Babe, I room with his suitcase." Unlike Hollywood movie stars like Fatty Arbuckle, whose reputations were dragged through the mud in gossip magazines, the press always portrayed Ruth in a positive light. Newspapers rarely published stories about his excesses, instead focusing on tales about his visits to sick children in hospitals. Ruth's worst season came in 1925, when he became ill during spring training and missed fifty-six regular-season games. That year, the Yankees finished in seventh place. Ruth's ailment was possibly caused by a sexually transmitted disease, but the press blamed it on intestinal problems. Calling it the "stomach ache heard 'round the world," newspapers reported that Ruth had eaten too many hot dogs before a game.

Ruth bounced back. Two years after his illness, Ruth and first baseman Lou Gehrig led the 1927 Yankees to the World Series. That year, Ruth set a new record by hitting sixty home runs in the regular season.

No other *team* in the American League had hit that many homers in 1927, and Ruth's regular-season record would stand until 1961, when it was broken by Roger Maris. Some baseball fans consider the 1927 Yankees to be the best team of all time. New York won 110 games against 44 losses that year, compiling a .714 winning percentage. The Yankees won the American League pennant by nineteen games over the second-place Philadelphia Athletics. In October, New York met the Pittsburgh Pirates in the World Series. The series was over before it even started. Pittsburgh players saw New York batters hit the ball out of the park during batting practice and became completely intimidated by the Yankees. The Yanks swept the series, four games to none.

In 1930, during the Great Depression, Ruth signed a new contract with the Yankees for $80,000. A reporter, pointing out that he was now making more money than President Herbert Hoover, asked Ruth if he thought it was okay that he made more money than the president. Realizing that many people were facing hard times, Ruth responded, "I had a better year." The Roaring Twenties permitted such hyperbole, especially from a star who ranked, in most Americans' eyes, higher than the chief executive of the nation.

8

Segregation and the Negro Leagues (1896 to 1949)

IN 1896 THE SUPREME COURT upheld the constitutionality of Jim Crow under the doctrine of "separate but equal," and by the early twentieth century, African Americans began moving north in search of jobs and economic opportunity, and to escape racial oppression and violence. The movement of 1.6 million African Americans from the rural South to the urban North between 1910 and 1930, known as the Great Migration, established black communities in northern cities like Chicago and Detroit and in the New York City neighborhood of Harlem. Black northerners and white northerners lived in separate neighborhoods and worked in different occupations, with black workers making less than their white counterparts, and their children attended separate schools. Despite some economic gains, for the most part African Americans lived on the margins of northern society. This oppression prompted black leaders to offer different visions for the future. Booker T. Washington accepted segregation as a temporary accommodation in exchange for white support for black efforts in education, social uplift, and economic progress. Others refused such a passive stance. W.E.B. Du Bois demanded the restoration of voting rights for black citizens, an end to segregation, and the removal of discriminatory barriers to African Americans. In 1909 he helped found the National Association for the Advancement of Colored People (NAACP), but its progress was slow. Following World War I, as racial problems seemed to worsen, Marcus Garvey called on African Americans to give up their hopes for integration and instead create an independent black nation in Africa. None of these competing African American movements, however, seemed to overcome segregation. As a result, black Americans responded with their own separate but unequal social institutions, including black churches, black fraternities, black political organizations, black schools and universities, and even a black film industry that produced race movies—movies made by black filmmakers and actors for an African American audience. A new black middle class of ministers, professionals, and businessmen served the needs of the community. African Americans established complex societies that contained a wide range of people, including workers, businessmen, professionals, intellectuals, artists, and entertainers. In the North, two distinct styles of black music—blues and ragtime—synthesized into jazz, a new musical genre that became popular among whites as well. And the Harlem Renaissance, a black literary and artistic revival paralleling the development of jazz music in northern cities, emerged in the 1920s. Embedded in this cultural ferment, black baseball established its own separate but unequal—and oftentimes thriving—organization that aimed, ultimately, to show whites that integration of the major leagues was morally necessary and pragmatically profitable.

Prior to a game against the Baltimore Elite Giants at Yankee Stadium in July 1942, a beautiful woman ordered Willie Wells, the player-manager of the Negro National League's Newark Eagles, to have his players watch her in the stands for instructions when they came to bat. She would pass along signs to the Eagles batters based on the way she crossed her legs. When Wells stepped to the plate with a runner on first, however, he did not understand the signal. He could not tell if the woman was calling for a bunt or the hit-and-run play. While Wells was still trying to figure out the sign, Baltimore pitcher Bill Byrd began his windup. Before Wells knew what happened, Byrd's pitch hit him in the head, knocking him unconscious. Wells returned to the lineup two days later, but only after borrowing a hardhat from a Jersey City construction site. The next time he came to bat, Wells wore the safety gear on his head—possibly the first time a player wore a batting helmet in a baseball game.

The woman was Effa Manley, the co-owner of the Newark Eagles. Her husband, Camden, New Jersey numbers king Abe Manley, started the team in 1935 as a vehicle for laundering the money he made from his gambling racket. When Abe married Effa later that same year, she became the co-owner of the Eagles. But while Abe concentrated on running numbers, Effa took control of the team. She signed the team's players, scheduled the team's games, and arranged the team's travel accommodations. She often drew up the starting lineup and, as the above anecdote indicates, she even tried to orchestrate strategy. Effa Manley also served as the Negro National League's treasurer. She became heavily active in the early civil rights movement of the 1930s and 1940s. In the thirties she served as the treasurer of the New Jersey NAACP, and she unsuccessfully lobbied Congress to adopt the Costigan-Wagner Act, an antilynching bill. She had more success with the "Don't Shop Where You Can't Work" boycott, which, in 1935, forced Blumstein's Department Store in Harlem to hire black employees.

Manley lived in a black world. But although she was raised by an African American stepfather and married to a black gangster, she was white. Most people at the time, however, assumed that she was a light-skinned African American. In the first half of the twentieth century, a sharp racial divide existed in America; one could not move freely between a black world and a white world.

As discussed in chapter 3, African American ballplayers, like black society at large, sought to find feasible alternatives to integration. Forced out of white baseball in the late nineteenth century, black athletes—like African Americans in other fields—responded by establishing their own organizations. As early as the 1880s, amateur African American teams like the Philadelphia Orions, the St. Louis Black Stockings, and the Baltimore Athletics began to play baseball. The first professional African American team, the Cuban Giants, played at a resort on Long Island in 1885. In the first two decades of the twentieth century, other professional black teams sprang up, including the Chicago Leland Giants in 1901, the Homestead Grays from the Pittsburgh area in 1912, and the Bacharach Giants of Atlantic City, New Jersey, in 1916.

In the 1890s an African American baseball team called the Waco Yellow Jackets passed through the tiny town of Calvert, Texas. There, the pitching of an eighth-grade student named Andrew Foster impressed the professional ballplayers. When the Yellow Jackets left town, Foster went with them. Foster soon pitched for some of the premier black teams in America, including the Cuban X-Giants, the Philadelphia Giants, and the Chicago Leland Giants. He earned the nickname "Rube" when he defeated Rube Waddell of the Philadelphia Athletics in an exhibition game in 1903. As the player-manager of the Leland Giants, Foster became disillusioned with the low pay he and his teammates received when playing against white teams. He was determined to run his own team, and in 1910 he and his white business partner, John Schorling, the son-in-law of Charles Comiskey, established a team called the Chicago American Giants. Schorling arranged for the American Giants to use South Side Park, the stadium abandoned by the White Sox when Comiskey Park opened the previous year.

As the operator of a baseball team, Foster discovered the same thing William Hulbert learned while running the Chicago White Stockings in the 1870s—it is hard to make a profit in baseball with a team that plays an irregular schedule. Like Hulbert before him, Foster realized that the key to success hinged on playing in a stable league. In 1920 Foster set up the Negro National League, a circuit of eight black teams based in the Midwest. To ensure balanced competition among member clubs, Foster arranged several trades between various teams to spread the talent around. To protect the club owners, Foster imposed a reserve clause, although it proved to be weak and ineffective.

Pleased with the success of the Negro National League, Foster encouraged African American teams on the East Coast to organize their own league, and the Eastern Colored League began play with six teams in 1923. Starting in 1924, the pennant winner of the Negro National League met the pennant winner of the Eastern Colored League in the Negro League World Series. Although the Negro League World Series would be played until 1927, it never became as popular as its promoters had hoped. Few African American fans had the resources to attend, or even follow, such a long series.

In the late twenties, the Negro leagues encountered a series of challenges. Foster stepped down from running the Negro National League after he suffered a mental breakdown in 1926. The league continued in a rudderless manner without his leadership. In the middle of the 1928 season, when a dispute over players' contracts broke out between clubs, the Eastern Colored League collapsed. Three years later, battered by financial losses caused by the Great Depression, the Negro National League went out of business. Many African American leaders, however, recognized the importance of baseball to black communities. To many black residents of northern cities, Negro league teams were a source of pride, providing African American communities a sense of identity and unity. In 1932 the vacuum left by the dissolution of the Negro National League was filled by two other Negro leagues: a minor black league in the South called the Negro Southern League, which in 1932 claimed major Negro league status, and a new league established by Homestead Grays owner Cumberland Posey called the East-West League. The East-West League stretched from Detroit to the East Coast, while the Negro Southern League extended from Louisiana to as far north as Chicago and Cleveland. Both circuits lasted only one year as major Negro leagues.

In 1933 a Pittsburgh businessman named Gus Greenlee revived the Negro National League. Greenlee owned the Crawford Bar & Grille, a nightclub on Crawford Avenue in Pittsburgh that attracted the biggest jazz stars of the time, including Duke Ellington, Lena Horne, and Count Basie. Most of the money Greenlee earned, however, came from running gambling operations and selling bootleg whiskey. In the black community, there was no stigma to Greenlee's profession; bookmakers and bootleggers were viewed as leaders. Numbers runners were especially respected and admired, as they offered an opportunity for a quick windfall for struggling members of the community. Gambling and bootlegging were two of the very limited opportunities open to industrious and ambitious African American men. Like Abe Manley, Greenlee established a Negro league baseball team to launder his income, and like Rube Foster, Greenlee recognized that his baseball team, the Pittsburgh Crawfords, would be more profitable if it played in an organized league.

In 1933 Greenlee also organized the East-West All-Star Game, an annual event that would be played at Chicago's Comiskey Park. The best players on Negro league teams in the East would play the best players on Negro league teams in the Midwest. Players were selected by fan voting conducted by the *Pittsburgh Courier* and the *Chicago Defender*, African American newspapers with nationwide readership. The East-West All-Star Game quickly became the most important event on the Negro leagues' calendar. Between 1933 and 1949, the game averaged more than thirty-five thousand fans, often drawing a larger crowd than Major League Baseball's All-Star Game. To meet the demand for transportation, railroads added extra cars to take fans from the Deep South to Chicago to attend the game.

In 1937 J. L. Wilkinson, the white owner of the Kansas City Monarchs, organized a rival Negro league. Wilkinson had first entered baseball in 1912, when he formed the All-Nations team, an independent club that included African American, Native American, Mexican, and Japanese ballplayers on its roster. In 1920 Foster invited Wilkinson to sponsor a team in the original Negro National League, so Wilkinson created the Kansas City Monarchs, a team that would last until 1965. After the original Negro National League collapsed during the 1931 season, the Monarchs struggled to remain solvent. Too far from most of the clubs in the new Negro National League, Wilkinson's team could not realistically join Greenlee's organization. Instead Wilkinson created a new circuit, based in the Midwest, called the Negro American League. With a second Negro league, the Negro League World Series was revived in 1942, but the same challenges encountered by the original Negro League World Series of the 1920s prevented the new championship series from surpassing the East-West All-Star Game in popularity.

In the twenties and thirties, the Negro leagues served as the center of black communities in northern cities. African American ballplayers, like black musicians and the stars of race movies, were celebrities whom the entire community admired. The Negro leagues represented the only real opportunity for black athletes to earn a living playing a sport. With the exception of boxing, which boasted a few black prizefighters, all other professional sports were closed to black athletes. Negro league baseball teams provided jobs for perhaps two hundred black baseball players, with about another two hundred jobs for African American athletes on independent teams. During the Great Depression, players in the Negro leagues could earn a decent living. Many players made around $400 a month, and even the least skilled players on the poorest teams in the Negro leagues earned a living wage. The impoverished Birmingham Black Barons paid a minimum salary of $60 a month, about what the average white laborer made during the Depression. And some Negro league stars did very well; Kansas City Monarchs pitcher Satchel Paige made $37,000 in 1942, four times the average white major leaguer's salary.

Black ballplayers earned their pay. The Negro league season was long and hard. The length of the schedule varied, as teams played between sixty and eighty league games in each season, but Negro league teams played many more games than that. In order to bring in enough revenue to pay decent salaries, Negro league teams barnstormed, traveling from town to town playing nonleague exhibition games. Teams often played two—and sometimes three—games a day. Negro league teams scheduled nonleague games against other Negro league teams, independent black teams, and teams of white professional players. Baseball researchers have determined that Negro league teams won 60 percent of the games played against white major league opposition. Following a drubbing by a team of Negro leaguers in Puerto Rico in 1936, the Cincinnati Reds vowed to no longer schedule exhibition games against black teams. When the weather became colder, Negro league teams toured the South and played there. In the winter, they often traveled to Mexico, Cuba, or Venezuela to continue playing.

Sporting goods dealers welcomed the business from the Negro leagues. For the Spalding Company, providing equipment to black ballplayers fit into the business model developed by Albert Spalding during his world tour, in which he tried to increase sales of his product by bringing baseball to more people. Sometimes major league teams worked with black teams. The Washington Senators often ordered bats for the Washington Grays, passing along their major league discount to the Negro league team. At the end of every season, the New York Yankees sold their used uniforms to the New York Black Yankees, a transaction that made a little extra money for the major league club while providing inexpensive, quality major league uniforms for the Negro league team. When possible, Negro league teams rented major league stadiums, using them when the major league tenants were out of town. Playing in major league stadiums gave black teams a quality facility and major league teams an additional source of revenue. A few Negro league teams had their own stadiums. Gus Greenlee built Greenlee Stadium in Pittsburgh, the only black-built stadium in the Negro leagues, to house his fabulous Crawfords, perhaps the best Negro league team of all time. In 1939 the New York Cubans played their home games on a baseball diamond under the 59th Street Bridge in Manhattan. Called the 59th Street Sandlot, the ballpark was technically baseball's first covered stadium. It was not glamorous like modern indoor stadiums, however, as grass could not grow on parts of the field without exposure to direct sunlight, so the infield was made up of dirt and cinders.

When playing in northern cities, Negro league teams stayed in the best hotels in black neighborhoods, just a notch below the best hotels in town. When traveling through the South or the hinterlands, however, African American ballplayers stayed in black-only hotels or boarding houses. If no lodging was available, they sometimes slept on the team bus or camped outside it. In the twenties, wealthier Negro league teams traveled by train. The Chicago American Giants had a Pullman sleeping car, a very luxurious way to travel at the time. Negro league baseball teams traveling by train had a significant impact on African Americans because the railroads were the largest employers of black workers, especially porters who carried luggage for railroad passengers. For a black porter who spent his day carrying the bags of countless white passengers, handling the luggage of an African American man traveling in luxury became a point of pride. In the 1930s, buses replaced rail travel. The buses were not as comfortable as the train, but because they were not tied to the rail line or the railroad schedule, they offered more flexibility for scheduling. A few wealthy clubs purchased new, modern buses. Gus Greenlee bought a bus for the Pittsburgh Crawfords in the 1930s, and in 1946 Effa Manley spent $15,000 on an air-conditioned Flxible Clipper bus for the Newark Eagles.

A multimillion-dollar industry, the Negro leagues represented one of the largest African American businesses in America during the first half of the twentieth century. Many of the owners of Negro league teams were black businessmen. Some, like Gus Greenlee, Abe Manley, and New York Cubans owner Alessandro Pompez, were bootleggers, racketeers, or number runners. Few other African American men could afford to own a baseball team. The Negro leagues also boasted two prominent white owners: J. L. Wilkinson and Effa Manley.

The style of play in the Negro leagues differed from that in the white leagues. Negro league teams did not rely on the long ball or the big inning, instead playing a scrappy game that emphasized stolen bases. With the arrival of Babe Ruth's home run, the stolen base became a lost art in the major leagues in the twenties and thirties. Former Negro leaguers reintroduced the stolen base when they entered the major leagues in the late forties and 1950s.

Many Negro league stars are recognizable to baseball fans today. James Thomas Bell, whose thirty-year career included stints with seven Negro league teams, was one of the fastest players in the game. Cool Papa Bell, as he was called, could circle the bases in twelve seconds. According to a popular legend, Bell was so fast that he could turn out the light and be in bed, under the covers, before it got dark. There was some truth behind the legend. According to his roommate Satchel Paige, one day

Bell noticed that the faulty wiring in the cheap black-only hotel where the Kansas City Monarchs were staying created a delay when the light switch was flipped. He turned to Paige and demonstrated that he could live up to his reputation.

The greatest slugger of the Negro leagues was probably catcher Josh Gibson of the Pittsburgh Crawfords and Homestead Grays. Although statistics from Negro league games are incomplete, by some estimates—counting nonleague exhibition games and games played during barnstorming tours—Gibson may have hit eight hundred or more home runs in his lifetime. The same estimates have him hitting as many as eighty home runs in a single season. Negro league legend states that Gibson is the only person to hit a fair ball completely out of Yankee Stadium, a feat he reputedly accomplished twice, though historians have not been able to verify those colossal hits. Sadly, doctors diagnosed Gibson with a brain tumor in 1943, and although he continued to play baseball, over the next three years Gibson complained of terrible headaches and checked into and out of hospitals. He died in January 1947, just three months before Jackie Robinson took the field for the Brooklyn Dodgers.

Pitcher Satchel Paige played twenty-two years in the Negro Leagues, starting in 1927. Perhaps the greatest pitcher of all time, he was also a showman. More than once he intentionally walked the bases full and then ordered the outfielders to sit down before striking out the next three batters. Paige was also a civil rights pioneer; while playing in the Negro leagues, Paige refused to pitch in towns where he could not get a meal or a place to sleep. After the collapse of baseball's color barrier, Paige pitched two seasons for the Cleveland Indians, contending for the 1948 American League Rookie of the Year Award at age forty-two. Starting in 1951, he pitched three seasons for the St. Louis Browns. Paige seemed ageless. Although his birth certificate confirms that he was born in 1906, rumors circulated that he was older. After hiring a private detective to dig into Paige's background, Indians owner Bill Veeck announced that Paige could not have been born in the twentieth century. In 1965, at age fifty-nine, Paige came out of retirement to pitch a game for the Kansas City Athletics.

Few people realized it at the time, but the arrival of Jackie Robinson on the Brooklyn Dodgers in 1947 put the nail in the coffin of the Negro leagues. Not only did the Negro leagues lose their stars, but they

Although the records are incomplete, counting non-league exhibition games and games played during barnstorming tours Negro League slugger Josh Gibson may have hit as many as 800 home runs. Sadly, Gibson died from a stroke at age 35 in January 1947, three months before Jackie Robinson broke the color barrier. National Baseball Hall of Fame and Museum. Cooperstown, N.Y.

also started to lose their fans as African Americans began to attend major league games. Railroads in the Deep South added extra cars to their trains in order to take black fans north to see the Dodgers play in Cincinnati or St. Louis. Unable to compete with the integrated Dodgers or Giants across the Hudson River, in 1949 Effa Manley moved the Newark Eagles to Houston, Texas, nearly eight hundred miles from St. Louis, the nearest major league competition. But even that was a stopgap measure. In 1949 the Negro National League went out of business. The Negro American League managed to hang on for another dozen years, but for the last decade of its life it no longer offered a quality product. For many black ballplayers, integration meant an end to their baseball careers. The major league teams integrated slowly, only adding the biggest Negro league stars to their rosters, and when the Negro leagues went out of business, most black ballplayers no longer had an employer. Rarely compensated for their players who joined white teams, the owners of Negro league teams also lost money. As black fans switched allegiance to major league teams, Negro league franchises became worthless. Still, African Americans took solace in the fact that they had integrated Major League Baseball, in part because the stellar play in the Negro leagues proved blacks could compete on an equal level with whites.

Twenty years after the integration of baseball, a growing movement emerged to remember Negro league players before they passed into obscurity. Starting in 1971, the National Baseball Hall of Fame began considering Negro league players for induction. Since then, nearly three dozen individuals associated with the Negro leagues—including Satchel Paige in 1971, Josh Gibson in 1972, Cool Papa Bell in 1974, and Effa Manley in 2006—have been enshrined in the Hall of Fame. In 1990 the Negro Leagues Baseball Museum, an institution dedicated to preserving the memory of the Negro leagues, opened in Kansas City.

9

Baseball and the Great Depression (1929 to 1940)

THE GREAT DEPRESSION, a severe economic downturn that started with the stock market crash of October 1929 and lasted through the 1930s, devastated America. By the end of 1929, stocks had lost half their value. By 1932, the worst year of the Depression, the value of stocks dropped another 30 percent, and by the next year thirteen million Americans—a quarter of the workforce—were unemployed. In the first four years of the Depression, industrial production fell by 50 percent and the Gross National Product dropped from $105 billion to $60 billion. And between 1929 and 1933, eleven thousand banks—44 percent of the US banking system—failed. In addition to numbers on a balance sheet, the Great Depression had a very real human cost. Without unemployment benefits, the jobless waited in breadlines or went to soup kitchens for food. In cities, the homeless lived in shacks or lean-tos on vacant lots, called "Hoovervilles," after President Herbert Hoover. In 1932, in response to the Great Depression, the country elected Franklin Delano Roosevelt, who promised a New Deal for the American people. During his first hundred days in office, Roosevelt signed fifteen major pieces of legislation, including bills providing aid to bankers, farmers, industrialists, workers, homeowners, and the unemployed. Mostly, however, Roosevelt restored hope among desperate Americans. Despite the economic crisis, he was confident and cheery. He promised Americans that the only thing they had to fear was "fear itself." The New Deal created the Works Progress Administration (WPA), a $5 billion jobs program that put unemployed people to work building thousands of public projects, including schools, post offices and other public buildings, roads, airports, and a number of minor league ballparks, including Roosevelt Stadium in Jersey City and War Memorial Stadium in Buffalo. The WPA also

erected a steel-and-concrete grandstand at Doubleday Field in Cooperstown,
New York. The Great Depression would continue for the rest of the decade,
until the United States returned to massive spending in anticipation of World
War II. During the Depression, baseball was forced to make some critical
adjustments to survive as well.

On July 6, 1933, the greatest names in baseball gathered at Comiskey
Park in Chicago to participate in the very first Major League All-Star
Game. In the third base dugout, a sturdy man in street clothes named
Cornelius McGillicuddy, better known as Connie Mack, stood at the
helm of the American League squad. Born in 1862, during the second
year of the Civil War, Mack spent his entire adult life in baseball. He had
been a major league catcher in the 1880s and 1890s before becoming the
manager of the Pittsburgh Pirates in 1894. Fired by Pittsburgh after his
third season, Mack ended up managing the Milwaukee Brewers of Ban
Johnson's Western League. When Johnson transformed his league into
a major league circuit in 1901, Mack signed on as the manager and co-
owner of the American League's new Philadelphia franchise.

Unlike Jacob Ruppert, the owner of the New York Yankees and the
Jacob Ruppert & Company brewery, producers of Knickerbocker beer,
or Philip K. Wrigley, the owner of the Chicago Cubs and the chewing
gum company, Mack had no source of income outside of baseball. But he
knew how to manage. In the mid-1920s Mack assembled a powerful team
built around four future Hall of Famers—catcher Mickey Cochrane, first
baseman Jimmie Foxx, outfielder Al Simmons, and pitcher Lefty Grove.
In 1929 his Philadelphia Athletics won 104 games, finishing 18 games
ahead of the second-place Yankees, and took the World Series from the
Cubs in five games. The A's repeated as World Series champs the following season, this time defeating the Cardinals in six games, and returned
to the World Series in 1931, only to lose to St. Louis in seven games.

By 1933 Mack stood at the top of the baseball world. Following his
1929 World Series championship, civic leaders honored Mack with
Edward W. Bok's Philadelphia Award for his service to the city. Major
League Baseball recognized his contribution to the game by selecting
him to manage the first American League All-Star team. But the Great
Depression had already started to take its toll. No longer able to afford
Al Simmons's $33,333 annual contract, Mack sold him, along with two

other players, to the Chicago White Sox for $100,000. Without Simmons, the A's slipped to third place in 1933. The Depression continued to decimate the team. In 1934 Mack traded Mickey Cochrane to the Tigers and Lefty Grove to the Red Sox. Two years later he sent slugger Jimmie Foxx to the Red Sox for $150,000. The Athletics continued to fall in the standings, finishing in sixth place in 1934 and falling to last place in 1935. The team would remain in last place through the 1943 season, and the Athletics would not become contenders again until the early 1970s—forty years and two cities later.

Just as it had on the economy and the American psyche, the Great Depression had a damaging impact on baseball. Many fans could no longer afford to go to a baseball game. And, like businesses in other industries, baseball teams and leagues that had been operating on a shoestring shut down. The Depression was especially hard on Negro league and minor league teams. The Negro National League folded in 1931, and half the minor leagues disappeared during the first four years of the Depression. In 1929, twenty-six minor leagues, consisting of 182 clubs, operated

The Great Depression forced Philadelphia Athletics owner Connie Mack to trade or sell four future Hall of Fame players. The Library of Congress Online Photo Archive

in the United States; four years later only fourteen leagues, with a total of 93 clubs, were still in business. No major league team went out of business during the Great Depression, but many were operating very close to the brink. Major league clubs experienced a steep drop in attendance. In 1929, 9.6 million fans attended major league games, but in 1933 only 6 million went to a game, a decline of 36 percent. Attendance at major league games would not return to 1929 levels until 1940.

The Great Depression, however, did not affect all major league teams equally. While some clubs barely made it through the hard times, other teams survived without much difficulty. The New York Yankees, a successful team that continued to win, prospered during the Depression. With Babe Ruth's leadership, the Yankees won the 1932 World Series. By 1934, however, Ruth was aging, so the Yankees sold him to the Boston Braves when the season ended. But with Lou Gehrig at first base, the Yankees kept winning. In 1936 a rookie named Joe DiMaggio joined the Yankees. That year, Gehrig hit forty-nine home runs, DiMaggio hit twenty-nine, and catcher Bill Dickey hit twenty-two. It was during this period that the Yankees were first called the "Bronx Bombers." Starting in 1936, the Yankees won four straight World Series. In 1940, however, Gehrig was diagnosed with amyotrophic lateral sclerosis (ALS, which would become known as Lou Gehrig's disease), which forced him to retire after playing in 2,130 consecutive games, a record that stood for fifty-six years. He died in 1942.

The New York Giants were another successful team during the Great Depression. In 1932 John McGraw, who had managed the Giants since 1902, retired. Giants first baseman Bill Terry replaced him as manager. Terry had been the last National League ballplayer to hit .400, hitting .401 in 1930. As manager, he led the Giants to the National League pennant in 1933, 1936, and 1937, and to the 1933 World Series championship over the Washington Senators. New York's pitching staff was led by Carl Hubbell, whose money pitch was a screwball, a curve ball that broke in the opposite direction.

The St. Louis Cardinals also thrived in the 1930s. The Cardinals paid lower costs for players as general manager Branch Rickey's farm system kept the stream of inexpensive talent flowing to St. Louis. The Cardinals won the 1931 and 1934 World Series and an additional National League pennant in 1930. The scrappy 1934 Cardinals were nicknamed the "Gashouse Gang," after plants that generated heating and cooking gas from coal. Pitcher Jay "Dizzy" Dean and his brother, Paul "Daffy" Dean, led the team in pitching, with thirty and nineteen wins, respectively. That season, Daffy Dean pitched a no-hitter in the second game of a doubleheader. Dizzy, who had pitched the first game of the day and was famous for his outlandish quotes, bragged to a reporter that he, too, would have pitched a no-hitter if he knew his brother was going to throw one. St. Louis also had a potent offense led by second baseman Frankie Frisch. Nicknamed the "Fordham Flash" after the university he attended, Frisch was a rarity in the 1930s: a college-educated ballplayer. Future Hall of Famer Joe "Ducky" Medwick roamed left field. In 1937 Medwick won the Triple Crown, leading the National League in home runs, batting average, and runs batted in.

Other teams, however, barely survived. As noted earlier, the Depression forced Connie Mack to trade or sell many of the stars of the Philadelphia Athletics. The St. Louis Browns also struggled. During the first two decades of the twentieth century, the Browns had been the most popular team in St. Louis, but in the thirties the Cardinals surpassed the Browns in popularity. The Browns, never having not won a single American League pennant, saw their total attendance drop from 280,697 in 1929 to 80,922 in 1935, an average of fewer than 1,100 fans per game.

The Brooklyn Dodgers were another team that faced hard times during the Great Depression. The Dodgers had been in disarray since owner Charlie Ebbets died in 1925. Having last won a National League pennant in 1920, by the 1930s the team was viewed as a joke by many people. The club's incompetence earned it the nickname the "Daffiness Boys." The Brooklyn faithful, however, affectionately referred to the team as "Dem Bums." Wilbert Robinson—nicknamed "Uncle Robbie"—managed the club from 1914 to 1931, a period when the team was usually called the Brooklyn Robins. Like Giants manager John McGraw, Robinson had played for the National League's notorious Baltimore Orioles of the 1890s. Even the Dodgers' stars seemed unprofessional. In one instance, due to blunders by Brooklyn base runners, according to some reports, what should have been a clean triple hit by slugger Babe Herman resulted in a triple play. By the late thirties, the Dodgers were deeply in debt. In 1938 the telephone company shut off the club's phone service for failure to pay the bill, and the Brooklyn Trust Company, to whom the

Dodgers owed more than a half million dollars, notified the club that they could not borrow any more money. The Dodgers were on the verge of bankruptcy.

Under severe financial pressure, many teams looked for ways to encourage people to come to the ballpark. Clubs adopted new innovations to bring out fans, some of which were merely gimmicks, but others would have a lasting impact on the game. In an effort to excite bored New England fans, in 1936 the last-place Boston Braves, a team that had finished 61½ games out of first place the previous season, changed its name to the Boston Bees. The gimmick did not work, as the new name never caught on, and by 1941 the team was again known as the Boston Braves. Other teams attempted to lure fans with newer, more colorful uniforms. In 1937 the Brooklyn Dodgers changed the color of its caps, stockings, and trim to Kelly green, a very nontraditional baseball color. In 1938 the Philadelphia Phillies added gold trim to their uniforms, and in 1940 the Pittsburgh Pirates placed a pirate head on the team's jerseys.

Some clubs tried to attract fans by adding famous old names to the roster. In the 1930s there was no ballplayer more famous than Babe Ruth, and after the 1934 season, the Boston Braves bought Ruth, who was well past his prime, from the Yankees. After struggling through the first two months of the season, Ruth retired from the game. In 1938 the Brooklyn Dodgers hired Ruth to be the team's first base coach. Hoping to attract fans who wanted to see Ruth swing a bat, the Dodgers let the slugger take batting practice before each game. Realizing that he was being exploited, Ruth quietly quit at the end of the season.

Some of the experiments attempted by baseball in the thirties were more than gimmicks; they became innovations that changed the game. In 1933 the city of Chicago hosted a world's fair, called the "Century of Progress International Exposition." The fair gave Arch Ward, the sports editor of the *Chicago Tribune*, an idea: If Chicago could host the fair of the century, why not stage the baseball game of the century? Ward organized the first Major League All-Star Game, in which the stars of the National League played the stars of the American League, which was played at Comiskey Park on July 6, 1933. The game was so successful that it became an annual tradition.

During the Depression, many unemployed fans could not afford to go to a ball game, while those who had jobs often worked during the daytime, when games were played. One way to increase attendance was to schedule games at night, when fans with jobs were free to attend. Night games were not new. In 1880, teams representing two Boston department stores played a night game in Hull, Massachusetts, to demonstrate lighting installed by the Northern Electric Light Company. Three years later a minor league night game was played in Fort Wayne, Indiana, and by the 1920s several minor league teams were playing night games. In 1930 the Negro leagues' Kansas City Monarchs traveled with portable lights so they could play at night. But the major leagues, believing that night games were a gimmick and not "real" baseball, resisted the trend to play games at night. The pressures caused by the Great Depression convinced some teams to change their position. In 1935 Larry MacPhail, the general manager of the Cincinnati Reds, installed lights at Crosley Field, where the first major league night game was played against the Philadelphia Phillies. A switch installed in the White House allowed President Franklin Roosevelt to turn on the lights for Major League Baseball's first night game. With their higher attendance, night games soon became a fixture of the major league schedule.

By 1938 the situation in Brooklyn had become desperate. The Brooklyn Trust Company was demanding payment from the Dodgers, and the club turned to the National League for help. National League president Ford Frick suggested the Dodgers hire Larry MacPhail to be the club's new president and general manager. The club took Frick's advice, and MacPhail, in turn, hired Leo Durocher to be the Dodgers' new manager. Durocher had a very volatile temper, but he turned Brooklyn into a contender. MacPhail also adopted innovations designed to bring fans back to the ballpark. Even though the club had little money to spare, MacPhail thought spending $75,000 to renovate Ebbets Field was an important investment. As a part of the renovation, MacPhail ordered lights installed in the ballpark, and on June 15, 1938, the Dodgers hosted MacPhail's old club, the Cincinnati Reds, in the first night game at Ebbets Field. Four days earlier, in his previous start, Cincinnati starting pitcher Johnny Vander Meer had pitched a no-hitter in Boston against the Bees. On June 15, in the first night game ever played in New York City, Vander Meer became the first and only pitcher to throw two no-hitters in a row.

MacPhail also put the Dodgers on the radio. Fearing the broadcasting of one team's games would hurt the attendance of the other two, all three New York City teams had previously agreed to keep off the radio. In 1939, however, MacPhail withdrew the Dodgers from the agreement. He brought Red Barber, the broadcaster he had employed in Cincinnati, to Brooklyn to broadcast Dodgers games. Barber was a southerner who had a gift for homespun language. With the club's games available on the radio, the Dodgers became very popular in New York City, giving the team a jump on the Yankees and Giants. Under MacPhail, attendance at Ebbets Field increased dramatically, from fewer than five hundred thousand fans a year before he took over the team to almost a million fans in 1940.

By the end of the thirties, the Great Depression was lifting. Still, in order to augment attendance, many major league teams continued to schedule night games. In 1941, Cubs owner Philip K. Wrigley decided to install lights at Wrigley Field. He bought the hardware and planned to have lights put up in early 1942. In the meantime, although the Depression was subsiding, the St. Louis Browns were finding it harder and harder to compete against the Cardinals. In late 1941 the Browns obtained permission from the American League to move to Los Angeles for the 1942 season. Shortly after that, on December 7, 1941, Japanese bombers attacked the US naval base at Pearl Harbor in Hawaii. After the attack, Wrigley decided to not install the lights, instead donating them to the government to be installed at an army or navy base. Lights would not be installed at Wrigley until 1988. And with the United States at war with Japan, the West Coast suddenly no longer seemed like an attractive location to play baseball. The Browns decided not to move to Los Angeles and remained in St. Louis, at least for the immediate future.

10

Baseball Goes to War (1941 to 1945)

THE JAPANESE ATTACK ON Pearl Harbor on December 7, 1941, drew America into World War II. In addition to a military comprising nearly sixteen million men, the government required a civilian labor force of about sixty million workers to manufacture the weapons, uniforms, and supplies needed by the troops. Many of the seven million workers who were unemployed in 1940 helped meet this need, as did retirees, African Americans from the rural South, and women. Six million women took jobs in defense plants, performing every kind of task, including tending to blast furnaces, running lathes, operating cranes, welding ship hulls, loading shells, and riveting airplane parts. In order to pay for World War II, the government borrowed money by issuing war bonds. To help sell the bonds, it recruited more than three hundred movie stars to appear at rallies staged at various venues, including ball fields, in more than three hundred cities across the United States. In addition, to overcome shortages due to military requirements, President Franklin Delano Roosevelt imposed rationing. Citizens also held scrap drives, collecting metal, rubber, and paper for reuse during the war. While Americans were fighting oppression abroad, racial unrest increased at home. The government rounded up 110,000 men, women, and children of Japanese descent, 40 percent of whom were American citizens, and shipped them to internment camps in the Rocky Mountain states. In May 1943, during the Zoot Suit Riots, named after a fashion popular with Latino men in California, sailors and marines on leave in Los Angeles attacked young Mexican American men. And throughout the war, the United States still denied equal rights to thirteen million African Americans at home. In January 1941, African American labor leader A. Philip Randolph, demanding the integration of the US military and an end to racial discrimination in the defense industry, threatened to lead black workers on a march on Washington. President Roosevelt established the Fair Employment Practices

Committee (FEPC), and in exchange, Randolph canceled the march. Racial tensions persisted, however. In June 1943, violence between whites and African Americans in Detroit erupted into a riot that left thirty-four people dead. Despite the unrest, the military remained segregated—as did baseball.

On the morning of September 28, 1941, before the start of a season-ending doubleheader against the Athletics, a nervous Ted Williams sat in the visitors' dugout at Shibe Park in Philadelphia biting his fingernails. Although the games had no bearing on the American League standings—the Yankees had clinched the pennant on September 4, more than three weeks earlier—for the Red Sox left fielder there was a lot riding on the final two games. Williams had woken up that morning batting .39955. No major leaguer had hit .400 since Bill Terry of the Giants did it in 1930. According to some reports, Red Sox manager Joe Cronin offered to let Williams sit out the last two games. As batting averages are rounded to three digits, if he did not play Williams would have ended the season with an average of .400. But Williams wanted to have more than his "toenails on the line." Williams played both games and collected six hits in eight at-bats that afternoon, finishing with a .406 batting average. As of 2016, no one has hit over .400 since.

After a decade of half-empty ballparks, the Depression had finally ended, and baseball had come back more popular than ever. In 1941 almost 9.7 million fans had attended a major league game, one hundred thousand more than had attended a ball game in 1929, the season before the Great Depression started. And in 1941, baseball gave fans plenty of excitement, and not just because of Williams's hitting performance. For more than two months, from May 15 through July 16, Joe DiMaggio of the Yankees managed to get a hit in every game he played. DiMaggio's feat of hitting safely in fifty-six straight games shattered the old record of forty-four games set in 1897 by Wee Willie Keeler of the National League's Baltimore Orioles. Indians pitchers Al Smith and Jim Bagly held DiMaggio hitless on July 17 in Cleveland, ending the streak. The next day DiMaggio began a new streak, collecting hits in each of his next sixteen games. DiMaggio took the streak in stride, however; as a member of the minor league San Francisco Seals in 1933, he had hit safely in sixty-one straight games. When the season ended, sportswriters had the difficult task of deciding whether Williams or DiMaggio should receive

Joe DiMaggio of the Yankees (left), who hit safely in 56 straight games, and Ted Williams of the Boston Red Sox, who finished the season with a .406 batting average, helped make the 1941 baseball season memorable. National Baseball Hall of Fame and Museum. Cooperstown, N.Y.

the American League's Most Valuable Player Award. Although hitting .400 is rare, no major leaguer before (or since) had hit safely in fifty-six consecutive games, so the sportswriters gave the award to the Yankee Clipper.

With the enthusiasm generated by Williams and DiMaggio, baseball's future seemed bright. But the United States' entry into World War II in December would create new challenges for the sport. As America entered the war, Major League Baseball faced three monumental questions: Was it appropriate for Major League Baseball to operate during the war? How could Major League Baseball promote patriotism and assist in the war effort? And if baseball did continue during the war, with so many players drafted into the military, where would the major leagues find players to fill the rosters?

Five weeks after Pearl Harbor, remembering the confusion surrounding the "work or fight" order of World War I, Commissioner Kenesaw Mountain Landis sent a letter to President Roosevelt asking if baseball should play the upcoming season. Roosevelt's immediate response to Landis is known as the Green Light Letter. The president, responding with his personal opinion rather than an official edict, replied that he believed baseball was important to American society. Roosevelt wrote, "I honestly feel that it would be best for the country to keep baseball going." He pointed out that because of the war, Americans would be working longer hours and would need a form of recreation to take their minds off work. Because ball games lasted two to two-and-a-half hours, which meant Americans would still have plenty of time to tend to their defense jobs, and because it was not expensive to attend a ball game, Roosevelt believed baseball was an ideal form of recreation for Americans during the war. He also expressed his hope for more night games, which would allow more workers to attend. Roosevelt stated that baseball players of military age could not be excused from military service, but he encouraged the use of older players, "even if the actual quality of the teams is lowered." Roosevelt, obviously including the minor leagues and Negro leagues in his calculation, acknowledged that professional baseball included about "600 teams with 5,000 or 6,000 players," which he said were a "definite recreational asset" to twenty million Americans.

Major league teams promoted patriotism during the war. Teams added a patriotic patch to the sleeves of their uniforms, and clubs admitted soldiers and sailors in uniform to games free of charge. Baseball teams also found ways to help with the war effort. They often donated used bats, balls, and uniforms to the military so that baseball could be a form of off-duty recreation for soldiers and sailors. As noted in chapter 9, Cubs owner Philip K. Wrigley even donated the lights he had planned to install at Wrigley Field to the war effort. Clubs encouraged fans to buy war bonds and found other imaginative ways to raise money for the war. In 1942, two days after defeating the National League in the All-Star Game, the American League all-stars played a benefit game against a team of major leaguers in the military. The game, held in Cleveland's Municipal Stadium, drew sixty-two thousand fans. The most unusual benefit game was held at the Polo Grounds in New York City on June 26, 1944. In the only tricornered game in major league history, the Yankees, Giants, and Dodgers all faced each other in the game. Each team played six innings, three against each opponent. The Dodgers won the game with five runs; the Yankees only scored one run and the Giants were shut out. More than fifty thousand fans attended the game, which raised $5 million for the war effort. The Negro league teams helped out, too. Effa Manley arranged for the Newark Eagles' team bus to take jazz musicians from Harlem to Fort Dix, New Jersey, to entertain the troops.

As baseball had come to represent America, it was often used in propaganda. The 1942 combat movie *Guadalcanal Diary* captured the impact of baseball in a scene where, after being cut down by Japanese machine gunfire, Corp. Taxi Potts, a Brooklyn cab driver fighting with the marines in the South Pacific, died happy because he had just heard on the shortwave radio that the Dodgers scored four runs in the ninth inning.

Baseball even had a role in combat. It not only offered soldiers a connection to home, but also provided American troops a means to confirm the nationality of strangers dressed in US uniforms. When encountering an unfamiliar soldier, American troops would often ask him who won the most recent World Series. There were only two possible correct responses—the Yankees in 1941 and 1943 and the Cardinals in 1942 and 1944—and German spies dressed in American uniforms did not know the answer, but presumably all true Americans did. Baseball could also cut the other way: In the jungles of the Pacific, Japanese soldiers taunted US Marines with chants of "To Hell with Babe Ruth," who was familiar to many Japanese baseball fans because he visited that country with a team of all-stars in 1934.

Anticipating that the United States might be drawn into the war, sixteen months before Pearl Harbor, Roosevelt convinced Congress to pass the Selective Training and Service Act of 1940, the first peacetime draft in American history. Hundreds of major league players were drafted during the war. In March 1941, Pirates pitcher Hugh Mulcahy became the first major leaguer conscripted under the new law. Mulcahy—who, because of his less than stellar won-loss record, had picked up the unfortunate nickname "Losing Pitcher"—applied for a deferment in order to finish the baseball season. The military, apparently believing he was more valuable in the battlefield than on the pitching mound, rejected his application. By August 1941, still more than three months before Pearl Harbor, nearly two hundred players had received a draft notice. By the end of the war, around five hundred big leaguers and more than four thousand minor league and Negro league players served. Two former major league players—Elmer Gedeon, who played five games for the Senators in 1939, and Harry O'Neill, who played a single game for the Athletics that same year—were killed in the conflict, as were 125 minor leaguers. Red Sox great Ted Williams enlisted in the military in May of 1942, becoming a navy pilot. The navy announced that Williams's physical exam indicated that he had 20/10 vision, which helps to explain his phenomenal hitting ability. Moe Berg, a catcher who bounced between six major league teams from 1923 to 1939—and was a Princeton graduate who spoke seven languages—became a spy with the Office of Strategic Information. Because he had twice visited Japan with traveling baseball teams, including the 1934 all-star team that featured Babe Ruth, the military intelligence service consulted him before the Doolittle Raid that bombed Tokyo in April of 1942. As a spy, Berg was dispatched to the Caribbean, Latin America, and even the Balkans during the war.

Cleveland Indians pitcher and future Hall of Famer Bob Feller became the first American athlete to voluntarily enlist in the military during the war when, hoping to become a fighter pilot, he joined the US Navy two days after Pearl Harbor. Denied his wings because he failed the hearing test, Feller became a gunner on the USS *Alabama*. As a crew member of the *Alabama,* Feller participated in a number of combat operations, including the Battle of Tarawa and the Battle of the Philippine Sea.

Ballplayers in the military continued to play when not on duty. After his combat tour ended in January 1944, Feller pitched for a team representing the Great Lakes Naval Station near Chicago, where Feller was assigned as a navy instructor. In 1945, major leaguers in the navy stationed in Hawaii played a seven-game all-star series that pitted stars from the American League against stars from the National League. Ted Williams of the Red Sox and Stan Musial of the Cardinals were among the airmen and sailors to play in the series.

The war hit all major league teams hard. The Cleveland Indians and Chicago Cubs got off easy, losing only twenty-three and twenty-four players, respectively, to the war, while the Washington Senators and New York Giants both had thirty-one players in the military. The Philadelphia Athletics were perhaps hit the hardest, with forty members of the A's in the service at some point during the conflict. But players were not the only people Major League Baseball lost to the war. In 1942, Brooklyn Dodgers president and general manager Larry MacPhail enlisted in the army, opening the door for St. Louis Cardinals general manager Branch

Rickey to take his place in Brooklyn. With so many players serving in the military, major league competition declined dramatically during the war, so much so that the perennial cellar-dwelling St. Louis Browns won their first and only American League pennant in 1944.

The greatest challenge facing big-league clubs during the conflict was finding players to fill the roster spots vacated by major leaguers serving in the war. With sixteen million men between the ages of eighteen and forty-four serving in the military, ball clubs resorted to employing teenagers too young for the draft, veteran ballplayers too old for the draft, and other men who were not healthy enough to join the military. Joe Nuxhall, a fifteen-year-old kid, became the youngest major leaguer of all time when he pitched for the Reds in 1944. The St. Louis Browns attracted some attention in 1945, when they signed a one-armed outfielder named Pete Gray. Gray, who had enjoyed two successful seasons with the minor league Memphis Chickasaws before advancing to the major leagues, could easily swing a bat with one hand. Playing defense proved to be a little more difficult, but Gray devised a technique where he would catch a baseball with an undersized glove, then stick the glove under the stump of his right arm while transferring the ball to his hand. Gray became proficient enough with his method to be able to catch a fly ball and return it to the infield almost as quickly as a two-armed player. The Browns released Gray at the end of the season—not because of his play in the outfield but because of his difficulty hitting a curveball. Gray may have inspired Senator William Langer of North Dakota in June of 1945 to introduce a bill in Congress that offered hope for wounded veterans by requiring 10 percent of major league players to be amputees.

Discharged ballplayers who returned to the major leagues received a special patch to wear on their baseball uniforms. The patch replicated the Honorable Service Lapel Button worn by former soldiers, sailors, and marines to indicate that they had been honorably discharged. The medal was important for recently discharged servicemen who did not have access to civilian clothes, as it indicated that the person in uniform was not absent without leave. Because of its unattractive design, former servicemen often referred to the medal as the "Ruptured Duck." For that reason, many World War II veterans declined to wear the patch on their baseball uniforms.

Major League Baseball, like the rest of America, also endured shortages and restrictions. Limits on travel forced the cancellation of spring training in Florida during the war, and major league teams instead prepared for the season in the North. In 1943 and 1944 the Red Sox held spring training at Tufts University in Medford, Massachusetts, while the Boston Braves held spring training at Choate Preparatory School in Wallingford, Connecticut. During the war, the Brooklyn Dodgers held training camp at Bear Mountain Inn in upstate New York, where the indoor athletic facilities of the nearby United States Military Academy at West Point were available during inclement weather.

Because of the war, Major League Baseball canceled the 1945 All-Star Game, ostensibly to save resources and avoid the need to travel. This excuse was bogus. Germany had already been defeated in May of 1945, and the major leagues had played the All-Star Game in 1942, 1943, and 1944, when the United States was fighting a war in two theaters. The real reason the 1945 All-Star Game was canceled is that there were not enough stars still playing baseball to hold a legitimate all-star contest. In place of the All-Star Game, Major League Baseball organized a series of interleague exhibition games to raise money for the war. In all but two cases, the games featured teams from the same city or the same state, with only the Brooklyn Dodgers–Washington Senators and Pittsburgh Pirates–Detroit Tigers games featuring teams that did not share the same market.

Despite the Green Light Letter, Cubs owner Philip K. Wrigley worried that a lengthy war might still shut down Major League Baseball. Wrigley was especially concerned about his ballpark not being able to generate revenue, so he decided to have a potential tenant ready if the Cubs stopped playing. Wrigley formed a new league called the All-American Girls Professional Baseball League (AAGPBL). The AAGPBL was not meant to rival Major League Baseball. The caliber of play would not equal even that of the men who played in the majors during the war, and the league did not place teams in major cities. Instead it was organized to be a ready substitute should the major league teams shut down. If the baseball season were canceled due to a lack of players, a team of women could move their games to Wrigley Field. If Rosie the Riveter could fill in for men in shipyards and airplane plants, Rosie the Right Fielder could fill in on the baseball diamond.

Wrigley wanted to groom the "right kind" of women to play in the AAGPBL. Because he wanted good athletes, he sent scouts across the

United States and Canada to find the best female baseball and softball players in North America. But he also wanted the women in his league to appear ladylike. He was afraid that Americans would be put off by women who dressed and acted like men, so he wanted his players to appear feminine and sexy. Even images of the famed Rosie the Riveter showed her with muscles and makeup, conveying the message that she was both tough and feminine. The women of the AAGPBL were not permitted to smoke or drink in public or to wear their hair short, and every player in the league was sent to charm school to be sure they knew how to "act like ladies." Wrigley ordered that the uniforms in his league feature skirts. He did not want the women in the AAGPBL to wear pants, even though skirts made it difficult to slide.

Rather than place AAGPBL teams in major league cities, Wrigley initially put the franchises in small midwestern cities. The league opened in 1943 with four teams—the Kenosha Comets and Racine Belles in Wisconsin, the Rockford Peaches in Illinois, and the South Bend Blue Sox in Indiana. The following year, the league expanded to six clubs, adding teams in Milwaukee and Minneapolis, two large minor league cities.

"Rosie the Right Fielder." With the threat that World War II might eventually shut down Major League Baseball, Cubs' owner Philip Wrigley formed the All-American Girls Professional Baseball League. Here AAGPBL star Mary "Bonnie" Baker takes a swing, while catcher Irene Hickson of the Racine Belles waits for the ball. National Baseball Hall of Fame and Museum. Cooperstown, N.Y.

The new teams, however, found it difficult to compete against high-level minor league baseball. In 1945 the Milwaukee Chicks moved to Grand Rapids, Michigan, while the Minneapolis Millerettes moved to Indiana and became the Fort Wayne Daisies. Wrigley gave the task of managing the day-to-day matters of the league to his associate Arthur Meyerhoff, a man best known for introducing America to the nonstick cooking spray PAM.

To manage its teams, the AAGPBL recruited former major leaguers, including Josh Billings, who managed the Kenosha Comets, and Max Carey, who managed the Milwaukee Chicks. Catcher Mary "Bonnie" Baker of the South Bend Blue Sox was perhaps the biggest star of the AAGPBL, which often used Baker, a former model and three-time all-star, in publicity photos and as a league spokesperson. Dottie Wiltse, a pitcher for the Minneapolis Millerettes and Fort Wayne Daisies, was probably the best pitcher in the league. She struck out 205 batters in her rookie year, compiling a 20-and-16 record with a losing team.

In 1945, with the war winding down and baseball still in operation, Wrigley decided the league was no longer necessary. But the women in the league were unwilling to put down their gloves just because the men were coming back—and neither was Meyerhoff. In 1945 Wrigley sold his interest in the league to Meyerhoff, who continued to run the league for another nine years. Although the league remained popular in the late forties—the combined attendance of ten teams exceeded nine hundred thousand fans in 1948—by the 1950s baseball no longer fit into the role most Americans envisioned for women. The AAGPBL went out of business after the 1954 season. Like the women who lost their jobs in the defense industry when the war ended, the athletes of the AAGPBL returned to their former lives.

But would the war's end usher in opportunities for baseball, and the nation as a whole, or would it bring a return to the struggles of the Great Depression? That was the key question as Americans—and baseball—readied themselves for the challenges and changes of the postwar world.

11

Jackie Robinson and Civil Rights (1946 to 1989)

JIM CROW BEGAN TO WEAKEN after the war, first in baseball and then across the country. In July 1948, President Harry Truman issued an executive order that ended segregation in the armed forces. The Supreme Court delivered the greatest blow to Jim Crow in May 1954 when it handed down its unanimous decision in the case of Brown v. Board of Education, *which ruled that the* Plessy v. Ferguson *doctrine of "separate but equal" did not apply to public education because "separate educational facilities are inherently unequal." Although southern states bitterly resisted the desegregation of schools, integration continued. In 1955, Rosa Parks, the secretary of the local NAACP chapter, refused to give up her seat on a Montgomery city bus to a white rider and was arrested for violating Alabama's Jim Crow law. The NAACP responded with a boycott of the bus lines, which launched the Reverend Dr. Martin Luther King Jr. into the national spotlight. In 1960, students at North Carolina Agricultural and Technical State University staged a sit-in to integrate the lunch counter at a Woolworth's department store in Greensboro, while Freedom Riders—both black and white—attempted to end segregation at southern bus stations. Presidents Dwight Eisenhower and John F. Kennedy were reluctant to get involved until circumstances forced their hands. In 1957, Eisenhower sent the 101st Airborne Division of the United States Army to integrate Little Rock Central High School. Six years later, Kennedy introduced a moderate civil rights bill that became the Civil Rights Act of 1964, signed into law by his successor, Lyndon B. Johnson. The following year, Johnson signed the Voting Rights Act of 1965. Some civil rights opponents resorted to violence, culminating in the murder of King in April 1968. Meanwhile, facing violent opposition and frustrated with the slow prog-*

ress of civil rights, some African Americans grew impatient with their own
nonviolent methods. As the decade continued, racial unrest, including the out-
break of riots, increased. By the end of the sixties, with disenchanted whites
fearing a breakdown in order, support for the civil rights movement was on
the wane. Since then, events such as the 1991 beating of motorist Rodney King
by Los Angeles police officers and the killing of unarmed African Americans
by police in Staten Island, Baltimore, and Ferguson, Missouri, in the 2010s
illustrate that racial problems remain. Still, the civil rights movement made
real advances, such as changes in voting rights that led to the election of more
black leaders, and Americans of all backgrounds embraced black actors and
actresses, black athletes, black rock stars, and black talk show hosts. But, sadly,
many white Americans today still harbor resentment toward the achievements
of African Americans.

With a cloudless sky and an afternoon high of 68 degrees, April 15, 1947,
seemed perfect for Opening Day at Ebbets Field in Brooklyn. As it was
every year, the air was tense with the anticipation of another baseball season, even more so because the previous year the Dodgers had finished the
regular season in a tie for first place, only to be swept by the Cardinals in
a special tie-breaking series. Brooklyn fans were extra nervous, however,
because just five days earlier, Commissioner A. B. "Happy" Chandler
had suspended Dodger manager Leo Durocher for the season for asso-
ciating with known gamblers, and the club had not yet named a permanent replacement. If that did not create enough tension for Dodgers fans,
a rookie would be playing first base—a former Negro leaguer named
Jackie Robinson, the first African American allowed to play baseball in
the major leagues in sixty-three years.

Twenty-six thousand fans, more than half of them black, gathered at
Ebbets Field that day. While the attendance was respectable, more than
seven thousand seats remained empty, and the crowd was smaller than
the nearly thirty-two thousand fans who had turned out the year before
for the home opener against the crosstown rival Giants. White fans in
the stands were polite but unenthusiastic about Robinson's arrival, and
the mainstream New York media, while acknowledging Robinson's
presence, downplayed its significance and focused instead on Durocher's
absence and the return to the lineup of the potent but injury-prone center
fielder Pistol Pete Reiser. The African American press, however, under-

scored the significance of the event, with the *Pittsburgh Courier* publishing a regular column, ghostwritten by black sportswriter Wendell Phillips under Robinson's byline, while New York's *New Amsterdam News* urged black patrons to moderate their excitement at Dodgers games lest they provoke a backlash from uncomfortable white fans.

The Boston Braves held Robinson hitless in three at-bats in his first major league game, and in the fifth inning, Robinson hit into a double-play, ending a nascent Dodgers rally. Yet his enormous talent still helped Brooklyn win. In the seventh inning, with Brooklyn trailing 3–2 and Eddie Stanky on first, Robinson dropped a bunt. First baseman Earl Torgeson scooped up the ball, but, hurried by Robinson's surprising speed, sent a wild throw toward pitcher Johnny Sain, who was covering first. The ball hit Robinson in the back and ricocheted into right field, sending Stanky to third and Robinson to second. A double by Reiser knocked in both runners, giving Brooklyn the lead.

As the fourteen thousand African American fans who attended Opening Day in Brooklyn demonstrated, Robinson had an immediate impact on baseball. Black fans, who previously had followed only the Negro leagues, started to attend Dodgers games, and not just in Brooklyn. Railroads in the Deep South had to add extra cars to trains heading to Cincinnati and St. Louis—the National League's two southernmost outposts—when the Dodgers were in town. But Robinson also had an impact across America. White fans in Brooklyn, who at first were indifferent to Robinson, began to appreciate his bat and speed. When Robinson first took the field in Brooklyn, white fans saw him as a black ballplayer, but as his talent emerged during the course of the season, his race started to matter less. If Robinson came to bat with two runners on base and the Dodgers down by a run, white fans saw him as simply the player who could win the game.

While the civil rights movement was changing America, baseball was changing as well. Since the 1880s, the color barrier had kept African Americans out of the major leagues. Some white Americans, however, believed segregation in baseball was wrong. In 1923 the *Sporting News*, the most important baseball newspaper, wrote an editorial calling for African Americans to be allowed in the major leagues. In the thirties, having been forced to sell his stars because of the Great Depression, Connie Mack considered signing Negro league players to restore competeness

Jackie Robinson, the first African American to play in the major leagues in six decades, joined the Brooklyn Dodgers in 1947, breaking the color barrier and changing America. National Baseball Hall of Fame and Museum. Cooperstown, N.Y.

to the Philadelphia Athletics at an inexpensive price. Ultimately, however, he decided not to do so because he did not want to challenge the other team owners.

With the United States' entry into World War II, more voices called for an end to segregation in Major League Baseball. New York mayor Fiorello LaGuardia, whose city boasted three major league teams, demanded an end to the color barrier. Boston city officials, threatening to repeal the law allowing baseball on Sunday, pressured the Braves and Red Sox to integrate. To appease the city, the Red Sox invited three Negro league players—Sam Jethroe of the Cleveland Buckeyes, Marvin Williams of the Philadelphia Stars, and Jackie Robinson of the Kansas City Monarchs—to Fenway Park to try out for the team. The Red Sox had no intention of signing the players; the audition was held strictly for show. Although Boston manager Joe Cronin was impressed with Robinson, nothing came from the tryout.

The color barrier nearly collapsed in 1943. For several years the Philadelphia Phillies had been operating on the brink of bankruptcy. At the conclusion of the 1942 season, Phillies owner Gerald Nugent put the club up for sale. In his 1962 autobiography *Veeck—As in Wreck*, Bill Veeck, who in 1942 owned the minor league Milwaukee Brewers but would later be a maverick owner of three different big-league teams, claimed that he had reached a deal with Nugent to buy the Phillies. Because of the war, it was difficult to find quality ballplayers, but Veeck had a solution. He planned to stock the Phillies with a virtual Negro league all-star team. On his way to Philadelphia to close the deal, Veeck stopped off in Chicago to pay a courtesy call on Commissioner Kenesaw Mountain Landis. Although Landis's racist views were widely known, Veeck divulged his plan to the commissioner. When Veeck arrived in Philadelphia, he discovered the team was no longer for sale; the National League had taken control of the club. In his book, Veeck accused Landis of arranging the takeover to prevent the integration of the team.

Also in 1942, Larry MacPhail, the president and general manager of the Brooklyn Dodgers, resigned to join the army. To replace MacPhail, the Dodgers hired Branch Rickey, the general manager of the St. Louis Cardinals. Rickey, who had invented the farm system in St. Louis, emphasized efficiency and profit, but he also possessed a strict moral temperament. He was a devout Methodist who did not drink or smoke. Rickey would not even attend ball games on Sundays, although he had no problem making money from Sunday games. From a moral perspective, Rickey was greatly troubled by the color barrier, but he also saw financial opportunity in integration—adding black players would make it easier to market the Dodgers to African American fans. Besides, black players could help the Dodgers win.

When Landis died in November 1944 and thus no longer presented an obstacle to ending the color barrier, Rickey began to consider ending segregation in baseball. In 1945 he announced the formation of a new Negro league, an organization he named the United States League. Rickey said he would own one of the franchises in the league, a club called the Brooklyn Brown Dodgers, which would play at Ebbets Field when the white

Brooklyn Dodgers were on the road. The African American press criticized Rickey's proposal; the existing Negro leagues were dominated by black businessmen, and they might not be able to compete against white owners like Rickey. The black press did not realize, however, that Rickey's announcement was a ruse. In August 1945 he invited Jackie Robinson, a shortstop for the Kansas City Monarchs, to come to Brooklyn to try out for the Brown Dodgers. When Robinson arrived at Ebbets Field, Rickey informed him that he was not there for the Brown Dodgers, but to try out for the Brooklyn Dodgers' top minor league team, the Montreal Royals of the International League.

Sportswriter Wendell Smith of the African American newspaper the *Pittsburgh Courier* had long championed Robinson as the best candidate to break the color barrier, and Rickey chose Robinson for more than his ability. The Dodgers owner wanted a ballplayer who was not only good (and Robinson was nationally known from his college days at UCLA as a top athlete in football and track as well as baseball), but who was mature and had "guts enough *not* to fight back." Robinson already had earned a reputation for fighting back. In 1944, while a member of the army, he had been court-martialed after he refused to move to the back of an army bus in Fort Hood, Texas. Because the military was not subject to Texas state law, an all-white panel cleared Robinson of wrongdoing. At their meeting in August 1945, Rickey tested Robinson by unleashing a string of racial epithets, then explained to the shocked ballplayer that he would face much worse from fans and from players on other teams. Rickey feared that if Robinson lost his temper on the field, his plan would fail. After extracting a promise that, at least for the first few years, Robinson would not react to racial taunts or even opponents' aggressive play, Rickey signed him to a minor league contract.

Although Robinson was good enough to play in the majors in 1946, he spent the season in Montreal, where he would not be subjected to racial taunts from American fans when the Royals were at home or when they played their closest International League rival, the Toronto Maple Leafs. The other six clubs in the league were in the United States, but three of them—the Buffalo Bisons, Rochester Red Wings, and Syracuse Chiefs— were in New York State, while two others, the Newark Bears and Jersey City Little Giants, were in New Jersey. Only the Baltimore Orioles were based south of the Mason-Dixon line. Robinson had a great season in Montreal, leading the league with a .349 batting average as the Royals took the pennant by 18½ games over Syracuse.

Following Robinson's season in Montreal, many people in baseball suspected that he would be promoted to Brooklyn in 1947. To prevent that from happening, major league team owners at the January 1947 winter meeting held a secret vote on Robinson that only became public years later. By a 15–1 margin, the club owners voted against allowing Robinson in the big leagues. Only the Dodgers voted to let him play. Commissioner Happy Chandler, however, overruled the vote. Chandler was a southerner who had served as the governor and US senator from Kentucky, and, like many southerners, he often used racist terms like "boy" when he spoke. But unlike Landis, he recognized that the color barrier was wrong. The war influenced Chandler's decision. He defended his decision by saying, "Plenty of Negro boys were willing to go out and fight and die for this country. Is it right when they came back to tell them they can't play the national pastime?" His religion also figured into his thinking, as the commissioner explained, "I'm going to have to meet my Maker someday. And if He asks me why I didn't let this boy play, and I say it's because he's black that might not be a satisfactory answer." Chandler would pay a price for letting Robinson play; when his term as commissioner expired in 1951, the owners refused to rehire him.

For the 1947 season, Rickey decided to hold the Dodgers' spring training in Havana, Cuba, far from the Jim Crow laws of Florida, and he invited the Montreal Royals to train alongside the Dodgers. Rickey hoped that once the Dodger players saw how good Robinson was, they would demand that he be promoted to Brooklyn. But there was no groundswell of support for Robinson. Instead the players circulated a petition refusing to play with him. Opposition was especially strong from the many southerners on the team. Manager Leo Durocher responded by saying, "I don't care if the guy is yellow or black or if he has stripes like a . . . zebra. I'm the manager of this team, and I say he plays. What's more, I say he can make us all rich." Although most players backed down after Durocher's rejoinder, one player, an outfielder from Alabama named Fred "Dixie" Walker, still resisted. Walker, who was so popular with Dodgers fans that, in their Brooklyn accents, they called him "The People's Cherce," asked to be traded. When the 1947 season ended, Rickey sent him to the last-place Pittsburgh Pirates. Walker later called his request to be traded the biggest mistake of his life.

On April 10, five days before the start of the season, Rickey promoted Robinson to the Dodgers. Because veteran Harold "Pee Wee" Reese was entrenched at shortstop, Robinson played first base in 1947. The following season he shifted to second base, the position he played for most of his major league career.

Opposing fans and players directed a great deal of abuse at Robinson when the Dodgers were on the road. In Philadelphia, the Phillies' bench, led by manager Ben Chapman, hurled an endless string of racial slurs at Robinson. Knowing he had promised not to fight back, opposing base runners slid at Robinson with their spikes high, and pitchers threw at his head. In Cincinnati, where the crowd at Crosley Field was especially brutal, Robinson received death threats.[1]

Before the Dodgers arrived in St. Louis, the entire Cardinals team threatened to go on strike if Robinson played. National League president Ford Frick responded quickly, warning that any player who went on strike would be permanently banned from baseball. Frick concluded by saying, "I don't care if it wrecks the National League for five years. This is the United States of America, and one citizen has as much right to play as another." The Cardinals backed down.

The Dodgers had a great season in 1947, winning the pennant with a five-game lead over St. Louis. At age 28, Robinson won the Rookie of the Year Award. Just as important to Rickey, the Dodgers drew 1.8 million fans and led the National League in attendance.

Robinson opened the door for other African American ballplayers. Eleven weeks after he joined the Dodgers, the Cleveland Indians, now owned by Bill Veeck, signed Larry Doby, the first black player in the American League. Doby had been the center fielder for the Newark Eagles of the Negro American League, and when Veeck tried to obtain him, Eagles owner Effa Manley insisted that Veeck buy his contract from Newark. Recognizing the Eagles as a legitimate club that owned the rights to Doby, Veeck agreed to compensate Manley's team, setting a precedent that major league clubs must respect Negro league contracts. Major league clubs, however, continued to ignore the Negro leagues' reserve clause.

In 1947 the St. Louis Browns signed third baseman Hank Thompson. The following year the Dodgers brought up two more black players, pitcher Don Newcombe and catcher Roy Campanella. The Giants signed two African American outfielders, Monte Irvin in 1949 and Willie Mays in 1950. But after that, integration seemed to hit a wall. To some, it appeared that major league teams had a quota of black ballplayers that they would not exceed, perhaps out of fear that too many African Americans on a team would keep white fans away. Other teams were very slow in signing black players. The Yankees claimed they were searching for a black ballplayer who represented the "Yankee image." The excuse did not sound plausible, as neither Babe Ruth nor Mickey Mantle were wholesome role models. Finally, the Yankees signed catcher Elston Howard in 1955. The Boston Red Sox were the last team to sign a black player. In July 1959, more than twelve years after Jackie Robinson took the field in Brooklyn, utility infielder Pumpsie Green joined the team.

By the 1960s, however, the color of baseball players stopped mattering to most people. In 1971, when the Pittsburgh Pirates played a game with nine black starting players, few people noticed. Many black players, including Robinson, were active in the civil rights movement, and African American integration opened the door wider to other minorities, particularly Latinos. But it would be a generation after Jackie Robinson's debut before major league clubs hired black managers. Finally, in 1975, the Cleveland Indians made Frank Robinson (no relation to Jackie) their manager. Still, by the mid-1980s only three black men—Robinson of the Indians and later the Giants, Larry Doby of the White Sox, and Maury Wills of the Seattle Mariners—had managed in the major leagues.

Table 11.1.   The Integration of Major League Baseball

1947	1951	1955
Brooklyn Dodgers	Chicago White Sox	New York
Cleveland Indians		Yankees
St. Louis Browns	**1953**	
	Philadelphia	**1957**
1949	Athletics	Philadelphia
New York Giants	Chicago Cubs	Phillies
1950	**1954**	**1958**
Boston Braves	Pittsburgh Pirates	Detroit Tigers
	St. Louis Cardinals	
	Cincinnati Reds	**1959**
	Washington Senators	Boston Red Sox

On April 15, 1987, on the fortieth anniversary of Jackie Robinson's first major league game, the ABC nightly news program *Nightline* dedicated the show to Jackie Robinson's historic first game. During the program, host Ted Koppel asked Los Angeles Dodgers general manager Al Campanis why there had been so few African American managers in the major leagues. Campanis replied that African Americans "may not have some of the necessities to be a field manager or a general manager." Suddenly Major League Baseball had a serious public relations crisis on its hands. The Dodgers immediately fired Campanis, while Major League Baseball worked overtime trying to repair its image. In 1989 the Toronto Blue Jays made Cito Gaston the fourth African American to manage a major league team. Gaston became the first African American manager to win the world championship as, under his leadership, the Blue Jays won the World Series in 1992 and 1993. Since then, African American managers have become so commonplace that few people remark on their color when they are hired or fired—although in baseball, as in other professional sports, a debate persists over why there are not more African Americans in top executive and ownership positions.

In many ways, the history of baseball reflects what happened in American society, but when it came to the civil rights movement, baseball helped lead the way. The collapse of baseball's color barrier had a significant influence on American society. It was probably baseball's most important contribution to American life. Jackie Robinson joined the Dodgers in 1947, more than a year before President Harry Truman integrated the military and seven years before *Brown v. Board of Education* integrated public schools. Robinson's arrival on the Dodgers marked the first major step of integration. It prepared America for civil rights. If a player helped a team win, that player's skin color no longer mattered to that team's fans. As Americans began to realize this, racial hatred lessened.

12

The Postwar American Century (1945 to 1964)

AMERICANS IN THE POSTWAR PERIOD *encountered a great deal of pressure to conform to a preconceived set of ideals and values, in large part because of the Cold War between the United States and the Soviet Union. A second Red Scare emerged after World War II in an anticommunist witch hunt that made Americans wary of bucking capitalist principles and Christian virtues. The other factor that defined America after World War II was affluence. Between 1945 and 1960 the gross national product soared 250 percent and per capita income rose 35 percent. Much of this growth was fueled by pent-up consumer demand. After a decade and a half of austerity, Americans craved new automobiles and appliances. Returning veterans, with money to spend and access to low-interest mortgages through the GI Bill, formed a large market of ready homebuyers. By 1960, with the growth of suburbia, 60 percent of Americans owned their own home. As middle-class white Americans left the cities, people with lower incomes, often people of color, moved in to take their place. Not only were middle-class city dwellers relocating to the suburbs, but, following the introduction of home air conditioning in the thirties and forties, many Americans left the Northeast and Midwest for the warmer climate of the Sun Belt. California's population nearly doubled between 1930 and 1950. With their newfound affluence and their homes in the suburbs, many Americans rediscovered their love affair with the automobile. By the 1960s, with the interstate highway system under construction, two-car families became the rule. As drive-in businesses, such as McDonald's and Holiday Inn, appeared, an automobile-based culture emerged. Americans also fell under the influence of the new medium of television. Eighty percent of American homes had a television by 1960. Television reinforced the image of the American family, depicting it as white, middle-class, and Christian. Despite the strong pressure to conform to the perceived parameters of American society, challenges to the status quo emerged during the fifties and became full blown in the revolutionary sixties. Baseball in the postwar period reflected America's obsession with conformity and affluence, while at the same time striving to adjust to America's new reality.*

In the spring of 1957, New York Yankees Mickey Mantle and Whitey Ford planned a birthday party for their friend, second baseman Billy Martin. Mantle and Ford were the megastars on a team filled with superstars. Mantle, the Yankees' center fielder, was probably the most popular baseball player of the fifties. The previous season he won the American League Triple Crown, the rare achievement of leading the league in three important categories: batting average, home runs, and runs batted in. When Mantle retired in 1968, his career 536 home runs trailed only Babe Ruth and Willie Mays. Ford was the ace of the New York pitching staff, the so-called Chairman of the Board. In 1956, Ford led the Yankees with nineteen wins and only six losses. When he retired after the 1967 season, the Yankee pitcher had compiled a career record of 236 wins and 106 losses. Mantle, Ford, and Martin socialized frequently, and they often drank to excess. Martin, who had gotten into a few well-publicized fights, also had a quick temper. To celebrate his birthday, on May 16, six Yankees—Mantle, Ford, and Martin, as well as pitcher Johnny Kucks, right fielder Hank Bauer, and catcher Yogi Berra—and their wives gathered at the Copacabana nightclub in Manhattan to eat, drink, and catch a performance by African American entertainer Sammy Davis Jr.

During the performance, a group of intoxicated members of a bowling team celebrating at the next table began heckling Davis and shouting racial slurs at him. When someone from the Yankees table asked the bowlers to quiet down, they began to taunt the ballplayers. Martin asked the loudest bowler to step outside with him. A few minutes later Bauer, heading outside to see if Martin was okay, claimed to have discovered the drunken heckler unconscious on the floor near the cloakroom. The next day the media reported that six Yankees were involved in a brawl at the Copacabana. Although the players maintained that the man was beaten up by bouncers, the victim, a Bronx deli owner, accused Bauer of assault. A Manhattan grand jury was convened to investigate the matter, but the

In 1961, the "M & M Boys," Mickey Mantle (left) and Roger Maris of the New York Yankees, challenged Babe Ruth's 34-year-old record of 60 home runs in a single season. Mantle fell short of the record, finishing with only 54, but Maris broke Ruth's mark with 61 homers, only to see his accomplishment diminished by Ford Frick, the commissioner of baseball, who put an asterisk next to Maris's record because the 1961 season was eight games longer than Ruth's 1927 season. National Baseball Hall of Fame and Museum. Cooperstown, N.Y.

judge dismissed the case because of a lack of evidence. Yankees management, however, fined five of the ballplayers $1,000 each (one of them, Johnny Kucks, because he made less than the others, was fined only $500), and a month later, citing his bad influence on Ford and especially Mantle, the Yankees traded Martin to the Kansas City Athletics.

The incident at the Copacabana and Martin's subsequent trade to the A's seemed to capture the spirit of America in the fifties. Like America in the postwar era, the Yankees were powerful and confident. New York seemed to be at the center of the world, and it certainly served as America's cultural heartbeat and economic engine. At the time of the brawl, the team had just won six World Series championships and seven American League pennants in eight years. The ball club responded to the incident at the Copacabana the same way American society responded to those who did not fit the preconceived set of Cold War ideals and values, discarding their second baseman because he did not conform to the club's ideal image.

Other sports would eclipse baseball in popularity during the 1960s and beyond, but for much of the 1950s baseball had very little competition. The National Football League did not explode in popularity until after the 1958 NFL championship game at Yankee Stadium. That contest, between the Baltimore Colts and the New York Giants, went into overtime, and the Colts' sudden-death victory on national television gave the league immense publicity. A second professional football circuit, the American Football League, formed in 1960, and the champions of both leagues began playing a postseason Super Bowl in 1967. In 1970 the NFL absorbed the AFL, creating the modern National Football League. In the fifties and early sixties, professional basketball was still a minor sport, with the National Basketball Association maintaining franchises in smaller markets like Fort Wayne, Indiana, and Syracuse and Rochester, New York. Baseball, however, was still enormously popular in the postwar era. If, as some historians have claimed, the 1920s represented baseball's Golden Age, then the fifties represented baseball's Silver Age. Just as the United States was at the peak of its power in the twenty years following World War II, baseball was at its peak as well.

In the fifties, baseball stars were national figures. Most Americans were familiar with Ted Williams, the left fielder of the Boston Red Sox, and Stan Musial, the first baseman of the St. Louis Cardinals, as well as

Jackie Robinson. And most Americans agreed that the best center fielder in baseball played in New York City—they just could not agree on which team. Countless arguments debated the merits of Yankees center fielder Mickey Mantle, who replaced Joe DiMaggio in 1951, versus those of Willie Mays of the Giants and Duke Snider of the Dodgers.

The fifties were a good time for baseball in general, but they were an especially good time for baseball fans in New York City. Just as New York was the heart of American culture in the 1950s, it was also the center of the baseball universe. Not only did New York have three major league teams, it had three very good major league teams. In the American League, the Yankees, owned by Del Webb, a builder of suburbia in the West, were the most dominant team, winning the pennant every year between 1947 and 1964 except 1948, 1954, and 1959. The Yankees won five straight World Series from 1949 to 1953, and they also won the series in 1947, 1956, 1958, 1961, and 1962. As one wag said, rooting for the Yankees was like rooting for US Steel. Of course, in the 1950s America also led the world in manufacturing.

In the National League, the Giants and Dodgers often competed for the National League pennant. The crosstown competition was the fiercest rivalry in sports, as the fans and players of both teams hated each other. When the Dodgers traded Jackie Robinson to the Giants after the 1956 season, the aging Robinson chose to retire rather than play for Brooklyn's archrival. Brooklyn won six pennants during the postwar period, capturing the National League flag in 1947, 1949, 1952, 1953, 1955, and 1956. In each of those seasons, the Dodgers faced the Yankees in the World Series. As the Yankees tended to win those contests, Dodgers fans consoled themselves with the defiant expression "Wait 'til next year." In 1955, Brooklyn finally won its first and only World Series championship. The Giants won the National League pennant in 1951 and 1954, sweeping the Cleveland Indians in the 1954 World Series.

One of the greatest pennant races of all time took place in 1951. The Dodgers held a large lead for most of the season—by August 11, they were 13½ games ahead of the Giants. But in the second half of the season the Giants started to creep up, at one point winning 15 games in a row. The two teams finished the season with identical 96-and-58 records. To determine the pennant winner, the National League staged a three-game tie-breaking series. The Giants won Game 1 at Ebbets Field by a score of 3–1. The Dodgers evened the series the next day, winning 10–0 at the Polo Grounds. The final game of the series, also at the Polo Grounds, was played on October 3. Going into the bottom of the ninth inning, the Dodgers held a 4–2 lead. With one out, third baseman Bobby Thomson came to bat with Whitey Lockman at second and Clint Hartung at third. Thomson had been hot, knocking in a run in the seventh inning and homering in Game 1. Willie Mays, who would end his career twenty-two years later with a total of 660 home runs but at the time was still an unproven rookie, stood on deck. Given that first base was empty, the conventional wisdom held that the Dodgers should have given Thomson an intentional walk and pitched to the rookie, hoping he would hit into a game-ending double play. Instead Dodgers manager Charlie Dressen called for relief pitcher Ralph Branca to replace starter Don Newcombe on the mound. Branca pitched to the Giants third baseman, and Thomson knocked a three-run home run over the wall in left field. Perhaps the most famous home run in baseball history, the "Shot Heard 'Round the World" gave the Giants the National League pennant. A week later the Giants would lose the World Series to the Yankees in six games.

Despite the popularity of baseball in the postwar period, the forces shaping American society presented new challenges to the game. For instance, the "Shot Heard 'Round the World" was literally heard around the world, as Armed Forces Radio broadcasted the game to bases on every continent. In May 1951, one month after being removed from command in the Korean War by President Harry Truman, General Douglas MacArthur threw out the first pitch at a game between the Phillies and the Giants at the Polo Grounds, where the general was enthusiastically cheered while the president was booed in absentia.

Baseball was even dragged into the postwar ideological fray. In an April 1949 speech at an international peace conference in Paris that was sponsored by the Soviet Union, African American folk singer and actor Paul Robeson announced that black Americans would not fight for the United States in a war against the Soviet Union. With his speech, Robeson, a former NFL football player and a star of segregated movies who had already made the transition to mainstream films, attracted the attention of the House Committee on Un-American Activities. In response, the committee summoned Jackie Robinson, perhaps the most famous African American in the country, to Washington, DC, to answer if black Americans would support the United States in a war against the Soviet

Union. Robinson was hesitant about testifying before the committee, but on the advice of Branch Rickey, he agreed to appear. In his statement, Robinson testified that he could not speak for the singer but he believed that most African Americans would "do their best to help their country win the war." Robinson added that African Americans were not going to stop fighting racial discrimination, but he believed that black Americans could "win our fight without the Communists." Thus, the Cold War influenced baseball. McCarthyism, the tactic of advancing politically by making accusations of disloyalty, subversion, or treason without proper evidence, named after Wisconsin senator Joseph McCarthy, who built a political career in the early 1950s on the practice, also cast its shadow on the sport. In 1954, fearing that the name of his ball club invoked images of Communist revolutionaries, Cincinnati Reds owner Powel Crosley changed the name of his team to the Cincinnati Redlegs. In 1961, with McCarthyism a distant memory, new owner Bill DeWitt restored the name Cincinnati Reds.

Other forces prevalent in postwar America affected baseball. Suburbanization, for instance, endangered baseball's stability. Ballparks were neighborhood institutions, often squeezed between existing streets and buildings. For instance, the outfield fence of Griffith Stadium, the home of the Washington Senators, followed strange angles that cut around a tree and an apartment building. Parking was scarce at most urban ballparks, which were built when neighborhood fans walked or took the bus, streetcar, or subway to the game, and the lack of parking threatened to keep suburbanites away. Fearing crime or succumbing to racism, many suburban fans became reluctant to travel to the city to attend a game, especially at night. And with the introduction of television, suburban fans found it easier to catch the game on TV—or forgo the game altogether for another program.

Baseball had not been keeping up with the demographic changes that were taking place in America, and by the end of World War II the major leagues and the US population had become seriously misaligned. For fifty years no changes had been made in the major league map—the same sixteen major league teams, representing the same ten cities, played baseball between 1903 and 1952. The major leagues were confined to the northeastern quadrant of the United States, with no team south of the Potomac and Ohio Rivers and with the two westernmost teams, both in St. Louis, on the banks of the Mississippi River. During the same period, however,

American demographics changed. The population doubled between 1900 and 1950, jumping from 76 million to 151 million. And the population shifted, with western and southern states gaining residents. California, which still did not have a major league baseball team when the war ended, jumped from the fifth most populous state in 1940 to second place in 1950. Technology also changed America, as commercial air travel made the West Coast seem less remote.

Minor league teams felt pressure from the changes taking place in America. In the first half of the twentieth century, large cities in the North that lacked a major league team, as well as cities along the West Coast, were content to support high-level minor league clubs. Starting in 1946, these leagues were classified as Triple-A. Cities in the South settled for teams in second-tier minor leagues, Class Double-A. With the advent of television, however, rather than going to a minor league game, some fans preferred to stay home and watch broadcasts of major league teams. Fans and civic leaders in large cities without big-league teams began to

Table 12.1. High-Level Minor League Teams, 1949

Class AAA		
American Association	International League	Pacific Coast League
Columbus Red Birds	Baltimore Orioles	Hollywood Stars
Indianapolis Indians	Buffalo Bisons	Los Angeles Angels
Kansas City Blues	Jersey City Giants	Oakland Oaks
Louisville Colonels	Montreal Royals	Portland Beavers
Milwaukee Brewers	Newark Bears	Sacramento Solons
Minneapolis Millers	Rochester Red Wings	San Diego Padres
St. Paul Saints	Syracuse Chiefs	San Francisco Seals
Toledo Mud Hens	Toronto Maple Leafs	Seattle Rainiers

Class AA	
Southern Association	Texas League
Atlantic Crackers	Beaumont Exporters
Birmingham Barons	Dallas Eagles
Chattanooga Lookouts	Fort Worth Cats
Little Rock Travelers	Houston Buffaloes
Memphis Chickasaws	Oklahoma City Indians
Mobile Bears	San Antonio Missions
Nashville Volunteers	Shreveport Sports
New Orleans Pelicans	Tulsa Oilers

demand major league clubs. At the same time, others questioned whether Boston, Philadelphia, and St. Louis could still support two teams and whether New York City could support three.

The fifty-year logjam finally gave way in Boston. By the fifties, the Braves were struggling at the box office. The Braves were not a terrible team. Led by starting pitchers Warren Spahn and Johnny Sain, Boston won the 1948 National League pennant. (The other two Braves starters, Bill Voiselle and Vern Bickford, were less memorable that year, inspiring the Boston faithful to lament, "Spahn and Sain and pray for rain.") But the Braves were losing out in popularity to the Red Sox. In 1952 they drew only 281,278 fans. Not happy with the low attendance and tired of playing second fiddle to the Red Sox, Braves owner Lou Perini announced in March 1953, one month before the start of the season, that the club was moving to Milwaukee. Milwaukee had once had an American League club, in 1901, but the AL Milwaukee Brewers had become the St. Louis Browns after only one season. In 1953 the Wisconsin city had just built a new ballpark, Milwaukee County Stadium, ostensibly for the minor league Brewers, but in reality the city hoped the new stadium would lure a major league tenant. The Milwaukee Braves thrived in their new location; in just their first eight games in Milwaukee, attendance at Braves games surpassed that of their entire 1952 season in Boston. When the season ended, Milwaukee had set a new National League attendance record, drawing 1,826,397 fans. And the Braves were successful in Milwaukee. Led by right fielder Hank Aaron and third baseman Eddie Mathews, Milwaukee won the National League pennant in 1957 and 1958, and the team beat the Yankees in the 1957 World Series.

Other teams followed the Braves' lead. In St. Louis, the Browns had trouble competing with the Cardinals. Bill Veeck, who had sold the Indians and then bought the Browns, tried to lure fans with promotions. Veeck once said, "You can draw more people with a losing team by giving them bread and circuses than with a losing team and a long, still silence." He made good on that principle. In 1951 Veeck signed a player with dwarfism to a contract with the Browns, and on August 19, the Browns sent the three-foot-seven Eddie Gaedel to pinch-hit against the Tigers. Gaedel, whose strike zone was only one and one-half inches high, walked on four pitches and was promptly replaced by a pinch runner. But even gimmicks did not help draw fans. Veeck tried to move the team to Los Angeles, but the American League, citing the distance from the other clubs, rejected his request. He also tried to move the team to Milwaukee, where he had once owned a minor league team, but Braves owner Lou Perini, who owned the minor league Brewers and was planning his own team move to Milwaukee, objected. Veeck then looked at Baltimore. Other American League owners, tired of his publicity stunts, refused to let the Browns move unless Veeck sold the team. At the end of the 1953 season, Veeck sold the Browns to a Maryland attorney named Clarence Miles, who moved the club to Baltimore and changed the name of the team to the Orioles.

In Philadelphia, the Athletics could no longer compete with the Phillies. The Phils, who had earned the nickname the "Whiz Kids" because of young stars like pitcher Robin Roberts and right fielder Richie Ashburn, won the 1950 National League pennant, while the A's had not finished in first place since 1931. The Athletics' aging owner, Connie Mack (who turned ninety-one in December 1953), had become too frail to operate the team. After fifty years at the helm, he had already stepped down from his managerial duties following the 1950 season. In November 1954 Mack sold the Athletics to Chicago stockbroker Arnold Johnson, who moved the club to Kansas City for the 1955 season.

The moves, or franchise shifts, of the Braves, Browns, and Athletics made sense. In each case, the club left a two-team city, and baseball's geography remained confined to the northeastern quadrant of the United States. But what happened in the late fifties radically redrew the baseball map and made Major League Baseball a truly national organization. Both the Brooklyn Dodgers and New York Giants needed new stadiums. Their existing facilities were old—Ebbets Field was built in 1913, while the Polo Grounds was built in 1911. Both were located in residential neighborhoods—the Flatbush neighborhood of Brooklyn and Harlem in Manhattan—and neither offered much parking. City officials in New York, however, were unwilling to help the Giants get a new stadium. The team's owner, Horace Stoneham, began to negotiate with officials in Minneapolis. Had the Giants moved to Minnesota, however, they would have remained in the northeastern quadrant of the country.

Across the East River in Brooklyn, the Dodgers were planning on building a new stadium. Walter O'Malley, a lawyer with the Brooklyn Trust Company, had taken over the ownership of the club after forcing

Branch Rickey out in 1950. O'Malley planned to construct a domed stadium in downtown Brooklyn at the terminal for the Long Island Railroad, the same location where the Barclays Center—home of the NBA's Brooklyn Nets—would eventually be built in the twenty-first century. O'Malley was willing to bear the construction costs if the city of New York condemned the land.

But city planner Robert Moses had a different idea. Moses, who was attempting to rebuild New York City, wanted to create a modern infrastructure. No tunnel or bridge was built in New York without his approval, and he was responsible for bringing the United Nations, the World Trade Center, and the 1939 and 1964 World's Fairs to the city. Moses wanted to build the new stadium for the Dodgers in the Flushing Meadows neighborhood of Queens, near the grounds of the 1939 World's Fair. O'Malley hated the location. The Dodgers owner still thought in terms of neighborhood fans, and with the proposed stadium site surrounded by water on three sides and a cemetery on the fourth, he feared the team would not attract walk-up customers. More troubling to O'Malley was the question of whether the team still could be called the *Brooklyn* Dodgers if they played in Queens.

While O'Malley was mulling his options, officials from Los Angeles approached him. They did not attempt to convince him to move the Dodgers to California. As Brooklyn was the most prominent team in the National League, Los Angeles officials did not believe they could do that. Instead they sought advice from O'Malley on how to buy the Washington Senators and move that team to Los Angeles. But O'Malley saw opportunity in the conversation. He knew that because of travel costs, the National League would not approve the move of only one team to California. O'Malley contacted Stoneham and convinced him to move the Giants to San Francisco rather than Minneapolis, and both clubs headed west following the 1957 season.

At the gate, the Los Angeles Dodgers and San Francisco Giants were an immediate success. The Giants, playing in the minor league–caliber Seals Stadium, drew 1,272,625 fans in their first season on the West Coast, double their attendance in New York in 1957. The team's new major league stadium, the windy Candlestick Park, which was built at the edge of the city in an area slated for industrial development, opened in 1960. For four years, the Dodgers played in the massive Los Angeles

Memorial Coliseum, which had a capacity of 92,500 for baseball. As the Coliseum was designed for football, the Dodgers made temporary modifications to the structure, erecting a fence across the football field to create a right field wall 300 feet down the line from home plate. Because the grandstand at the left field foul pole was only 251 feet from home plate, the club also installed a forty-two-foot-high screen along the left field wall. The Dodgers drew 78,672 fans in their first home game in Los Angeles and 1,845,556 for the year, 800,000 more than the team attracted in Brooklyn the previous season. In 1962 the team moved into Dodger Stadium, which was built on the site of what had been a formerly vibrant Mexican American neighborhood called Chavez Ravine. Because it destroyed a neighborhood, the location caused controversy—both at the ballot box and in the minority community—but in the end, voters approved the stadium. Both stadiums were designed with acres of parking. The two teams were also successful on the field. Los Angeles won the 1959 and 1963 World Series, while the Giants won the 1962 National League pennant, only to lose the series to the Yankees in seven games.

While West Coast fans celebrated the arrival of major league baseball, fans back in New York struggled with the hole left by the loss of the city's two National League teams. Former Giants and Dodgers fans could not bring themselves to root for the Yankees. Unexplainably, without the competition from two other major league teams, the Yankees actually drew sixty-five thousand *fewer* fans in 1958 than they had the year before. The city immediately attempted to attract another National League team, only to be rebuffed by the Reds, Phillies, and Pirates. The National League rejected city leaders' request for the creation of a new National League team in New York. Mayor Robert F. Wagner Jr. assigned the task of luring another team to the city to attorney William A. Shea, who adopted a different strategy. In 1959 Shea announced the formation of a third major league called the Continental League, which he said would begin play in 1961. The league would feature franchises in New York as well as seven other large cities that lacked a major league team—Atlanta, Buffalo, Dallas–Fort Worth, Denver, Houston, Minneapolis–St. Paul, and Toronto. To give the league credibility, former Brooklyn Dodgers owner Branch Rickey was named president of the Continental League.

The threat posed by the Continental League forced Major League Baseball to act. In July 1960 the National League unanimously agreed to expand to ten clubs. Two weeks later, confident that New York would receive one of the new franchises, the Continental League dissolved without ever playing a game. In October the National League announced that it would add teams from two Continental League cities, New York and Houston, both of which would start playing in the 1962 season. By the end of the twentieth century, every Continental League city except Buffalo would have a major league team.

At its October meeting a week later, the American League gave Washington Senators owner Calvin Griffith permission to move his team to Minneapolis–St. Paul before the start of the 1961 season. At the meeting, the American League also added two new clubs, although neither was placed in a Continental League city. To replace the team leaving Washington, the league added a new franchise, which would also be called the Washington Senators. And with the National League competing with the Yankees in New York, the American League decided to return the favor by placing an expansion team in Los Angeles. To get a jump on the National League, the American League announced that its two new teams would begin playing in 1961.

The teams in baseball's four new cities represented the triumph of the suburbs. Because the Minneapolis–St. Paul franchise represented two cities, Griffith originally wanted to name the club the Twin Cities Twins (the team's cap still bears a "TC" logo), but before they ever played a game he instead christened them the Minnesota Twins. Rather than play in one city or the other, the Twins would play their home games at Metropolitan Stadium in suburban Bloomington, on the site of the future Mall of America. The new National League team in Texas, called the Houston Colt .45s because of the state's Old West heritage, would play at Colt Stadium, a temporary facility quickly erected in Houston's suburban Medical Center District, until the club's permanent stadium, being built on adjacent land, was ready. The other new National League team, called the New York Mets after the nineteenth-century New York Metropolitans of the old American Association, would play at the Polo Grounds in Manhattan until 1964, when a new stadium, named after William A. Shea, was ready in Flushing Meadows, Queens—the same site Robert Moses had wanted for the Dodgers. Not only was Shea Stadium accessible from two interstate highways, but because it was not built in the crowded boroughs of Manhattan or Brooklyn, it had enough room to provide parking for thousands of cars.

The American League's new West Coast team, called the Los Angeles Angels after that city's former minor league club, perhaps best represented suburbanization. In the club's first season, the Angels played in a ballpark called Wrigley Field, which had served as the home to the city's minor league Angels. In 1962 the team temporarily moved into the newly constructed Dodger Stadium, although the American League club referred to the facility as Chavez Ravine rather than by its official name. In 1966 the Angels' permanent home was ready. The new stadium was not built in Los Angeles, but in suburban Anaheim, near Disneyland in Orange County. On September 2, 1965, in preparation for the club's 1966 move to Anaheim Stadium, the team officially changed its name to the California Angels, becoming the only twentieth-century baseball team to change its name in midseason. The owner of the Angels, singing cowboy movie star Gene Autry, did not believe the team could be known as "Los Angeles" if it played in a suburb thirty miles away.

Expansion created new challenges for baseball. With the addition of two new clubs in each league, the major leagues had to change their schedule. Under the old 154-game schedule, every team played 22 games against each of its opponents. With ten clubs in 1961, the American League expanded its schedule to 162 games, with every team playing 18 games against league teams. Expansion also diluted major league talent, especially pitching. Pitchers who would not have made a major league roster when there were only sixteen teams now found themselves on big-league staffs.

Still, the level of play remained exciting. In 1961 two Yankees—center fielder Mickey Mantle and right fielder Roger Maris, called the "M & M Boys" by the press—challenged Babe Ruth's thirty-four-year-old record of sixty home runs in a season. Both players—but especially Maris—received a great deal of hate mail for threatening a record many people held as sacred. On the last day of the season, Maris hit his sixty-first home run. While the hit should have broken the record, Commissioner Ford Frick announced that because Maris took eight more games than Ruth to set the record, his record would not replace Ruth's. Instead, Maris would hold the record for a 162-game season while Ruth would continue to hold the record for a 154-game season. Many saw Frick's decision as a slap in Maris's face, as he essentially placed an asterisk next to the new record.

The following year, with the addition of the Mets and the Colt .45s, the National League adopted the 162-game schedule. While the Colts were creating new traditions in Houston, the Mets drew on nostalgia, adopting Dodgers blue and Giants orange for team colors. The club brought in former Yankees manager Casey Stengel to skipper the team. Stengel had led the Yankees to seven World Series titles from 1949 to 1958, but the Yankees fired him after he lost the 1960 World Series. Many people, including Stengel himself, believed the Yankees had fired the seventy-year-old manager because of his age.

In their first season, the Mets were one of the worst teams in baseball history. Even Stengel's skill could not overcome the club's lack of talent. The first run the Mets surrendered scored on a balk, and the club lost its first nine games. The Mets finished the 1962 season in last place, losing 120 games and winning only 40. But even as a terrible team, the Mets immediately became very popular in New York, as former Dodgers and Giants fans embraced the young team. The Mets drew almost a million fans in 1962 and surpassed a million the following year, and in 1964, in their new home at Shea Stadium, the Mets outdrew the Yankees, even though the Yanks would win their fifth straight pennant that year. The Mets were not as successful on the field, remaining in the cellar for most of the decade. The club finished in last place from 1962 to 1965, and again in 1967. In 1966 and 1968 the team managed to climb to ninth place. Then something miraculous happened—in 1969 the "Amazin' Mets" won the World Series in five games! America had changed, and, miraculously, so had the Mets.

13

Change and Revolution (1960 to 1975)

THE SIXTIES WERE A PERIOD OF *political unrest that unleashed various protest movements that were still active through the 1970s. These reform movements transformed American society. The most significant social movement of the era was the civil rights movement, discussed in chapter 11, but other crusades—including the women's movement, which sought to end gender discrimination; the antiwar movement, which opposed US involvement in the Vietnam War; and the counterculture and youth movement, which promoted individuality over conformity—also shaped the sixties and seventies. These protest movements left their imprints on the era and on baseball.*

In October 1969 center fielder Curt Flood received a call from someone in the St. Louis Cardinals office informing him that he had been traded to the Philadelphia Phillies. Flood, a three-time all-star who had helped lead the Cardinals to the 1967 and 1968 National League pennant and to the 1967 World Series championship, responded with stone-cold silence. He did not want to go from a perennial pennant contender to a team that finished thirty-seven games out of first place. Accustomed to the comforts of Busch Memorial Stadium, which had opened in 1966, he did not want to play in Philadelphia's antiquated Connie Mack Stadium. And Flood, an African American, did not want to play before Philadelphia's notoriously belligerent and often racist fans. He was also angry that the call had come from an underling, rather than from general manager Bing Devine.

Frustrated, Flood turned to Marvin Miller, the executive director of the new players' union, the Major League Baseball Players Association. Miller, who had only recently turned the thirteen-year-old MLBPA into a bona fide labor union, assured Flood that if he wanted to sue Major League Baseball, the union would bear the legal costs, but he warned the ballplayer that because of Major League Baseball's antitrust exemption and the history of courts favoring baseball team owners, there was not "a chance in hell of winning." More importantly, Miller advised him that even if he did win, Flood would not benefit from a lawsuit, as he would likely be driven out of baseball. Flood asked Miller if a lawsuit would benefit others, and when Miller informed him that it would help existing and future players, Flood agreed to pursue litigation. "You're a union-leader's dream," Miller remarked as the two planned their strategy.

In December, Flood sent a letter to Baseball Commissioner Bowie Kuhn protesting that he was not "a piece of property to be bought and sold." Acknowledging that he had received a contract offer from the Phillies, Flood stated that he believed he had the right to consider offers from other teams before making a decision, and he asked the commissioner to inform the other major league teams of his availability for the 1970 season. Citing the reserve clause, Kuhn rejected Flood's bid for free agency. Flood went ahead with the lawsuit, and in 1972, in the case of *Flood v. Kuhn*, the United States Supreme Court upheld the reserve clause and rejected Flood's assertion that he was a free agent. Miller not only correctly predicted the outcome of the case, but he also prophesied Flood's future. Rejecting the contract from the Phillies, Flood sat out the 1970 season. The Phillies traded Flood to the Washington Senators for the 1971 season, where he would play thirteen games before leaving baseball for good.

Flood later explained that the civil rights movement had inspired him to challenge the reserve clause. His claim is not surprising. The reform movements of the sixties and seventies exerted a substantial influence on baseball, as did other elements from the era. In late 1963 NASA moved its manned space program to Houston from Cape Canaveral, Florida. A year later, because the ball club had been receiving complaints from Colt's Manufacturing Company which made the Colt .45 revolver, Judge Roy Hofheinz, the president of the Houston Colt .45s, announced that, in honor of NASA, starting in 1965 the team would be known as the Houston Astros. When that season started, the Astros moved into baseball's first domed stadium—the Astrodome, which was hailed as the "Eighth Wonder of the World." The climate-controlled facility featured a glass

Marvin Miller, the executive director of the Major League Baseball Players Association, turned the organization into a bona fide labor union. National Baseball Hall of Fame and Museum. Cooperstown, N.Y.

roof that allowed sunlight to nurture the ballpark's natural grass surface. During the season, however, ballplayers discovered that they could not follow fly balls in the glare coming through the glass. To rectify that problem, the sunlight was blocked by painting the roof white—which, unfortunately, killed the grass, and for the rest of the season, the Astros played home games on dead grass that had been painted green. Before the 1966 season began, workmen replaced the grass with an artificial surface called AstroTurf. AstroTurf offered a number of advantages for grounds crews, including less maintenance, better drainage, and truer bounces of ground balls. But AstroTurf also presented a number of disadvantages: It was as hard as concrete and, because it lacked the spring found in natural surfaces, over time it damaged players' knees. And players found that ground balls traveled faster over the surface. Many ball clubs, however, believed its benefits outweighed its drawbacks. By the midseventies, seven baseball teams that played in outdoor stadiums had replaced natural grass with an artificial surface.

Like America, baseball endured a period of turmoil in the 1960s. In the fifties, five economically troubled baseball teams had left their traditional homes for greener pastures. As baseball franchises became less grounded in their home cities, owners of losing teams discovered that the easiest way to attract more fans was to move the team. Because of the novelty of watching a major league game and the pride of living in a major league city, even second-rate teams initially drew well in new cities. But if that team did not improve quickly, in a few years many of the new fans became discouraged.

Although the Braves initially seemed to strike gold in Milwaukee, by the 1960s the club was in decline. After 1961 Milwaukee did not finish higher than fifth place, and attendance suffered. In 1954 the Braves became the first National League team to draw two million fans, but in 1962 attendance slipped below a million and in 1965 the team barely attracted a half million fans. In the meantime, civic leaders in Atlanta were seeking a major league baseball team. The Georgia city had just built a new multipurpose stadium, which had already attracted an NFL expansion team. City leaders believed that a major league baseball team would solidify Atlanta's status as a major league city. In 1965 the Braves attempted to move to Atlanta during the middle of the season. Although the National League blocked the midseason move, it allowed the Braves to move to Atlanta in time to start the 1966 season.

The Kansas City Athletics were also in trouble. The team was abysmal, both on the field and at the gate, when it left Philadelphia in 1955, and it did not improve in Kansas City. By the mid-1960s, the A's began to investigate other possible locations. After considering Seattle, New Orleans, and Dallas–Fort Worth, in 1964 the team owner, Charles O. Finley, signed an agreement with the state of Kentucky to move the Athletics to Louisville. He had planned to change the team's name to the Kentucky Colonels, which would have allowed the club to continue to use the "KC" logo it had adopted in 1963. But the American League, fearing that Louisville was no longer a major market, vetoed the move. The A's did not stop looking for a new home and, at the conclusion of the 1967 season, the American League allowed the team to move to Oakland, across the bay from San Francisco, where they would play in the Oakland–Alameda County Coliseum, a new multipurpose stadium built for pro football's Oakland Raiders. Beginning in 1968, the A's would also make that stadium home.

The loss of teams in Milwaukee and Kansas City upset political and business leaders in both cities. Kansas City, which had already approved the construction of a new baseball stadium, sued the American League. Fearing the lawsuit might threaten baseball's antitrust exemption, Major League Baseball agreed to expand to twenty-four teams in 1969. To replace the Athletics, the American League added a new team, the Kansas City Royals. It also placed a team—the Seattle Pilots—in the Pacific Northwest. The National League was expected to put expansion teams in Milwaukee and Buffalo, but instead it added the San Diego Padres in Southern California and the Montreal Expos in Canada. At the time, Montreal was Canada's largest city, and it had once been the home of the Brooklyn Dodgers' top farm club. Named after Montreal's recently held World's Fair, Expo '67, the Expos were the first major league team located outside of the United States.

Remembering the struggles of the twelve-team National League of the 1890s, both leagues split into two divisions. And with the creation of an Eastern Division and Western Division in each league, Major League Baseball established a new postseason playoff series—the League Championship Series—with the series winner from each league meeting in the World Series. When the LCS began in 1969, a team had to win three games out of five to advance to the World Series, but starting in 1985 the series was extended to a best-of-seven series.

Table 13.1. Major League Baseball, 1969

American League	
Eastern Division	*Western Division*
Baltimore Orioles	California Angels
Boston Red Sox	Chicago White Sox
Cleveland Indians	Kansas City Royals
Detroit Tigers	Minnesota Twins
New York Yankees	Oakland Athletics
Washington Senators	Seattle Pilots

National League	
Eastern Division	*Western Division*
Chicago Cubs	Atlanta Braves
Montreal Expos	Cincinnati Reds
New York Mets	Houston Astros
Philadelphia Phillies	Los Angeles Dodgers
Pittsburgh Pirates	San Diego Padres
St. Louis Cardinals	San Francisco Giants

But baseball had still not returned to stability. Civic leaders in Milwaukee, disappointed at not receiving an expansion team, convinced the Chicago White Sox to play a number of home games in Milwaukee in 1968 and 1969. The handful of games played in the city (roughly 12 percent of the White Sox home schedule) represented more than a third of Chicago's home attendance in both years. In 1969 the Milwaukee group, led by car dealer Allan Huber "Bud" Selig, reached a deal with the White Sox to buy the club and move it to Wisconsin. The American League, however, not wanting to abandon what was still the country's second-largest city, blocked the sale. In the meantime, the Seattle Pilots were experiencing severe problems in the Pacific Northwest. The team was undercapitalized, and although the city had begun the process of building a new domed stadium, it would not be ready for years. Sick's Stadium, the minor league ballpark the Pilots settled on for the interim, was inadequate for a major league team. After one season, the Pilots declared bankruptcy and the team was put up for sale. Without a loan of $600,000 from the American League, the Pilots would not have been able to conduct spring training in 1970. In April, only a week before the start of the new season, the group of businessmen who had attempted to buy the White Sox purchased the Pilots, renamed them the Milwaukee Brewers, and moved them to Wisconsin.

The Washington Senators were also experiencing financial difficulty. Washington had not won a pennant since the original American League Senators finished in first place in 1933. When the 1971 season ended, Senators owner Bob Short announced that the team would move to Dallas–Fort Worth for the 1972 season. Short renamed the team, which would play halfway between Dallas and Fort Worth in the suburban community of Arlington, the Texas Rangers. In order to balance out the divisions geographically, the Rangers joined the American League's Western Division, while the Brewers switched to the East. The Senators' move had at least one negative effect on baseball: Without a team in Washington, DC, Major League Baseball could no longer stage an annual season-opening ceremony in which the president threw out the first pitch. Only on rare occasions would the president be available to travel to Baltimore or another city for Opening Day.

In the 1970s, differences developed between the National League and the American League. The game played by National League teams stressed speed and defense, while the American League relied on power and home runs. This was partly due to the facilities in which each league played. By 1971, half the stadiums in the National League—including the Astrodome, Candlestick Park, and new multiuse stadiums in St. Louis, Philadelphia, Pittsburgh, and Cincinnati—featured an artificial playing surface, while all twelve American League teams still played on grass. (Artificial surface would finally appear in the American League with the opening of Royals Stadium in Kansas City in 1973 and the establishment of expansion franchises in Seattle and Toronto in 1977.) A rule change was also responsible for the different styles of play. As most pitchers are poor hitters, in 1973 the American League adopted the designated hitter, a tenth player who would come to bat for the pitcher. The designated hitter rule also provided a roster spot for aging sluggers who had become too old and slow to play defense. When New York Yankee Ron Blomberg came to bat at Fenway Park in Boston on April 6, 1973, he became the first designated hitter in baseball history. In the National League, however, pitchers continued to take their turn at bat.

Another difference between the two leagues emerged in 1977. Threatened by a lawsuit from the city of Seattle, the American League added two more teams. To appease officials in the Pacific Northwest, the league placed the Seattle Mariners in its Western Division. The Mariners would play in the American League's first domed stadium, the Kingdome. To remain balanced, the American League added a team to its Eastern Division, the Toronto Blue Jays. The Blue Jays became the American League's first team outside the United States, although Toronto had nearly become a National League city when the Giants threatened to move there in 1976. Many people looked to the National League to follow suit by adding new teams to Washington, DC, and New Orleans. The nation's capital, which was still looking for a team to replace the Senators, had nearly lured the Padres to Washington in 1974, but McDonald's founder Ray Kroc stepped forward to buy the team and keep it in San Diego. And New Orleans had just opened a domed stadium called the Louisiana Superdome, which—although it had been built for the New Orleans Saints of the NFL—could also hold sixty-five thousand fans for baseball. But the National League resisted all pressure to expand and continued to operate as a twelve-team league. With the expansion of the American League to fourteen clubs in 1977, baseball had returned to a state of stability not seen since the early fifties. Owners realized that constantly shifting teams from one city to another would hurt baseball, and after 1977, baseball clubs were strongly discouraged from moving. As a result, the major league baseball map remained unchanged from 1977 through 1992.

The protest movements of the sixties and seventies also left their mark on the game. By the midsixties, many young people began to see themselves as alienated from their parents' generation, and, with their rejection of materialism, a generation gap appeared. As young people encouraged each other to express their individuality through dress, music, and behavior, a counterculture emerged. Many in the younger generation wore long hair, facial hair, colorful clothing, and even beads. The counterculture created its own set of values, which often included drug use and "free love." Baseball did not experience the same countercultural wave as society at large, but elements of the counterculture still infiltrated the game. While many stars, including Mickey Mantle and Roger Maris, wore crew cuts, other players—like Joe Pepitone of the Yankees, whose locks hung over his ears, and Oscar Gamble of the Indians, whose Afro burst out from underneath his cap—expressed their individuality through their hairstyles. Illegal drug use was not uncommon among ballplayers. Red Sox pitcher Bill Lee, an admitted marijuana smoker, was nicknamed "Spaceman" by his teammates, while Dock Ellis of the Pirates later claimed that he was high on LSD when he threw a no-hitter against the Padres in 1970. But the influence of the counterculture was perhaps best captured through the Athletics and their eccentric owner, Charles O. Finley.

Finley, a wealthy insurance agent from Gary, Indiana, purchased the Kansas City Athletics in 1960. Upon buying the team, Finley vowed that the Athletics, a club that had finished last in the eight-team American League, would not finish in eighth place in 1961. Finley kept that promise—with two new teams added to the American League in 1961, Kansas City finished in ninth place. In order to attract fans, Finley changed the color of the A's uniforms. Traditionally baseball clubs wore crisp white uniforms at home and gray uniforms on the road, while baseball caps, stockings, undersleeves, and trim had always been blue, black, or red. When the Athletics took the field in 1963 wearing bright gold uniforms with Kelly green caps, stockings, undershirts, and trim, opposing players compared the uniforms to that of a softball team. But the colorful uniforms worn by the A's would eventually revolutionize the look of many major league teams, who would adopt brightly colored—some might say gaudy—uniforms in the 1970s. The flashy uniforms would be taken to their extreme when Bill Veeck, who reentered baseball when he bought the Chicago White Sox the previous year, outfitted his team in short pants in 1976. The shorts, which were unpopular with the players because they made sliding very difficult, were quietly abandoned midseason.

Finley promoted the counterculture in other ways, too. Rock music had experienced a surge of popularity among young people with the arrival in America of the Beatles. With Beatlemania sweeping the country in 1964, Finley personally paid $150,000—almost $5,000 a minute—for the Beatles to play a concert at Kansas City's Municipal Stadium, the home of the Athletics. In the seventies, he encouraged the A's to grow long hair, and in 1972 he promised a bonus to his poorly paid players if they grew facial hair. Eager for a few extra bucks, the entire squad sported mustaches that year.

A strong supporter of the designated hitter rule, Finley attempted to get Major League Baseball to adopt other innovations. His pet project was his attempt to convince baseball to create a designated runner position: a runner who would step in for the slowest player in the lineup each time he got on base without forcing him out of the game. To prove his point, in 1974 Finley added world-class sprinter Herb Washington to his roster. Playing under the existing substitution rules, in a little more than a full season in the majors, Washington appeared in 105 games, stealing thirty-one bases and scoring thirty-three runs without ever coming to bat. Nonetheless, the other major league teams—perhaps discouraged when Washington was picked off first base in the bottom of the ninth inning of Game 2 of the 1974 World Series—remained unconvinced. And in an era when tennis was transitioning from white to fluorescent-colored tennis balls, Finley tried to change the color of baseballs. Believing that batters had difficulty following white baseballs, Finley obtained permission from Major League Baseball to experiment with orange baseballs in two 1973 spring training games. Although the human eye can recognize orange more quickly than it can most other colors, the orange baseballs proved even more challenging for hitters than white ones. Unable to distinguish the orange leather from the red stitching while the ball was in flight, batters could not detect the ball's spin, and therefore could not determine if the pitch was a curveball.

Before the start of the 1968 season, Finley moved the Athletics to Oakland, across the bay from San Francisco and only five miles from Berkeley, a major center of the counterculture. Finley never quite accepted the name Athletics because it was too closely associated with former team owner Connie Mack. In 1971 Finley officially changed the club's name to the Oakland A's, banishing the word Athletics from team uniforms, pennants, programs, and all signage at the Oakland–Alameda County Coliseum. The club would not resume using the name Athletics until after Finley sold the team in 1981. In Oakland, Finley finally put together a winning team. With stars like right fielder Reggie Jackson, starting pitcher Jim "Catfish" Hunter, and closer Rollie Fingers, the A's won five straight division titles between 1971 and 1975, as well as the 1972, 1973, and 1974 World Series.

Although limited in its impact, the women's movement of the sixties and seventies also exerted an influence on baseball. In 1963 journalist Betty Friedan wrote *The Feminine Mystique*, in which she argued that suburban domesticity left women with feelings of emptiness and no sense of accomplishment. To escape the mystique, Friedan advised women to seek independent careers. Friedan's influence can be seen in baseball, as four different women owned major league teams in the last four decades of the twentieth century. Two of them—Jean Yawkey of the Red Sox in 1976 and Joan Kroc of the Padres in 1984—inherited their teams when their husbands died, but two other women became club owners on their own. Joan Whitney Payson, who held a small stake in the Giants, had voted against the team's move to San Francisco in 1957. She subsequently sold her share and worked to acquire a replacement team. When the National League awarded an expansion team to New York in 1962, it named her the owner. Cincinnati auto dealer Marge Schott purchased a controlling interest in the Reds in 1984. Schott became one of the most visible and vocal owners in baseball, but, unfortunately, not always with positive results. In 1999, after she made flattering comments about Adolf Hitler and the Nazi Party, Major League Baseball finally forced her out of the game. Women also have achieved success as baseball executives. Katy Feeney, the daughter of former National League president Charles "Chub" Feeney, took a temporary secretarial job in the National League office in 1977 and eventually ascended to the position of senior vice president of Major League Baseball.

American women seemed to be on the verge of making major gains in the seventies. When Congress passed the Education Amendments of 1972, Title IX banned sexual discrimination in educational programs receiving federal assistance, requiring public schools and universities to offer equal educational and athletic opportunities to students of both genders. One unexpected benefit of Title IX was the explosion of female high school and college athletic programs. And with more women engaged in amateur athletics, interest in professional opportunities naturally increased. In 1972, Congress also approved the Equal Rights Amendment (ERA), which stated that "[e]quality of rights under the law shall not be denied or abridged by the United States or by any State on account of sex." In order to become a part of the US Constitution, the amendment needed to be ratified by thirty-eight states within seven years. At first the amendment's adoption appeared certain, as thirty states ratified it in its first two years, but by the end of the decade, support for the ERA cooled. Only thirty-five states approved it before the deadline expired.

As with the ERA, women were not totally successful in achieving their goals. In 1977, a woman named Pam Postema obtained a job as a minor league umpire. Although she had the opportunity to call a few major league spring training games, Postema never was promoted to the major leagues. After twelve years in the minors, including six at the Triple-A level, Postema was fired. Claiming gender discrimination, Postema sued and reached an out-of-court settlement with her former employer, the Pacific Coast League. A decade later, a second woman, Ria Cortesio, also became a minor league umpire. Like Postema, Cortesio called a major league spring training game, but after nine years in the minors, she was also fired without being promoted to the major leagues.

More than two decades after the All-American Girls Professional Baseball League ceased operating, women returned to the diamond. In 1976 two icons of women's sports, Billie Jean King and Joan Joyce, along with sports promoter Dennis Murphy, established the International Women's Professional Softball Association (IWPS). Joyce had been the star pitcher on a perennial national amateur champion softball team, while King, a top-ranked tennis player, was probably the most famous female athlete in the world. King also had a connection to baseball, as her brother, Randy Moffitt, was a relief pitcher for the Giants. The IWPS first began play in 1976 with ten teams and a 120-game schedule made up of sixty doubleheaders. The league, however, failed to attract much interest. Among other problems, it suffered from a lack of competition, as Joyce's team, the Connecticut Falcons, won all four league championships and all but one of the league's world series games. By 1979 only six teams remained. In early 1980 the league's chief corporate sponsor, the BIC Corporation, withdrew its support, and the IWPS, like the ERA, quietly died.

While baseball was not immune to the effects of the counterculture movement and the women's movement, it perhaps best reflected the radicalism of the 1960s and 1970s by pursuing its own protest movement—the players' rights movement. Although there had been several unsuccessful attempts to create players' unions in the first half of the twentieth century, major league players had largely been unorganized since the collapse of the Brotherhood of Professional Base Ball Players in the 1890s. In the 1950s, ballplayers formed the Major League Baseball Players Association (MLBPA), electing Cleveland Indians pitcher Bob Feller the group's first president in 1956. At first Major League Baseball welcomed the creation of the MLBPA, even agreeing to stage a second all-star game each year from 1959 to 1962 to subsidize the association's pension fund. As issues between the players and owners grew more complicated, however, the MLBPA hired Marvin Miller in 1966 to become the organization's executive director.

Miller was born in New York City two weeks after the United States entered World War I. With a father who was a member of the Amalgamated Clothing Workers of America and a mother who was one of the first members of the United Federation of Teachers, Miller learned the importance of labor unions at an early age. He was still a child when he participated in his first picket line. After graduating from New York University with a degree in economics in 1938, Miller worked as a hearing officer for the National War Labor Board. After the war he took jobs negotiating for the International Association of Machinists and the United Auto Workers before becoming the chief economic adviser to the United Steelworkers in 1950. As executive director for the MLBPA, Miller turned the players' association into a bona fide labor union. Red Barber, baseball's pioneer radio broadcaster, once called Miller—along with Babe Ruth and Jackie Robinson—"one of the two or three most important men in baseball history." Yet, as of 2017, he still has not been named to baseball's Hall of Fame.

When Miller first took over the MLBPA, ballplayers, many of whom were young and inexperienced in life, tended to believe that they were lucky to be allowed to play baseball for a living. Miller sought to change this perception. He established a program to educate players about the fundamentals of organizing and union solidarity. He also took steps to shore up the union's financing by implementing a group licensing program. Miller succeeded in removing morality clauses from players' contracts, representing players who belonged to minority groups, and winning recognition of mental issues suffered by players. During his tenure, Miller brought base salaries to new levels. In 1968 he negotiated the first collective bargaining agreement in professional sports history. The agreement raised the minimum salary of major league players, which had been $6,000 since the 1940s, to $10,000. In 1970 Miller negotiated the right of players to seek arbitration to resolve grievances. When baseball club owners refused to increase their contribution to the players' pension fund, the MLBPA organized its first strike. The 1972 Major League Baseball strike, which lasted thirteen days, delayed the start of the season; after eighty-six games were canceled, the owners gave into the demands of the union.

The players' union, however, set as its ultimate goal the elimination of the ninety-year-old reserve clause, which kept salaries down by binding players to the same team for their entire career. In 1970 Miller and the MLBPA supported Curt Flood in his unsuccessful suit against Commissioner Bowie Kuhn. The impact of the reserve clause became apparent in 1974, when Oakland A's owner Charles Finley failed to make a $50,000 payment into an insurance annuity fund as required by the contract of starting pitcher Catfish Hunter. Hunter took the matter to arbitration, and the arbitrator ruled that because Finley had violated his contract, Hunter was a free agent who was welcome to offer his services to the highest bidder. Hunter agreed to a $3.35 million, five-year contract with the New York Yankees, demonstrating to everyone the income potential of ballplayers not bound by the reserve clause.

The following year, pitchers Andy Messersmith of the Los Angeles Dodgers and Dave McNally of the Montreal Expos did not sign new contracts. Instead, because of the reserve clause, they played the entire season under the terms of their expired contracts. When the 1975 season ended, however, both players declared themselves free agents. When Kuhn disagreed, Messersmith and McNally took the matter to arbitration, and in December, arbitrator Peter Seitz ruled that the reserve clause bound a player for only one season—the reserve year—and that because they had played the reserve year without signing new contracts, both Messersmith and McNally were, in fact, free agents. Major League Baseball appealed the *Seitz* decision, but in February 1976 a US District Court upheld the ruling.

Later that year, after Major League Baseball's appeals were exhausted, the players' union and Major League Baseball signed a new collective bargaining agreement that recognized free agency. Under the new agreement, a player who had six or more years of major league experience would become a free agent one year after his contract expired. In effect, the reserve clause continued to stand, as it does today, but it held a player to his team for only one year; then, after "playing out his option," a player was free to sign a contract with any major league team. After ninety-six years of impeding free agency, the reserve clause would no longer hold down players' salaries. Baseball was about to face its own revolution—this one financial.

14

Baseball in Postindustrial America (Since 1975)

BY THE MID-1970S, *the post–World War II boom had started to fizzle. The median family income stopped growing: Two-income families were earning what one-income families used to make. In 1973, 20 percent of all American workers earned less than $20,000 (in 2015 dollars); just six years later, 30 percent of Americans made less than that amount, and by 2015, nearly 40 percent earned less than that paltry sum. In the 1980s, political economists referred to these developments as the Great U-Turn. The decline was largely due to changes in the world's economy. By the seventies, competition was reemerging from Europe and Japan. This foreign competition raised costs while decreasing prices, which squeezed the profits of American companies. National borders began to lose their importance in economic relationships, as globalization—the development of an increasingly integrated world economy characterized by free trade, free flow of capital and information, and the exploitation of cheaper foreign labor sources—incorporated regional economies into a global economy. American businesses responded by restructuring their organizations, including the elimination of many middle management positions. They also attempted to increase productivity, especially through the adoption of automation, and to decrease their costs by reducing their labor force, cutting wages and benefits, and outsourcing formerly in-house jobs to contracted outsiders. In an effort to cut costs further, many businesses left their traditional homes in the Rust Belt, first for places in the Sun Belt and then eventually for Latin America or overseas—places that had lower wages, less stringent environmental regulations, fewer laws protecting workers, and weaker unions or no unions at all. In their wake, these companies left behind increased unemployment, which resulted in a shrinking local population, and* *often a host of environmental problems. The government under President Ronald Reagan also tried to help businesses withstand the Great U-Turn by lowering corporate taxes, eliminating or ignoring federal regulations, and taking the side of business during labor disputes. Starting in the mid-1980s, corporate profits (although not personal income) started to rise again, and no one seemed to care that the rules were not being followed and regulations had been eviscerated—at least not until the outbreak of the Great Recession in 2008. That downturn, the largest since the Great Depression, was severely exacerbated by slack regulatory enforcement and years of economic struggle. Baseball, too, struggled to adjust to a new economic reality during this era.*

On the evening of September 8, 1998, anticipation filled the air as a crowd of nearly fifty thousand packed into Busch Memorial Stadium in St. Louis hoping to see history in the making. Sammy Sosa, right fielder for the visiting Chicago Cubs, was entering the game with fifty-eight home runs, just three shy of the record set by Roger Maris in 1961. But the throng was not there to see Sosa. The day before, Cardinals first baseman Mark McGwire had tied Maris's record with his sixty-first home run. All summer long, McGwire and Sosa had chased Maris's home run record, stirring memories of Maris and Mickey Mantle pursuing Babe Ruth's record thirty-seven years earlier. On August 19, in the fifth inning of a game against the Cardinals, Sosa pulled ahead of McGwire by hitting his forty-eighth home run, but the Cardinals first baseman homered in the sixth and eighth to retake the lead. Now the two teams faced each other again, with McGwire on the threshold of setting a new record. For Major League Baseball, the home run race could not have happened at a better time. Baseball's popularity had been in decline since a labor dispute canceled the 1994 World Series, and for the first time in five years, fans had become excited about the game.

With two outs and nobody on base in the bottom of the fourth—and with the Cardinals down by two runs—McGwire lifted a pitch from Steve Trachsel 341 feet down the line into the left-field stands. For eleven minutes afterward, fireworks illuminated the Missouri sky. As he crossed the plate, his teammates and his ten-year-old son, Matt, a St. Louis batboy, congratulated the slugger, while Sosa dashed in from right field to join the celebration. When the season ended nineteen days later,

McGwire held the new record with seventy home runs, but Sosa also had eclipsed Maris, hitting sixty-six dingers.

To many people, however, something seemed wrong. In August, McGwire had admitted to an Associated Press reporter that he had been taking a muscle enhancement called androstenedione. At the time, the substance, which was available over the counter, had not been classified by the Food and Drug Administration as an anabolic steroid, and although the drug was banned in many sports, it had not yet been prohibited by Major League Baseball. As rumors circulated about baseball stars taking performance-enhancing drugs (PEDs), many fans again became disillusioned with the game. Records that were formerly held sacred now appeared tainted. Suspicions heightened in 2001, when Barry Bonds of the San Francisco Giants hit his seventy-third home run of the season, establishing a new record. In 2007, when Bonds hit the 756th regular-season home run of his career—breaking Hank Aaron's lifetime record—fashion designer Marc Ecko purchased the record-setting ball, branded it with an asterisk, and then donated it to the Baseball Hall of Fame.

Although it undermined the confidence of many fans, baseball's doping scandal was only part of the challenge facing the sport in the late twentieth and early twenty-first century. Baseball, like America, had been struggling under the new economic paradigm that emerged in the mid-1970s. Solutions to the challenges facing baseball, like the challenges facing the United States, still seemed elusive.

In the late twentieth and early twenty-first century, baseball struggled with a number of problems that first emerged in the mid-1970s. After the allowance for free agency, ballplayers were no longer bound to the same team for their entire career. After a player's contract expired, he could "play out his option" and become a free agent, selling his services to the highest bidder. Free agency affected all major league teams. Poorer clubs in smaller cities often could not afford to re-sign a player when he became a free agent. As a result, they often traded away players whose contracts expired so they would at least get *something* for the player they were about to lose. Other teams in pennant races were willing to acquire a potential free agent, even if they knew they could not afford to sign the player, because the player's bat or pitching arm might be just what the team needed to make the playoffs. Wealthy teams were also willing to acquire players in their option year, as they might be able to re-sign the player before he became a free agent.

Charlie Finley was one owner who could not afford to keep his stars once free agency took effect. Oakland was the smallest city in the major leagues, and although the San Francisco Bay Area was one of the largest metropolitan areas in the country, the A's shared the market with the Giants. Before the 1976 season began, Finley traded Reggie Jackson, along with two other players, to the Baltimore Orioles for three major leaguers. In June 1976, faced with the prospect of losing left fielder Joe Rudy and closer Rollie Fingers, Finley sold both players to the Boston Red Sox for $1 million each. He also sold starting pitcher Vida Blue to the Yankees for $1.5 million. Three days later, however, Commissioner Bowie Kuhn voided all three deals, claiming they were not in the best interest of baseball because the transactions decimated the A's while strengthening two already powerful teams. At the end of the season, Fingers signed a free-agent deal with the Padres, while Rudy jumped to the California Angels. (Blue, who had agreed to a contract extension as a condition of his sale to New York, remained on the A's. Finley finally sold the pitcher to the Giants in 1978.)

While free agency made it difficult for teams in small cities to retain players, it became a boon for teams in large cities like New York. In 1973 a prosperous Cleveland shipbuilder named George Steinbrenner purchased the Yankees. Having last won the American League pennant in 1964, New York was in the midst of a twelve-year dry spell when Steinbrenner took command. The club was wealthy, based in the largest city in the United States, with an enormous fan base and a huge television market. Now the team had an owner committed to spending money. Steinbrenner already had entered the free-agent market by signing pitcher Jim "Catfish" Hunter to a five-year, $3.35 million contract in 1975, after the pitcher was declared a free agent because Finley had failed to make a payment to his insurance annuity account. After the *Seitz* decision, Steinbrenner became totally committed to free agency. Following the 1976 season, the Yankees signed Reggie Jackson to a five-year, $3 million contract, and then won the next two World Series. Jackson, who also had been on the three-time World Series champion Oakland A's, picked up the nickname "Mr. October" when he hit five home runs in the 1977

World Series against the Dodgers. Three of those homers came in Game 6, tying Babe Ruth's fifty-one-year-old record for the most home runs in a World Series game.

The Yankees benefited from free agency, but most major league owners hated it, claiming that it was impossible for teams in smaller cities—like Oakland—to compete. When the collective bargaining agreement (CBA) with the Major League Baseball Players Association expired, the major league team owners insisted that free agency be changed. The players refused, and when the two parties could not reach an agreement, the ballplayers went on strike in June 1981. The 1981 Major League Baseball strike lasted fifty days, from June 12 until July 31, and 712 games were canceled. Finally, the day after their strike insurance policy ran out, the owners gave in and agreed to a CBA that kept free agency in place. Because the strike wiped out the middle of the season, the owners feared that fans, especially supporters of less competitive teams, would not come back. Therefore, for the 1981 season, the owners adopted a split season similar to the one the National League had used way back in 1892. When the season ended, the division winners of the first half played the division winners from the second half in a best-of-three division playoff series. Not everyone, however, was satisfied with the temporary playoff format adopted in 1981. When both halves of the season were combined, the St. Louis Cardinals had the best record in the National League's Eastern Division and the Cincinnati Reds had the best record in all of baseball—yet neither team qualified for the playoffs.

Free agency continued, and with it, major league salaries increased dramatically. Between 1970 and 1990, the major league minimum salary rose from $12,000 a year to $100,000, while the major league average shot up from under $30,000 to nearly $600,000. But not all the news was bad for club owners. Because of the excitement free agency brought to many clubs, fans seemed to be more interested in the sport, and attendance nearly doubled between 1970 and 1990. In 1986, for the first time ever, all twenty-six major league teams drew more than a million fans. Not only were major league teams attracting crowds, but so were the minor leagues. The Triple-A Louisville Redbirds of the American Association drew more than a million fans in 1983, while their intraleague rival, the Buffalo Bisons, drew more than a million fans in six straight seasons from 1988 to 1993.

Table 14.1. Major League Salaries, 1970–1990

Year	Major League Minimum	Major League Average
1970	$12,000	$29,303
1975	$16,000	$44,676
1980	$30,000	$143,756
1985	$60,000	$371,571
1990	$100,000	$578,930

And despite the dire predictions that free agency would kill base-ball in smaller cities, the small-market teams did not disappear. In fact, free agency seemed to bring parity to baseball. During the fifteen seasons between 1979 and 1993, twelve different teams won the World Series, and none of them were named the Yankees. Five World Series champions during this period—the Pirates, Royals, Twins, Athletics, and Reds—came from small-market cities. And only three teams—the Dodgers, Twins, and Blue Jays—won the World Series twice between 1979 and 1993.

In the 1980s, baseball enjoyed a surge in popularity. Sales of licensed caps and jerseys increased dramatically, while the baseball card industry exploded. From the 1950s to the 1970s, only one company, Topps Chewing Gum, regularly issued baseball cards. But the business became so lucrative in the 1980s that other companies entered the market, including Fleer, Donruss, and Upper Deck. And the cards were no longer being purchased only by young boys, as adults also began collecting them as an investment. Even Hollywood recognized baseball's popularity, producing films like *The Natural* (1984), *Bull Durham* (1988), *Field of Dreams* (1989), and *A League of Their Own* (1992).

During the eighties, fantasy baseball—the first of the fantasy sports—was invented. Originally called Rotisserie League Baseball, after the New York City restaurant where the first fantasy league was formed, the pastime quickly gained popularity, and publishers issued books explaining league rules, while newspapers ran weekly statistics for fantasy league participants. For some fans, obsession with baseball went beyond fantasy. In 1971 a group of baseball enthusiasts formed a semischolarly baseball historical society called the Society for American Baseball Research (SABR). Although SABR members explored all aspects of the game's history, some concentrated on an empirical analysis of the sport's statistics. This approach, called sabermetrics, analyzed stats for new insights into baseball, including, for instance, why a team wins or loses a specific number of games. Starting in 1977, Bill James, a night watchman with an economics degree and one of the pioneers of sabermetrics, issued an annual statistical evaluation of current major leaguers called *The Bill James Baseball Abstract.* Although his books sold only a few hundred copies in the seventies, James's yearly abstract had reached a mass audience by the 1980s—so much so that, citing burnout, he discontinued it in 1988. With his statistical approach, James has become one of the most influential minds in baseball, having authored more than two dozen books on baseball statistics.

Much of the increased popularity of baseball was fueled by nostalgia. In the 1980s, many teams discarded their gaudy uniforms for a return to the classic styles of the fifties. Clubs began to build new ballparks in urban neighborhoods rather than in the suburbs. Starting with Oriole Park at Camden Yards in Baltimore, which opened in 1992, ball clubs started building "retro parks" inspired by the grand ballparks of the first half of the twentieth century. Both Coors Field, which opened in Denver in 1995, and Citi Field, which replaced Shea Stadium in 2009, shared design features once found in Brooklyn's old Ebbets Field. Although the new stadiums replicated the atmosphere of old-fashioned ballparks, they featured modern amenities, including electronic scoreboards, luxury boxes, on-site restaurants, and perhaps the greatest ballpark innovation since floodlights—cup holders. Baseball teams were no longer content to share multipurpose stadiums with NFL teams, and with the opening of Marlins Park in Miami in 2012, the Oakland Athletics was the only team in Major League Baseball to share its facility with a football team.

There was trouble in paradise, however. Just as the prosperity Reagan's America enjoyed in the second half of the 1980s benefited businesses at the expense of workers, the success enjoyed by baseball teams in the 1980s was based on a rigged system that denied players the full benefits of free agency. In 1985 Peter Ueberroth became the commissioner of baseball. As the head of the Los Angeles Olympic Organizing Committee, Ueberroth had successfully orchestrated the 1984 Summer Olympics. Over the following three years, in a deal that smacked of the government response to the Great U-Turn, he secretly worked out an agreement with the twenty-six major league clubs in which the teams agreed to not outbid each other for free agents. The arrangement, known as collusion, not only kept salaries down, but it also violated the CBA the clubs had with the Major League Baseball Players Association. When the agreement became public, the MLBPA took the matter to an arbitrator, who ruled that Major League Baseball had violated its contract with the union. The arbitrator awarded the players' union $38 million in damages, and Ueberroth, who only had a year left on his contract as commissioner, resigned in disgrace. The club owners replaced him with National League president, and former president of Yale University, A. Bartlett Giamatti.

Giamatti was a lifelong Red Sox fan who had long coveted the position of commissioner, but he entered the job as a major scandal was about to break. Early in the 1989 season, rumors were circulating that Cincinnati Reds manager Pete Rose had been betting on baseball games. Rose had been a star player for the Reds' "Big Red Machine" of the sixties and seventies, and in 1985 he had surpassed Ty Cobb's record of 4,192 hits. When Rose retired as a player in 1986 with 4,256 hits, the major league record, he remained with the Reds as their manager. Giamatti ordered an investigation, which determined that Rose had been betting on games involving the Reds, a practice that violated rules that had been in place since the Black Sox Scandal. Although there was no evidence that Rose had ever bet against the Reds, simply betting on games involving his team was a serious violation. As a result, in August 1989 Giamatti imposed a lifetime ban on Rose. The controversial decision to expel baseball's all-time hit leader undoubtedly weighed on Giamatti, who died eight days later from a massive heart attack.

To replace Giamatti, major league club owners turned to his close friend, Francis Thomas "Fay" Vincent, who had been serving in the newly created position of deputy commissioner. Vincent's tenure as commissioner proved to be short and tumultuous. No longer able to keep salaries down through collusion, when the CBA with the players' union expired in 1990, the team owners demanded that the new contract include a salary cap to limit the amount of money a team could spend on players' salaries. Believing this would limit the opportunities available to free agents, the union rejected the offer, and during spring training, the club owners responded with a lockout. Vincent intervened to negotiate a new CBA, but it did not contain a salary cap. Because of the lockout, the

1990 season began a week late, but every game was played. Many owners, however, resented Vincent for undermining their attempt to force the adoption of a salary cap.

Vincent continued to irritate the club owners. Realizing that the cities of Chicago and St. Louis are farther west than Atlanta and Cincinnati, he attempted to have the Reds and Braves switch divisions with the Cubs and Cardinals, a proposal rejected by the National League clubs. He also favored eliminating the designated hitter rule, a rule the American League clubs were unwilling to abandon. Fearing a decrease in television revenue once Major League Baseball's lucrative four-year television contract with CBS expired in 1993, the owners also did not trust Vincent to negotiate a new network agreement. In September 1992, following a no-confidence vote among major league owners, Vincent resigned. Club owners named Milwaukee Brewers owner Bud Selig acting commissioner, and Major League Baseball would continue without an official commissioner until 1998, when Selig was permanently given the job. By naming a sitting owner as commissioner, however, baseball dropped the illusion that the commissioner put the best interests of the sport ahead of the best interests of the owners.

The increased popularity of baseball in the eighties led the National League to finally consider matching the American League by expanding to fourteen clubs. In 1985, Major League Baseball invited representatives from thirteen cities to New York to present their case to be considered for a National League expansion team. After hearing from the potential groups, baseball narrowed the field to six finalists—Buffalo, Denver, Miami, Orlando, Tampa–St. Petersburg, and Washington, DC. The collusion ruling forced baseball to speed up the expansion process in order to defray the $38 million fine. Charging each club $95 million to join, the National League placed a team in each division: In Miami, the Florida Marlins joined the Eastern Division, and in Denver, the Colorado Rockies joined the Western Division. Both teams began play in the 1993 season.

But after only one year, Major League Baseball decided to realign each league into three divisions—Eastern, Western, and Central. The new format allowed for another round of playoffs—a best-of-five League Division Series. The three division winners in each league qualified for the Division Series, as did a fourth team—the nondivision winner with the best record, which was awarded a wildcard playoff berth. As a result

Table 14.2.   Major League Baseball, 1994–1997

American League		
Eastern Division	*Central Division*	*Western Division*
Baltimore Orioles	Chicago White Sox	California Angels
Boston Red Sox	Cleveland Indians	Oakland Athletics
Detroit Tigers	Kansas City Royals	Seattle Mariners
New York Yankees	Milwaukee Brewers	Texas Rangers
Toronto Blue Jays	Minnesota Twins	
National League		
Eastern Division	*Central Division*	*Western Division*
Atlanta Braves	Chicago Cubs	Colorado Rockies
Florida Marlins	Cincinnati Reds	Los Angeles Dodgers
Montreal Expos	Houston Astros	San Diego Padres
New York Mets	Pittsburgh Pirates	San Francisco Giants
Philadelphia Phillies	St. Louis Cardinals	

of the realignment, for the first time since the Temple Cup series of the 1890s, teams that did not finish in first place could qualify for postseason play.

The 1994 baseball season promised to be exciting. With an extra round of playoffs, baseball offered twice as many pennant races. And individual players were having banner years, including Tony Gwynn of the Padres, who was flirting with hitting .400, a mark that had not been reached since Ted Williams did it in 1941, and Matt Williams of the Giants, who was on track to break Roger Maris's thirty-three-year-old record of sixty-one home runs in a season. Neither Gwynn nor Williams, however, would have the opportunity to set a record. The CBA between Major League Baseball and the players' union was set to expire at the end of the year, and both sides had dug in their heels. The club owners once again demanded that the Major League Baseball Players Association agree to a salary cap, which the players refused to accept under any circumstances. Recognizing that the owners had always caved in to the players in the past and believing that a mid-August date would allow a work stoppage to be resolved in time to resume the season, the union set a strike date for August 12. This time the players were wrong: The owners held fast in a rare display of unity and the season was never completed.

The 1994–1995 Major League Baseball strike shut down baseball. In September, Major League Baseball canceled the postseason, including the World Series, a ninety-year-old annual tradition that had survived the Great Depression and two world wars. Gwynn had to settle for a .394 batting average, while Williams belted only forty-three home runs. In December, with the collective bargaining agreement about to expire, Major League Baseball unilaterally adopted a salary cap—one that was so low that the salaries on 75 percent of major league teams had already exceeded it. And with no settlement in sight, the owners arranged to conduct spring training with replacement players—minor leaguers and other nonunion players. The MLBPA filed an unfair labor practices grievance with the National Labor Relations Board, and in late March requested an injunction with federal district court judge (and future Supreme Court justice) Sonia Sotomayor to stop the use of replacement players. Sotomayor, stating that "[y]ou can't grow up in the South Bronx without knowing about baseball," granted the injunction. The players agreed to return to the diamond under the terms of the expired collective bargaining agreement until a new agreement could be reached, which would not happen until 1997. The 1995 season began three weeks late, with a 144-game schedule, but baseball was back.

But would the fans return? Many fans, perceiving the strike as a disagreement between millionaires and billionaires, felt betrayed by the cancellation of the World Series. On Opening Day at Yankee Stadium, fans booed MLBPA executive director Donald Fehr. In Cincinnati, some fans chartered a small plane that dragged a banner in the sky above Riverfront Stadium with the message "Owners & Players: To hell with all of you!" And at Shea Stadium, three angry fans showed their contempt for the ballplayers by showering them with 160 one-dollar bills. When play resumed, baseball took a beating at the ticket office. After the strike, an average of six thousand fewer fans were attending each game. Major league attendance, which fell from 70 million in 1993 to 50 million in 1995, did not return to 70 million until 1998, but even that was partially due to the addition of two more teams. The average attendance at a major league game would not climb above thirty-one thousand until 2005.

Of all the major league teams, the Montreal Expos were hit the hardest by the strike. When the strike began on August 12, the Expos had the best record in baseball, and many fans of the Canadian team were confident that Montreal would play in the World Series. But with their team denied a chance to appear in the playoffs, Expos fans became disillusioned. Attendance, which had averaged more than twenty-two thousand per game in 1994, slipped to below twenty thousand in 1995, and in 1999 the Expos drew less than half that. In 2001 Major League Baseball took over ownership of the team.

Major League Baseball had both a public relations challenge and an economic problem. It had to improve its image to attract fans and it had to recover its financial losses from the strike. In an attempt to bring more fans to the ballpark, Major League Baseball instituted interleague play in 1997, which allowed fans in every city to see players from the other league. But although interleague play became very popular in the four markets that had a club in each league—New York, Chicago, Greater Los Angeles, and the San Francisco Bay Area—it was not the expected godsend in other major league cities. While the Yankees, Red Sox, and Dodgers drew well wherever they played, few fans in cities in the other league were anxious to see the last-place Phillies or Royals. Purists, who already disliked the designated hitter rule and the wildcard berth, hated interleague play. To make interleague games seem special, Major League Baseball originally scheduled them only during a short period in late June and early July, limiting the intraleague contests to teams from the same region. Eventually, however, because of the demand for games against popular teams like the Yankees and Red Sox, baseball revamped the interleague schedule so that each team played every team in the other league over the course of a three-year span.

To relieve its financial losses, Major League Baseball fast-tracked two more expansion teams, one in Phoenix and one in the Tampa–St. Petersburg area, charging each a $130 million franchise fee. The Tampa Bay Devil Rays were placed in the American League's Eastern Division, while the Arizona Diamondbacks joined the National League West. After it awarded a franchise to each league, Major League Baseball, realizing that fifteen is an odd number, asked the Diamondbacks to switch to the American League. The owners of the Diamondbacks, however, refused to switch leagues because they believed that Phoenix, which had been the home of a Giants farm team, had a National League tradition. Remembering that the old Milwaukee Braves had been a National League club and noticing that Milwaukee drew well when hosting interleague games against the Chicago Cubs, Brewers owner Bud Selig agreed to transfer his team to the National League's Central Division. To make room for the Devil Rays in the American League's Eastern Division and to fill the hole left by the Brewers, the Detroit Tigers switched to the Central Division. As a result, when the Diamondbacks and Devil Rays began play in 1998, the National League boasted sixteen clubs, while the American League had only fourteen.

Even with interleague play and extra playoff berths, fans were slow in coming back to the game. Then baseball unwittingly stumbled upon a solution. Performance-enhancing drugs had been used in baseball for decades, as ballplayers like Mickey Mantle were rumored to have taken amphetamines known as "greenies." In the late twentieth century, more powerful substances, such as steroids and human growth hormone, became available. In free agency, players who put up big numbers commanded higher salaries, so many players took PEDs. Some marginal players, realizing that a little extra output would mean the difference between playing in the majors or playing in the minors, also began to take drugs. "Juicing," as the practice was called, was against the rules and often illegal, but it seemed like a victimless crime. In 1997 first baseman Mark McGwire hit fifty-eight home runs, only three shy of Roger Maris's single-season record. The following year, McGwire and Sammy Sosa began their season-long pursuit of the record, and the excitement continued three years later as Barry Bonds surpassed McGwire's mark.

As the number of home runs increased, so did the number of fans following the game—and all the while, Major League Baseball remained suspiciously silent. Baseball might not have known about the players who were taking PEDs, but then again, it might not have wanted to know. Baseball benefited from the use of PEDs because more broken records meant more excited fans. And just as federal regulators looked the other way when banks and Wall Street firms ignored regulations, Major League Baseball did not act, failing to even adopt a league-wide testing program for PEDs until 2003. Fans, however, noticed that sluggers like McGwire, Sosa, and Bonds were significantly bulkier than they had been only a few years earlier. The scandal finally broke in 2005 with the publication of *Juiced*, a tell-all autobiography by former Oakland Athletics slugger Jose Canseco. In his book, Canseco not only admitted

Mark McGwire's 70 home runs
in 1998 were tainted by his
use of performance enhancing
drugs. National Baseball
Hall of Fame and Museum.
Cooperstown, N.Y.

taking steroids himself, but he also implicated other major leaguers,
including McGwire and pitcher Roger Clemens.

Just as the failure to enforce financial regulations considerably aggravated the Great Recession in 2008, by failing to enforce PED bans, Major
League Baseball did more harm to the game, as records once deemed
sacred were now tarnished. Fans, who were only just starting to return to
the game, once again became disillusioned. In 2005 Major League Baseball tapped former US senator George Mitchell of Maine to investigate
the use of steroids and human growth hormone in baseball. The Mitchell Report, issued in December 2007, named eighty-nine major leaguers
accused of using banned substances. As new lists of additional players
taking banned substances appeared, sportswriters and fans speculated
about what other major leaguers might be implicated. Following the
release of the report, Major League Baseball adopted a stricter drug testing policy. Once considered shoo-ins, McGwire, eligible since 2007, and
Sosa, Bonds, and Clemens, eligible since 2013, have been denied induction into the Hall of Fame.

The Montreal Expos presented additional problems. In 2001, the year Major League Baseball took over ownership of the club, the Expos drew fewer than eight thousand people per game. Two days after the conclusion of the World Series, Commissioner Bud Selig announced that club owners had agreed to reduce their financial losses by contracting to twenty-eight teams. Although the identities of the teams targeted for contraction were never disclosed, media reports indicated that the teams in question were the Expos and the Minnesota Twins, whose owner, Carl Pohlad, had agreed to sell the team to Major League Baseball for $250 million. Twins and Expos fans hated the proposal, and so did both the players' union, fearing fewer jobs for major league players, and the Metropolitan Sports Facility Commission, which managed the Hubert Humphrey Metrodome, the Twins' home stadium. The union and the commission both filed lawsuits to prevent contraction, and baseball abandoned the plan. In 2004 Major League Baseball announced that the Expos—renamed the Nationals—would move to Washington, DC, for the 2005 season. The Washington Nationals provided an additional benefit for baseball: the return of Major League Baseball to the nation's capital revived the annual tradition of a presidential first pitch to start the season.

Moving the Expos to Washington solved baseball's problems in Montreal, but other teams still faced challenges. Given the new economic realities of baseball's free-agent-driven salaries and its apparently shrinking fan base, some clubs looked for new approaches to deal with the crisis. Like American businesses that pursued creative solutions to the Great U-Turn, poorer teams sought a cheaper, more efficient way to win games. Sabermetrics seemed to offer an answer. Although the Texas Rangers and the New York Mets utilized computers to evaluate opposing players in the early 1980s, sabermetrics did not gain a real foothold in the major leagues until after 1997, when Billy Beane became the general manager of the Oakland Athletics, the team in the smallest city in the major leagues. Recognizing that he could not afford to compete with the Yankees or Red Sox in the free-agent market, Beane evaluated players based on the number of potential wins they could bring his ball club. Writer Michael Lewis chronicled Beane's approach in the 2003 book *Moneyball: The Art of Winning an Unfair Game*, which was made into a movie starring Brad Pitt in 2011. Many traditionalists in baseball scoffed at Beane's unusual method, but others saw merit in it. In 2003 Red Sox owner John Henry, seeking to end his club's eighty-five-year championship drought, hired Bill James, the father of sabermetrics, as a special adviser to his team. The following year, Boston won its first World Series championship since 1918. But although it helped turn the Athletics into a competitive team, without the financial resources of a team like the Red Sox, sabermetrics did not help Beane bring a championship to Oakland.

Economics was not the only problem facing baseball. As the twenty-first century unfolded, several baseball teams struggled with an identity crisis. In early September 1965, in preparation for the club's move to suburban Anaheim, owner Gene Autry had changed the name of his team from the Los Angeles Angels to the California Angels. When the Walt Disney Company purchased the club in 1997, in an attempt to rebrand Anaheim, the home of Disneyland, as a destination city, the company changed the team's name to the Anaheim Angels. In 2003 Disney sold the club to businessman Arturo Moreno. Moreno, hoping to tap into the massive Los Angeles market, wanted the club to return to its original name, but Anaheim city officials objected, pointing out that the club's lease with the city-owned stadium required it to use "Anaheim" in its name. To meet the requirement of the lease, in 2005 Moreno renamed the club the Los Angeles Angels of Anaheim.

To the surprise of many, baseball had trouble developing a strong following in South Florida. In 1997 the Florida Marlins became the first wildcard team to win a World Series, but the following year Marlins owner Wayne Huizenga, preparing to put his team on the market, sold off most of the team's star players. Under the leadership of a new owner, art dealer and former Montreal Expos owner Jeffrey Loria, the Marlins again won the World Series as a wildcard entry in 2003, but after that, the team slowly slipped out of contention. The team's ballpark—the massive Sun Life Stadium, which the club shared with the NFL's Miami Dolphins—had poor sight lines for baseball, and the seating configuration made fans feel too far removed from the game. In 2012 a new baseball-only stadium built by Miami–Dade County opened on the former site of the Orange Bowl. In exchange for the stadium, the club agreed to change its name to the Miami Marlins when it moved into the new ballpark.

Although it won the pennant in 2008 and has remained competitive since then, the American League's entry in Florida has also struggled to attract fans. Part of the problem is the team's home, Tropicana Field, a domed stadium built by the city of St. Petersburg in the 1980s, before Florida even had a promise of a team. The city built the stadium to get a jump on its larger cross-bay rival, Tampa, but the gamble nearly failed. Although the White Sox and the Giants both considered moving to the facility—in 1988 and 1992, respectively—neither team did, and even after the National League added two expansion teams in 1993, the facility remained empty. The dome finally obtained a tenant when the American League placed an expansion team in Tampa–St. Petersburg in 1998, but, by almost all accounts, the stadium ranks as the least attractive in baseball. Also problematic is the stadium's location. Not only is St. Petersburg smaller than Tampa, but it sits on a peninsula on the other side of Tampa Bay, inconvenient to fans in Tampa and farther from other Florida metropolitan areas such as Orlando. The club also suffered from an identity complex. The team's original owner, Vince Naimoli, wanted to name the club the Tampa Bay Sting Rays, but could not because the name had already been trademarked by the Maui Stingrays, a team in the Hawaii Winter Baseball League. So Naimoli settled on Devil Rays. The name, however, drew the ire of fundamentalist Christians who thought it conjured up visions of Satan. In 2008 the team's new owner, Stuart Sternberg, dropped the word "Devil" from the name, allowing Tampa Bay Rays' logos to represent both sunrays and stingrays.

Baseball as a whole was also dealing with an identity crisis. After a century of competition, in 2000 the American League and National League merged—the league offices were closed, the league presidents stepped down, and all thirty teams came under the direct authority of Major League Baseball. For a dozen years, fans hardly noticed a difference, but in 2013 the Houston Astros jumped to the American League, and Major League Baseball realigned into two leagues of three five-team divisions. The new alignment required interleague play to take place all season long. The year before, Major League Baseball added a second wildcard berth to each league and established an additional playoff round—a Wild Card Game in each league—with the winners advancing to the Division Series.

By the second decade of the twenty-first century, baseball, in some ways, had come full circle. A few teams, including the Astros, Blue Jays, Braves, and Brewers, had revived their colorful uniforms of the seventies. And in 2017 the Atlanta Braves left downtown Atlanta—and a park barely two decades old—for a new stadium built in suburban Cobb County. Both the owners and players seemed to recognize the damage caused by the 1994 strike, agreeing to new collective bargaining agreements in 1997, 2002, 2007, 2012, and 2016 without a work stoppage. The negotiations in 2002 came down to the wire. Only hours before the August 30 deadline set by the players, the owners and union accepted a collective bargaining agreement that included steroid testing, a luxury tax, and a significant increase in revenue sharing. The agreement also took contraction off the table, at least for the time being. The threat of a work stoppage has been averted for the foreseebale future, as the current CBA does not expire until December 2021. Major League Baseball also took a more serious attitude toward juicing, suspending Dodgers outfielder Manny Ramirez for fifty games in 2009. In 2014 baseball suspended Yankees third baseman Alex Rodriguez for the entire season when it was revealed that he had obtained human growth hormone from Biogenesis of America, an antiaging clinic in South Florida.

Despite improved relations between players and owners, in the twenty-first century, baseball, like America, faced other challenges. Television ratings were down, with the World Series drawing about a third of the viewers it had drawn in the mid-1980s. Attendance fell as well. After reaching a peak of more than seventy-nine million fans in 2007, attendance had fallen to less than seventy-four million fans by 2014. In public opinion polls, 34 percent of respondents listed football as their favorite sport, while baseball came in a distant second at 14 percent. The core of baseball's fan base was aging, and many young sports fans had forsaken baseball altogether, favoring other sports. Particularly troubling was the decline of the number of African American athletes playing the sport, falling from about 19 percent of players in the late 1970s to less than 8 percent by 2015.

The situation, however, was not as dire as cynics claimed. Because of changes in television—including more channels, on-demand programming, and internet streaming—TV ratings declined for many programs, not just baseball. Yet broadcasts of hometown teams in local markets were still very strong. In 2014, baseball games were the most-watched programs in eleven of the twenty-six television markets that had a team.

And although baseball attendance declined since 2007, the number of people attending major league games remained level, at between seventy-three and seventy-four million, since 2009; the NFL, with its shorter schedule, consistently attracted seventeen million fans a year during the same period. And, in any case, new technology such as Internet streaming was becoming a major source of revenue for the sport.

Each year, two million American boys and girls played Little League Baseball, while only a quarter of a million children from the same age group played in youth football leagues. In 2013 Major League Baseball launched a task force charged with developing programs to increase interest in the sport among African Americans. Reviving Baseball in Inner Cities, an outreach program for young people established in 1989, saw participation increase by 80 percent since 2009.

Baseball was still recovering from the 1994 strike and the subsequent doping scandal, but there were signs that baseball was bouncing back. In 2015 the Kansas City Royals won their first World Series championship in thirty years, generating renewed interest in the sport in the Midwest. And when the Chicago Cubs and the Cleveland Indians—two teams who had not won a World Series in a combined 176 years—met in the

Table 14.3.   Major League Baseball Today

American League		
Eastern Division	*Central Division*	*Western Division*
Baltimore Orioles	Chicago White Sox	Los Angeles Angels of Anaheim
Boston Red Sox	Cleveland Indians	Houston Astros
New York Yankees	Detroit Tigers	Oakland Athletics
Tampa Bay Rays	Kansas City Royals	Seattle Mariners
Toronto Blue Jays	Minnesota Twins	Texas Rangers
National League		
Eastern Division	*Central Division*	*Western Division*
Atlanta Braves	Chicago Cubs	Arizona Diamondbacks
Miami Marlins	Cincinnati Reds	Colorado Rockies
New York Mets	Milwaukee Brewers	Los Angeles Dodgers
Philadelphia Phillies	Pittsburgh Pirates	San Diego Padres
Washington Nationals	St. Louis Cardinals	San Francisco Giants

2016 Fall Classic, television ratings soared, making the 2016 Series the highest-rated seven-game World Series in fifteen years and the highest-rated World Series of any length since 2004. As it had after the Players' League of 1890, the Black Sox Scandal, the Great Depression, and two world wars, baseball survived.

15

A Global Game (Since 1865)

WITH THE RISE OF GLOBALIZATION, the significance of international boundaries in economic transactions has declined. From almost the beginning of its history, baseball has overcome barriers. Not only has baseball helped immigrants assimilate into American society, but it has also spread to the rest of the world, becoming a truly international game.

More than fifty thousand Giants fans spent a Saturday evening in September at the ballpark, hoping to see history in the making. In the third inning, the man they came to see stepped up to the plate. Wearing the familiar white Giants uniform with black-and-orange trim, the batter, only one home run away from setting a new record, calmly worked the count full. Then, raising his right leg in his trademark swing, he connected on the next pitch, a sinker that he lined into the right-field bleachers. Fifty thousand fans exploded into applause as the scoreboard boasted of the achievement.

The batter, however, was not Barry Bonds or even Willie Mays, and the ballpark was not AT&T Park, Candlestick Park, or the Polo Grounds. Instead, the game took place in 1977 at Korakuen Stadium in Tokyo, where first baseman Sadaharu Oh of the Yomiuri Giants (often called the Tokyo Giants by Americans) had just eclipsed Hank Aaron's all-time record of 755 home runs. Before he retired in 1980, Oh would hit 868 home runs in his career—106 more than Barry Bonds, 113 more than Hank Aaron, and 154 more than Babe Ruth—to become the world's greatest home run champion. Today, however, few Americans recognize—or even know about—Oh's accomplishment.

CHAPTER 15

When Oh surpassed Aaron in 1977, globalization had already started
to lessen the importance of international borders in economic transactions. By the 1970s, baseball, too, had become an international game, but
during its early history it had been recognized as an institution that was
uniquely American. In the early twentieth century, while industrialization was underway in the United States, Albert Spalding argued that
because of its egalitarian nature, baseball represented American ideals.
Even as late as the 1950s, during the height of the Cold War, French-
born historian and philosopher Jacques Barzun said that "[w]hoever
wants to learn the heart and mind of America had better learn baseball."

Baseball has helped define American culture, even infiltrating the
language. "Hitting a home run" has come to mean an unqualified success, while "striking out" means failing and "throwing a curve ball"
means trickery. A bizarre idea might come "out of left field." Baseball
metaphors, such as "getting to first base," are even used by teenagers to
describe their success in sexual situations.

Sadaharu Oh hit more home runs
than any other human being, belting
868 homers in his 22 seasons with
Japan's Yomiuri Giants. National
Baseball Hall of Fame and Museum.
Cooperstown, N.Y.

Because baseball had become so intertwined with America, immigrants used it as an assimilation tool; by playing baseball, they were adopting an American identity. A generation or two after various immigrant groups arrived in the United States, their children or grandchildren started to appear in the major leagues. Irish immigrants started to arrive in the United States in the 1840s and 1850s, and in the 1880s Mike "King" Kelly of the White Stockings, James "Tip" O'Neill of the Browns, and Hugh Duffy of the Beaneaters were among the stars of the game. Italian immigrants arrived in America in large numbers in the 1880s and 1890s; by the twenties and thirties, major league teams included players like Tony Lazzeri of the Yankees, Ernie Lombardi of the Reds, and the three DiMaggio brothers—Joe of the Yankees, Vince of the Pirates, and Dominic of the Red Sox. Polish immigrants began coming to America after 1900, and by the fifties and sixties, Ted Kluszewski of the Reds, Bill Mazeroski of the Pirates, and Carl Yastrzemski of the Red Sox were playing in the big leagues.

Perhaps the most ironic example of baseball as assimilation can be found among the Japanese Americans living in internment camps during World War II, where inmates often played baseball to pass the time. The Japanese Americans playing baseball in internment camps were expressing their American character while being denied their American identity by the government.

During the first half of the twentieth century, other ethnic groups were denied a place in the major leagues, the most notable example being African Americans. But the arrival of Jackie Robinson and Larry Doby not only paved the way for black players but also opened the door for Latino and Hispanic ballplayers, who, confronting the same type of discrimination faced by African Americans, found a place on major league rosters in the fifties and sixties. When Hall of Fame right fielder Roberto Clemente, who played eighteen years for the Pittsburgh Pirates, died in a plane crash in 1972 while on a humanitarian mission to bring relief supplies to earthquake victims in Nicaragua, he became a national martyr in his native Puerto Rico. Other noteworthy Latino players from the sixties included pitcher Juan Marichal of the Giants and the three Alou brothers—Felipe, Matty, and Jesus. For a very brief period of time in 1963, all three Alou brothers were even on the same team—the San Francisco Giants—and, in three games, played together in the same outfield.

Since the 1990s a number of Asian players have entered the major leagues, including Chan Ho Park of the Dodgers, who is from South Korea, and Ichiro Suzuki of the Mariners and Hideki Matsui of the Yankees, both of whom are from Japan. And when South African native Gift Ngoepe of the Pirates took over second base in the fourth inning of a game against the Cubs on April 26, 2017, baseball could boast that players born on six different continents have appeared in major league games. The arrival of Latino and Asian players demonstrated a change in baseball. These players were not children of immigrants assimilating through baseball; they were skilled players in other countries (or, in the case of Puerto Rico, a US commonwealth with a distinct culture that maintains its own sports organizations for international competition) who were recruited by major league teams to play in the United States. Globalization had arrived in baseball.

Although baseball, a descendant of the English game of rounders, first matured in the United States, it quickly spread to other places. Albert Spalding's 1888–1889 world tour and the around-the-world trip undertaken by the Philadelphia Athletics and New York Giants in 1913–1914

In 1972, future Hall of Famer Roberto Clemente became the eleventh major league player to collect 3,000 hits, a feat he accomplished in his last at-bat of the season. Three months later, Clemente, a national hero in his homeland of Puerto Rico, was killed in a plane crash while on a mercy mission to bring relief supplies to earthquake victims in Nicaragua. National Baseball Hall of Fame and Museum. Cooperstown, N.Y.

failed in their deliberate attempts to spread baseball throughout the globe, but through spontaneous actions, baseball did take hold in foreign places. Missionaries teaching in Japan in the 1860s taught baseball to their students. From these students, the game spread in Japan and eventually to Korea, Taiwan, and even Brazil. Cuban students who studied in New York City introduced the game in their homeland after they returned home. Baseball often spread without American influence, as Cubans also brought the game to Puerto Rico and the Dominican Republic.

In Canada baseball seemed to develop spontaneously with its emergence in the United States. In the 1870s the Tecumseh Base Ball Club, a team from London, Ontario, applied to join the National League. The league rejected the application because London did not have the league's minimum population of seventy-five thousand. London's chances were probably also hurt by its location in Canada, as the National League did admit Syracuse and Troy, New York, in 1879 and Worcester, Massachusetts, in 1880—all of which had populations of fewer than seventy-five thousand people. In 1877 the International Association, baseball's first minor league, was formed, with five clubs in the United States and two in Canada—the Tecumseh club of London and a second club in Guelph, Ontario.

Other North American teams outside the United States played in the minor leagues in the twentieth century. The International League, one of baseball's top minor leagues, has truly been international, as, for more than fifty years, the league boasted two teams in Canada—the Toronto Maple Leafs, which joined the circuit in 1896, and the Montreal Royals, which joined the following year. Almost a half century later, Jackie Robinson would play for the Royals on his way to the major league Dodgers. In the middle of the century, the league also moved into the Caribbean when it admitted the Havana Sugar Kings, a team in Cuba, in 1954. The Havana club would become the top farm team of the radical-sounding Cincinnati Reds, but the Cuban Revolution forced the league to move the team to Jersey City, New Jersey, in the middle of the 1960 season. Given that Cuban leader Fidel Castro was a fanatic about baseball, one wonders whether an American League expansion team for Havana in 1961 might have changed US-Cuban relations in the sixties. In 1961 the International League returned to the islands when its Miami Marlins franchise moved to San Juan, Puerto Rico. The Pacific Coast League also took on an international look in 1956, when the Oakland Oaks moved to Vancouver, British Columbia.

The National League expanded into Canada in 1969 with the creation of the Montreal Expos. Eight years later, the American League placed another expansion team—the Toronto Blue Jays—in Canada. In the 1980s Vancouver was one of the eleven North American cities that unsuccessfully sought a National League expansion team, and with the Expos' 2005 move to Washington, DC, the Blue Jays (winners of two World Series) remained the only major league team based outside of the United States.

Still, high-level professional leagues exist in other countries. In 1936, two years after a barnstorming American baseball team featuring Babe Ruth toured Japan, the professional Japan Baseball League was established in the Tokyo area. The Japanese government banned baseball and other Western institutions during World War II, but the occupying American army reinstated the sport after the war ended. Interest in baseball increased in 1949 when Lefty O'Doul, the manager of the minor league San Francisco Seals, brought his team to Japan to play a series of games against Japanese teams. Japanese baseball promoters set up the Central League in 1949 and a second circuit, the Pacific League, in 1950. A postseason championship, the Japan Series, between the annual champions of each league, began in 1950. When Sadaharu Oh surpassed Hank Aaron's home run record in 1977, many Americans dismissed it as a weak home run in an undersized park against minor league–caliber pitching. Since 1995, however, more than fifty Japanese stars have proven their ability on major league teams. The arrival of Japanese ballplayers in the United States has increased Japanese interest in American baseball.

South of the border, interest in baseball grew following visits to Mexico by the Chicago White Sox in 1906 and Cuban teams in 1917 and 1918. In 1925 sportswriter Alejandro Aguilar Reyes, who had spent a year in the United States observing American baseball, founded the Mexican League, a semiprofessional circuit. In the 1930s Jorge Pasquel, a wealthy Veracruz cigar manufacturer and customs broker, converted the organization into a full-fledged professional league. Pasquel entered the league by buying the Azules de Veracruz (the Veracruz Blues) in 1938, and his ownership of Mexico City's Delta Park, the premier baseball stadium in the country, widened his influence in the league. Plagued by internal disagreement, the league split into two circuits in 1940. With Pasquel's backing, the league that included the Azules survived, while the other circuit collapsed. Because of his strong political connections—he had been married to the daughter of one Mexican president and was a close friend to a second—Pasquel became the league president in 1946. Almost from the start, Pasquel began pouring his resources into the league, luring Negro league stars—including future Hall of Famers Martin Dihigo, Satchel Paige, and Ray Dandridge—to play in Mexico. Some scholars have argued that the success of the integrated Mexican League convinced many white Americans that baseball's color barrier was unnecessary. Pasquel implemented a plan to transform the Mexican League into a major league, signing about a dozen players from the big leagues, including pitchers Sal Maglie of the Giants and Max Lanier of the Cardinals, as well as Dodgers catcher Mickey Owens. Perceiving the defections as a serious threat to the major leagues, Commissioner Happy Chandler announced that any player who broke the reserve clause to play in Mexico would face a five-year ban from the major leagues. When former Giants catcher Danny Gardella, who had jumped to the Mexican League in 1946 for more than double the salary the Giants had offered, petitioned Chandler for reinstatement, Chandler rejected the request. Gardella sued. At first, a federal judge, citing the 1922 *Federal Baseball Club* case, dismissed the lawsuit, but an appellate court ordered a full trial. The prospect of going to court—and perhaps losing base-ball's antitrust exemption—convinced Chandler to lift the suspensions.

After losing most of its former major leaguers, the Mexican League teetered near bankruptcy in the early 1950s. In 1955, shortly after Pasquel died in a plane crash, league officials reorganized the circuit and secured its admission into the National Association of Professional Baseball Leagues (NAPBL), the organization of minor leagues under the author-ity of the commissioner of Major League Baseball. Initially, the Mexican League entered the minor league system as a Double-A league, but in 1966 the league upgraded to Triple-A, the same level as the International League and the Pacific Coast League. Today, the Mexican League is the only circuit in Minor League Baseball, as the NAPBL is now known, located outside of the United States.

In 1979, Caribbean baseball promoters attempted to create another high-level minor league, this one almost completely outside of the United

States. The Inter-American League comprised six teams—two in Venezuela and one each in the Dominican Republic, Puerto Rico, Panama, and the United States. The lone American team, the Miami Amigos, was managed by Davey Johnson, who in 1986 would lead the New York Mets to the World Series championship. The league's backers had hoped to obtain Triple-A minor league status, but financial difficulties caused by the expensive travel costs forced the Inter-American league to fold after only three months.

In the mid-twentieth century, winter leagues—which start play in November, after the World Series is over—formed in Latin America. Today these leagues operate in Mexico, Puerto Rico, the Dominican Republic, Venezuela, and Cuba. Many winter leagues offer the highest caliber of play in their country and provide an opportunity for local athletes to play baseball. Today, major leaguers from Latin America often play on winter league clubs in their home countries, either to hone their

In the twenty-first century, more than a quarter of the players on major league rosters are foreign born. Major leaguers from other countries included former Red Sox star David Ortiz, often called "Big Papi," who was born in the Dominican Republic. Today, Dominicans make up the largest number of foreign-born players, with about ten percent of all current major leaguers coming from that country. Boston Red Sox Photo Archive

skills in the off-season or to display their talents before their compatriots. In February, following the winter league season and prior to the start of spring training for North American clubs, the champions of the Latin American winter leagues meet annually in a round-robin Caribbean Series.

In most sports, the highest level of international competition can be found in the Olympics; baseball, however, was never a stalwart of the Olympic Games. Although not a medal event, an Olympic exhibition baseball game was first staged at the 1904 Games in St. Louis, the first Olympics held on US soil. Exhibition games were played at other Olympics as well, including the 1936 Olympics in Berlin, the same games in which African American track star Jesse Owens embarrassed Adolf Hitler by defeating German athletes in track and field events. In Berlin, a crowd estimated at around 90,000 watched an exhibition game played between two American teams. In 1956, 114,000 people in Melbourne watched an Australian baseball team play an American team in an exhibition game.

Countries hosting Olympic Games often include demonstration sports that have special cultural value to the country. While not official medal events, demonstration games include a tournament in which teams from a number of countries compete. When the Olympics were held in Los Angeles in 1984, the United States chose baseball as one of its demonstration sports. Boasting many future major leaguers—including Will Clark, Barry Larkin, Mark McGwire, and B. J. Surhoff—some have suggested that the 1984 US Olympic team was among the best baseball lineups ever assembled. Topps Chewing Gum even included cards featuring US Olympians in its 1984 baseball card set. In baseball, however, sometimes the best team does not win; the US team lost the gold medal to Japan. Four years later, when the Olympics were held in Seoul, the South Korean Olympic Committee also added baseball, a sport that had been played in Korea for over eighty years, as a demonstration sport. This time the US team won the gold medal in the baseball competition.

Baseball and its sister sport, women's softball, became official medal sports in the 1992 Olympic Games in Barcelona. There, Cuba became the first country to win an official Olympic gold medal in baseball; the US team did not even medal. Four years later, at the 1996 Olympics in Atlanta, the team from the United States won the bronze medal, while

Cuba again won the gold. In the 2000 Olympics in Sydney, Australia, future Twins first baseman Doug Mientkiewicz's home run over South Korea gave the United States its only official Olympic gold medal in baseball. Four years later, at the 2004 Olympics in Athens, the United States did not medal, while Cuba again won the gold. In 2008 in Beijing, the United States settled for the bronze medal, while South Korea won the gold medal.

In 2005 the International Olympic Committee (IOC) voted to eliminate baseball and softball from the Olympic Games, starting in 2012 with the games in London. The two sports were replaced by golf and rugby. The IOC claimed that it was removing baseball because Major League Baseball would not interrupt its season to allow big-league players to compete in the games. Some critics, however, have suggested that the elimination of baseball and softball reflected an anti-American sentiment on the committee following the United States' 2003 invasion of Iraq. In 2016, however, the IOC had a change of heart, voting to restore baseball as an Olympic sport starting in 2020.

In response to the removal of baseball from the Olympics, Major League Baseball and the International Baseball Federation established its own international baseball competition. Based on the World Cup soccer tournament, the World Baseball Classic began in 2006 as a competition between sixteen countries. Initially held every three years, the tournament was scheduled for late March, before the major league season starts, to allow major league players to represent their home countries in the competition. Starting in 2013, the World Baseball Classic was rescheduled to take place every four years. Japan won the gold medal in the 2006 and 2009 tournaments, while the team from the Dominican Republic won the gold in 2013. The United States did not qualify for a medal in the first three World Baseball Classic tournaments, but in 2017 Team USA won the gold medal.

In the nineteenth and early twentieth centuries, baseball was truly an American game. But today, players on major league rosters come from all over the world. And as the United States' record in the Olympics and the World Baseball Classic demonstrates, American athletes no longer dominate the sport. Baseball has become a world game.

Epilogue

Traditions

ON AUGUST 25, 1990, THE Cincinnati Reds released a forty-year-old outfielder named Ken Griffey to make room on their roster for a younger player. The Reds were in first place, with a 6½-game lead over both the Giants and Dodgers, and with just over a month left in the season, Cincinnati had its eyes on the playoffs. Griffey had been an important cog in the Big Red Machine, Cincinnati's World Series championship teams of the 1970s, but he had spent several years playing for the Yankees and the Braves before returning to the Reds in 1988. For Griffey, the opportunity awaiting him more than made up for the disappointment of leaving a contender (the Reds would sweep the Athletics in four games in that fall's World Series). The previous year, his son, Ken Griffey Jr., had joined the Seattle Mariners, making the Griffeys the first father-son combination to play in the major leagues at the same time. Now, in an arrangement worked out by the Reds and Mariners and approved by the National League, Griffey would sign with Seattle after being released by Cincinnati, making the Griffeys the first father-son combination to play on the same team.

On Friday, August 31, at the Kingdome in Seattle, the Griffeys played their first game together—a night game against the Kansas City Royals. When the game started, father and son took side-by-side positions in the outfield, with Junior in center field and his dad in right. Ken Griffey Sr. batted second in the lineup; his son came up right behind him. In the bottom of the first inning, the older Griffey got the first hit of the game, a single to center field off pitcher Storm Davis. Moments later, Junior cracked a single into right. In their first at-bat of their first game together, the Griffeys became the first father-son teammates to register back-to-back hits. Exactly two weeks later, in a game in Anaheim against the California Angels, the Griffeys became the first father and son combo to hit back-to-back home runs in a major league game.

On one level, the Griffeys' experience as teammates is a curiosity—an interesting anecdote about two of the many colorful characters who played the game. But on another level, the Griffeys illustrated something more profound: the meaning of the game. While baseball has served as a pillar of nationalism, a tool of assimilation, a battleground of labor and business, and a vehicle of globalization, it has mostly been a source of unity, bringing communities and families together as its lore and traditions are passed from one generation to the next. Parents sometimes grab a mitt and play a game of catch with their children. They take their kids to major and minor league games. Children and their parents have been following major league baseball for decades. Poet Carl Sandburg, recalling his nineteenth-century childhood, wrote in 1953 that he could "from day to day name the leading teams and the tail enders in the National League and the American Association."

Baseball has served to unite communities, and even the country. For instance, except for areas on the fringe of New England—such as western Connecticut, where the Yankees enjoy a significant following—virtually everyone in the region lives and dies with the Red Sox. In Brooklyn, the Dodgers broke down ethnic and even class lines. In *The Boys of Summer*, former sportswriter Roger Kahn recalled an incident that took place when he was seven: His father, a well-respected high school history teacher, took him to a Dodgers game at Ebbets Field, where, to the younger Kahn's amazement, Gordon Kahn became engaged in conversation about the Dodgers with a jacketless fan in suspenders and a straw hat who lacked a front tooth. Baseball not only united fans who followed the same team, but it also provided common ground for fans of rival teams. Historian Doris Kearns Goodwin, in her memoir *Wait Till Next Year,* described how, as a young Brooklyn Dodgers fan in suburban Rockville Centre, on Long Island, she enjoyed the frequent give-and-take with a pair of Giants fans who ran the local butcher shop. After the terrorist attacks of September 11, 2001, destroyed the World Trade Center in New York City, President George W. Bush threw out the first pitch in the World Series at Yankee Stadium. The act—undertaken at the national pastime—symbolized the determination of the country to survive terrorism, the unity of the country at that time, and the strength of American culture.

Baseball also brings families together, as the tradition of rooting for a particular team is passed from generation to generation. Kahn wrote about the bond he developed with his father over their mutual love for the Brooklyn Dodgers, and in Goodwin's case, the Dodgers united the whole family. When she was six, her father taught her how to keep score while listening to Dodgers games on the radio. For years afterward, she would spend her afternoons listening to the game on the radio and recording the action in a red scorebook. When her father returned from work, Goodwin recreated the game for him, play by play, not realizing that he could have read an account of the game in the afternoon newspaper.

Keeping score is one of the many rituals associated with attending a ball game. Although modern electronic scoreboards trace players' performances throughout the game, the demand for scorecards is still high enough that ballpark vendors sell them. Scorekeeping is a skill passed from generation to generation, and some fans have adopted elaborate systems to track the game. The attraction of keeping score remains strong today because baseball is a statistics-driven game. Every run, hit, and error is added up at the end of the game. Every at-bat is counted toward a player's average. Batting above or below .300 is the difference between a superior player and an average one, while winning twenty games is the mark of a pitcher who is having an excellent season. Is it any wonder that some fans became disillusioned when baseball records appeared tainted?

Baseball has developed its own set of rituals, many of which revolve around the first day of the season. The Opening Day ceremony is repeated annually in almost every major and minor league ballpark. Red, white, and blue bunting decorates the stadium. A local dignitary—often a mayor or governor, and sometimes the president—throws out the first pitch. As a military band performs the national anthem, fighter jets fly over the field. Other traditions are maintained throughout the season. The seventh-inning stretch, during which fans stand up and sing "Take Me Out to the Ball Game," interrupts every game.

Even the consumption of certain foods has become a part of baseball's tradition. Hot dogs and beer, consumed at ball games since the nineteenth century, as well as peanuts and Cracker Jack, mentioned in the lyrics of the century-old "Take Me Out to the Ball Game," have long been considered baseball cuisine. Many stadiums also offer their own specialty—traditional local favorites not available in many other parks—including cheesesteak sandwiches in Philadelphia, bratwurst in Milwaukee, fish tacos in San Diego, and Rocky Mountain oysters (deep-fried bull testicles) in Denver. Several ballparks even serve kosher hot dogs.

Ballplayers have developed their own traditions, many based on superstitions. When a pitcher is working on a no-hitter, the other players, not wanting to break his concentration, avoid him in the dugout. And, because it might jinx the effort, under no circumstances should players, or anyone else employed by the team, including radio and television broadcasters, mention that a no-hitter is underway. Many players avoid stepping on the foul lines while walking on the field. Some players on a hot streak attempt to repeat their daily routine without any changes until the streak is over. Red Sox third baseman Wade Boggs, known for his many superstitions, ate a chicken dinner before every game.

Fans of individual teams have developed their own traditions that are passed down from generation to generation. On Opening Day in Cincinnati, where the first professional baseball team took the field in 1869, schools are closed and a parade is held for the Reds. Despite the almost universal excitement of catching a home run ball, fans at Chicago's Wrigley Field throw the ball back if the home run was hit by a member of the visiting team, a practice that can get fans ejected in most other ballparks. Between innings, some ballparks stage mascot races. In Washington, DC, mascots wearing large masks of presidents run around the base paths. In some places, mascot races are tied to food. The Milwaukee Brewers stage a "sausage race" during each game, in which the contestants are dressed as a hot dog, a bratwurst, a kielbasa, a chorizo, and an Italian sausage, while the Pittsburgh Pirates hold a pierogi race.

Music has also become identified with some baseball teams. In the early twentieth century, a group of intransigent Red Sox fans—including Boston mayor John F. "Honey Fitz" Fitzgerald, the grandfather of President John F. Kennedy—established a fan club called the Royal Rooters. The Royal Rooters adopted the Broadway song "Tessie" as their own. Today, Red Sox fans have embraced the Neil Diamond song "Sweet Caroline" (a song Diamond later claimed was inspired by a photo of President Kennedy's daughter), which the Fenway faithful sing in the middle of the eighth inning. At the conclusion of every game in Yankee Stadium, the public address system plays a recording of the "Theme from *New York, New York*"—the Frank Sinatra version if the team wins and the Liza Minnelli version if the team loses. At Chicago's Wrigley Field, following a tradition started by the late broadcaster Harry Caray, a celebrity leads the crowd in singing "Take Me Out to the Ball Game." Unlike the Yankees, however, the Cubs have adopted a simpler way to inform the neighborhood of the result of the game, raising a flag with a "W" when they win and a flag with an "L" when they lose.

Support for individual teams has fueled the sale of baseball caps, jerseys, and pennants. Kahn reported that as a kid, he was given a child's Dizzy Dean uniform, a gift he rejected because Dean played on the Cardinals rather than on his beloved Dodgers. Goodwin admitted to owning a Brooklyn Dodgers cap when she was a teenager in the fifties. Baseball clubs have encouraged the collection of team merchandise by scheduling promotions in which caps, T-shirts, and even bobblehead dolls are given away.

Collecting baseball cards has been a pastime of young fans since the nineteenth century, when tobacco companies produced such cards. A 1909 card depicting Pirates shortstop Honus Wagner is now worth more than $2 million because Wagner, who objected to tobacco use, ordered the American Tobacco Company to cease production after only forty were issued. Since the 1950s, baseball cards have been big business.

Tabletop baseball games, some based on simple pinball machines, have been around since the nineteenth century. In 1961 a Bucknell University math student introduced a statistics-based game called Strat-O-Matic, in which fantasy games are played based on players' actual statistics. With the publication of Glen Waggoner's *Rotisserie League Baseball* in 1984, which demonstrated how to organize an imaginary pennant race utilizing players' current statistics, fantasy leagues formed in many offices across the country.

Perhaps the epitome of a tapping into a fan's imagination, however, was the introduction of fantasy camps in the 1980s. At these camps, fans—mostly middle-aged men—pay thousands of dollars to play baseball with their retired heroes at spring training facilities in the weeks before the current major leaguers report.

Baseball's reach into American culture extends well beyond the grasp of the major or minor leagues. In 1937 a man named Carl Stotz formed a youth league in Williamsport, Pennsylvania. Today the organization formed by Stotz, Little League Baseball, operates in all fifty states and in eighty countries. In 1947 a tournament of all-star teams from every member league was established, culminating in an annual Little League World Series played in Williamsport. Many future major leaguers, including Boog Powell of the Orioles, Gary Sheffield of the Marlins, and Jason Varitek of the Red Sox, have participated in the Little League World Series. Other Little League players have also made history. Thirteen-year-old Mo'ne Davis, representing a team from Philadelphia, pitched a two-hit shutout against a team from Nashville in the 2014 Little League World Series. Fresh off her victory, *Sports Illustrated* ran her photo on the magazine cover, making her the first Little League player to earn that honor.

Adults play the game, too. For decades, millions of grown men and women have spent their summer evenings participating in a less demanding version of the sport called slow-pitch softball. Other adults play by standard baseball rules. In the first half of the twentieth century, amateur and semiprofessional teams flourished in almost every town in America. Some of them, called company teams, were sponsored by major employers like the Great Western Sugar Company, Southern Bell Telephone, and Baldwin Piano. Every summer from 1915 until 1947, ten teams not affiliated with Major League Baseball—including amateur, semipro, and even Negro league teams—were invited to Denver to participate in the Denver Post Tournament.

In 1994, during the reorganization of exhibits, workers at the National Baseball Hall of Fame in Cooperstown discovered an old photograph of a baseball player hidden under one of the display cases. On the back of the photo, someone had written, "You were never too tired to play catch. On your days off, you helped build the Little League field. You always came to watch me play. You were a Hall of Fame Dad. I wish you could share this moment with me." The curator of the museum passed the photo along to *Sports Illustrated*, which published a story about it. A journalist for a small-town newspaper in upstate New York recognized that the baseball uniform belonged to a defunct company team representing Wellsville Sinclair Oil, and he eventually discovered it to be a photo of Joe O'Donnell, a former player on the team who died in 1966. The photo had been hidden in the Hall of Fame in 1988 by O'Donnell's son, Pat, who believed that players on company teams also should be honored by the Hall. Hall of Fame officials agreed, and hid the photo once again, near where it was first discovered. The hidden photo honors the thousands of invisible men and women who played for company teams—but it also shows a son's love for his father, illustrating the bond formed between generations of baseball fans.

Bibliographic Essay

FOR DECADES THE LITERATURE on baseball history was dominated by books written by journalists, sportswriters, and general authors. Professional scholars ignored baseball and other sports, concentrating instead on political, social, economic, and diplomatic developments. Consequently, research on baseball was pioneered by nonscholars. In the past two generations, however, professional historians have begun to examine the impact of baseball on American culture. With *Baseball: The Early Years* (New York: Oxford University Press, 1960), Harold Seymour produced the first scholarly book on baseball. The book traced the evolution of baseball in the nineteenth century. Seymour's thesis was that professional baseball is not a sport; it is a commercial amusement business. A decade later, Seymour published a sequel, *Baseball: The Golden Age* (New York: Oxford University Press, 1971), which, at the expense of developments on the field, concentrated on the business aspect of baseball between 1900 and 1930. *Baseball: The Golden Age* was especially insightful on the 1919 Black Sox Scandal and the ensuing creation of the commissioner's office, but Seymour chose to ignore the creation of the Negro leagues. In the introduction, he promised a discussion of Negro league baseball in his next volume, but nearly twenty years passed before Seymour's third volume appeared, and by then, others had already explored the Negro leagues. With the publication of his third volume, *Baseball: The People's Game* (New York: Oxford University Press, 1990), however, Seymour returned to the nineteenth and early twentieth centuries. This time he looked at amateur baseball—including sandlot baseball, high school baseball, college baseball, industrial league baseball, baseball in the military, even baseball in prisons—as well as the Negro leagues and women's leagues during the period between the Civil War and World

War II. While still maintaining that professional baseball was a business, Seymour had come up with nearly a dozen other levels of baseball that still fit the definition of a sport. After Seymour's death in 1992, his widow, Dorothy Seymour Mills, revealed that she had been a significant collaborator on all three of his baseball books, and thus subsequent editions of the books credit her as a coauthor. Despite its pioneering effort, however, the Seymour trilogy lacks citations.

In between the publication of Seymour's first two volumes, David Q. Voigt, a sociologist from Albright College in Pennsylvania, published a two-volume history of baseball. The first volume, *American Baseball: From Gentleman's Sport to the Commissioner System* (Norman: University of Oklahoma Press, 1966), surveyed the history of baseball from its origins to the Black Sox Scandal, while the second book, *American Baseball: From the Commissioners to Continental Expansion* (Norman: University of Oklahoma Press, 1970), covered the history of baseball from the 1920s through the 1960s. Voigt took an even more scholarly approach than Seymour, examining the intersection between play (the unrestricted pursuit of leisure) and sport (with its rules, regulations, and officials). Voigt argued that baseball set the pattern for other team sports. As a child's game, baseball would begin as play, become sport with the emergence of formal rules and organized leagues, and then return to play as it developed a spectator following. The late historian Jules Tygiel linked baseball history to America in *Past Time: Baseball as History* (New York: Oxford University Press, 2000). *Past Time* is not a comprehensive history of baseball but a collection of separate essays that connect various aspects of baseball history with trends in American history. For other general and survey treatments, see John P. Rossi, *Baseball and American Culture* (Chicago: Ivan R. Dee, 2000); Charles C. Alexander, *Our Game: An American Baseball History* (New York: Henry Holt, 1991); George Vecsey, *Baseball: A History of America's Favorite Game* (New York: Modern Library, 2006); and Mitchell Nathanson, *A People's History of Baseball* (Urbana: University of Illinois Press, 2012).

A number of American historians have looked at the United States before the Civil War. For the economic, political, and social changes taking place in America when baseball emerged in the first half of the nineteenth century, see Thomas C. Cochran's *Frontiers of Change: Early Industrialization in America* (New York: Oxford University Press, 1981) and Charles Sellers's *The Market Revolution in America: Jacksonian America, 1815–1846* (New York: Oxford University Press, 1993). Alexis de Tocqueville's two-volume *Democracy in America*, originally published in 1835 and 1840, has been republished in a number of different editions, including an English translation by Gerald E. Bevan (New York: Penguin Books, 2003). For a look at the egalitarianism and vitality of nineteenth-century New York City, where modern baseball developed, see Mary P. Ryan's *Civic Wars: Democracy and Public Life in the American City during the Nineteenth Century* (Berkeley: University of California Press, 1997) and Sean Wilentz's *Chants Democratic: New York City & the Rise of the American Working Class, 1788–1850* (New York: Oxford University Press, 1984).

Several baseball historians have explored the origins of the game. Robert W. Henderson's *Ball, Bat and Bishop: The Origins of Ball Games* (New York: Rockport Press, 1947) disproved the Abner Doubleday myth. Since the publication of Seymour's first book, additional scholarship has reexamined the origins of modern baseball in nineteenth-century New York City. Warren Goldstein's *Playing for Keeps: A History of Early Baseball* (Ithaca, NY: Cornell University Press, 1989) looked at baseball's capitalist roots during the game's amateur era. David Block, in *Baseball before We Knew It: A Search for the Roots of the Game* (Lincoln: University of Nebraska Press, 2006), argued that "rounders" was a regional name for a game that had been called "base ball" in other parts of England for centuries. John Thorn's *Baseball in the Garden of Eden: The Secret History of the Early Game* (New York: Simon & Schuster, 2012), by de-emphasizing the contributions of Alexander Cartwright, Henry Chadwick, and the Knickerbocker Base Ball Club, corrected errors recorded by Seymour and passed along by other historians. Thorn also investigated the importance of gambling in giving baseball a wider audience in the first half of the nineteenth century. Both Thorn and Block also looked at the connection Albert Spalding, Pirates owner William C. Temple, and Abner Doubleday had with a spiritualism movement called Theosophy.

George Kirsch, in *Baseball in Blue and Gray: The National Pastime during the Civil War* (Princeton, NJ: Princeton University Press, 2003), and William J. Ryczek, in *When Johnny Comes Sliding Home: The Post-Civil War Baseball Boom, 1865–1870* (Jefferson, NC: McFarland, 2006), examined the impact of the Civil War on baseball. Marshall D. Wright's

The National Association of Base Ball Players, 1857–1870 (Jefferson, NC: McFarland, 2000) cataloged every team and player who competed in baseball's first league, the amateur National Association of Base Ball Players, and provided short summaries for each NABBP season. *The Red Stockings of Cincinnati: Base Ball's First All-Professional Team and Its Historic 1869 and 1870 Seasons*, by Stephen D. Guschov (Jefferson, NC: McFarland, 1998), looked at baseball's first openly professional team. Two biographies of Alexander Cartwright appeared in 2009—Jay Martin's *Live All You Can: Alexander Joy Cartwright and the Invention of Modern Baseball* (New York: Columbia University Press, 2009) and Monica Nucciarone's *Alexander Cartwright: The Life behind the Baseball Legend* (Lincoln: University of Nebraska Press, 2009).

For information on industrialization, urbanization, and the arrival of immigrants in the second half of the nineteenth century, see Raymond A. Mohl's *The New City: Urban America in the Industrial Age, 1860–1920* (Arlington Heights, IL: Harlan Davidson, 1985) and Herbert Gutman's *Work, Culture, and Society in Industrializing America* (New York: Knopf, 1976). The definitive biography of John D. Rockefeller is still Allan Nevins's two-volume work, *A Study in Power: John D. Rockefeller* (New York: Scribner's, 1953), while Joseph Frazier Wall's massive *Andrew Carnegie* (New York: Oxford University Press, 1970) offers a detailed look at that mogul.

Harvey Frommer reviewed professional baseball in the nineteenth century in *Old Time Baseball: America's Pastime in the Gilded Age* (Boulder, CO: Taylor Trade Publications, 2005). William J. Ryczek's *Blackguards and Red Stockings: A History of Baseball's National Association, 1871–1875* examined baseball's first professional league, while Edward Achorn looked at the American Association's 1883 pennant race in *The Summer of Beer and Whiskey* (New York: Public Affairs, 2013). David Nemec's *The Great Encyclopedia of 19th Century Major League Baseball* (New York: Penguin Books, 1997) explored every professional baseball season between 1871 and 1900. Short biographies of 135 nineteenth-century players appeared in an anthology edited by Robert L. Tiemann and Mark Rucker called *Nineteenth Century Stars* (Kansas City, MO: Society for American Baseball Research, 1989). David L. Fleitz's *Cap Anson: The Grand Old Man of Baseball* (Jefferson, NC: McFarland, 2005) offered a biography of the nineteenth century's biggest baseball star.

Eric Foner's *Reconstruction: America's Unfinished Revolution, 1863–1877* (New York: Harper Collins, 1988) is the most thorough modern examination of Reconstruction. *The Strange Career of Jim Crow*, by C. Vann Woodward (New York: Oxford University Press, 1955), argued that segregation laws had not always existed in southern states but were adopted in the 1880s and 1890s. Leon Litwack's *Been in the Storm So Long: The Aftermath of Slavery* (New York: Vintage Books, 1979) looked at the impact of freedom on former slaves.

James E. Brunson's *The Early Image of Black Baseball: Race and Representation in the Popular Press, 1871–1890* (Jefferson, NC: McFarland, 2009) examined black baseball in popular culture in the nineteenth century. Biographies of two nineteenth-century African American players are available—David W. Zang's *Fleet Walker's Divided Heart: The Life of Baseball's First Black Major Leaguer* (Lincoln: University of Nebraska Press, 1995), which looked at the nineteenth century's best (and most famous) black player, and Jeffrey Michael Laing's *Bud Fowler: Baseball's First Black Professional* (Jefferson, NC: McFarland, 2013), which presented the life of the first known African American to play professional baseball.

The New Empire: An Interpretation of American Expansion, 1860–1898, by Walter LeFeber (Ithaca, NY: Cornell University Press, 1963), examined the creation of the American empire and the political and business motivation behind it. Louis A. Perez Jr.'s *The War of 1898: The United States and Cuba in History and Historiography* (Chapel Hill: University of North Carolina Press, 1998) looked at the Spanish-American War, arguing both that the United States acted against the wishes of the Cuban people and that American historians have largely left Cuba out of the history of the war.

The 1888–1889 World Baseball Tour was chronicled by Thomas W. Zeiler in *Ambassadors in Pinstripes: The Spalding World Baseball Tour and the Birth of the American Empire* (Lanham, MD: Rowman & Littlefield, 2006), who argued that Spalding's tour anticipated the creation of an American empire. Albert Spalding's history of baseball, *America's National Game* (New York: American Sports Publishing, 1911), claimed that the game of baseball represents the American character. Peter Levine presented a biography of Spalding in *A. G. Spalding and the Rise of Baseball: The Promise of American Sport* (New York: Oxford University

Press, 1985). James E. Elfers examined baseball's next big tour in *The Tour to End All Tours: The Story of Major League Baseball's 1913–1914 World Tour* (Lincoln, NE: Bison Books, 2003).

A number of historians have looked at the labor unrest of the Gilded Age. Leon Fink's *Workingmen's Democracy: The Knights of Labor and American Politics* (Urbana: University of Illinois Press, 1983) investigated the impact of the Knights of Labor in five American cities. Julie Greene's *Pure and Simple Politics: The American Federation of Labor and Political Activism* (New York: Cambridge University Press, 1998) looked at the political role the AFL took under Samuel Gompers. The major strikes of the period are covered in Robert V. Bruce's *1877: Year of Violence* (Indianapolis, IN: Bobbs-Merrill, 1959), which examined the Great Railroad Strike; Almont Lindsey's *The Pullman Strike: The Story of a Unique Experiment and of a Great Labor Upheaval* (Chicago: University of Chicago Press, 1943); and Paul Kahan's *The Homestead Strike: Labor, Violence, and American Industry* (New York: Routledge, 2013). *The Haymarket Tragedy*, by Paul Avrich (Princeton, NJ: Princeton University Press, 1986), studied the Haymarket riot and America's fear of European radicalism.

Robert P. Gelzheiser looked at the Gilded Age labor struggle in baseball in *Labor and Capital in 19th Century Baseball* (Jefferson, NC: McFarland, 2005). The growing tension between the players and owners during the 1889 season, and the season itself, was examined in two books—Daniel M. Pearson's *Baseball in 1889: Players vs. Owners* (Madison, WI: University of Wisconsin Press, 1993) and Jean Pierre Caillault's *A Tale of Four Cities: Nineteenth Century Baseball's Most Exciting Season in Contemporary Accounts* (Jefferson, NC: McFarland, 2004). Scott D. Peterson looked at the press coverage of the players' revolt in *Reporting Baseball's Sensational Season of 1890* (Jefferson, NC: McFarland, 2015). Bryan Di Salvatore offered a biography of the founder of the Brotherhood of Professional Base Ball Players in *A Clever Base-Ballist: The Life and Times of John Montgomery Ward* (Jefferson, NC: McFarland, 1999).

Other historians have looked at the reform movements of the late nineteenth and early twentieth centuries. Lawrence Goodwyn's *Democratic Promise: The Populist Movement in America* (New York: Oxford University Press, 1976) provided a broad history of the populist move-

ment, while *American Populism: A Social History, 1877–1898*, by Robert
C. McMath Jr. (New York: Hill & Wang, 1993), looked at populism in
the context of rural society. *Progressivism*, by Arthur S. Link and Richard
L. McCormick (Arlington Heights, IL: Harlan Davidson, 1982), is an
excellent introduction to the Progressive movement. Edmund Morris's
massive three-volume biography of Theodore Roosevelt—*The Rise of
Theodore Roosevelt* (New York: Coward, McCann, & Geoghegan, 1979),
Theodore Rex (New York: Random House, 2001), and *Colonel Roosevelt*
(New York, Random House, 2011)—provided a thorough examination
of the life of the twenty-sixth president. H. W. Brands also offered a
comprehensive biography of Roosevelt in *T. R.: The Last Romantic* (New
York: Basic Books, 1997).

Steven A. Riess looked at the relationship between baseball and urban
America during the Progressive Era in *Touching Base: Professional Base-
ball and American Culture in the Progressive Era* (Lincoln: University of
Nebraska Press, 1983). A number of good biographies exist of Ty Cobb,
the biggest star of the early twentieth century, including *Ty Cobb*, by
Charles C. Alexander (New York: Oxford University Press, 1984); *Ty
Cobb: A Terrible Beauty*, by Charles Leerhsen (New York: Simon &
Schuster, 2015); and *War on the Basepaths: The Definitive Biography of Ty
Cobb*, by Tim Hornbaker (New York: Sports Publishing, 2015). War-
ren N. Wilbert examined Ban Johnson and the creation of the American
League in *The Arrival of the American League: Ban Johnson and the 1901
Challenge to National League Monopoly* (Jefferson, NC: McFarland, 2007).

David M. Kennedy, in *Over Here: The First World War and American
Society* (New York: Oxford University Press, 1980), examined America
during World War I. In *From Progressivism to Prosperity: World War I and
American Society* (New York: Holmes & Meier, 1986), Neil Wynn looked
at the impact of World War I on American society, while Ellis Hawley, in
*The Great War and the Search for a Modern Order: A History of the American
People and Their Institutions* (New York: St. Martin's, 1979), investigated
how the First World War spurred the growth of managerial institutions.
The domestic turmoil that followed the war was the subject of *Race
Riot: Chicago and the Red Summer of 1919*, by William M. Tuttle (New
York: Atheneum, 1970), and Robert K. Murray's *The Red Scare: A Study
in National Hysteria, 1919–1920* (Minneapolis: University of Minnesota

Press, 1955). Stanley A. Coben's biography *A. Mitchell Palmer, Politician* (New York: Columbia University Press, 1963) outlined the life of the US attorney general who directed the Palmer Raids, while Kendrick A. Clement, in *The Presidency of Woodrow Wilson* (Lawrence: University of Kansas Press, 1992), offered a sympathetic biography of Wilson.

Mark Okkonen authored *The Federal League of 1914–1915: Baseball's Third Major League* (Garrett Park, MD: Society for American Baseball Research, 1998), a SABR publication that reviewed the last circuit to actively challenge Major League Baseball. Although more than a half century old, Eliot Asinof's *Eight Men Out: The Black Sox and the 1919 World Series* (New York: Henry Holt, 1963) is still the definitive look at the Black Sox Scandal; John Sayles directed a film adaptation of the book, starring John Cusack, in 1988. Daniel A. Nathan, in *Saying It's So: A Cultural History of the Black Sox Scandal* (Urbana: University of Illinois Press, 2003), examined the changing perceptions and memories of the scandal over the years. A number of biographies of the individuals involved in the scandal have appeared. Most biographies of Shoeless Joe Jackson are sympathetic, either mitigating his involvement because he was illiterate or minimizing it because of his immense talent. In *Say It Ain't So, Joe! The Story of Shoeless Joe Jackson* (Boston: Little, Brown, 1979), Donald Gropman, citing Jackson's flawless record in the 1919 World Series, doubted his involvement in the scandal. Harvey Frommer, in *Shoeless Joe and Ragtime Baseball* (Dallas: Taylor Publishing, 1992), also questioned Jackson's guilt, pointing not only to his performance in the World Series but also to minor inconsistencies in newspaper accounts of Jackson's testimony before the grand jury. The most recent biography of Jackson, David L. Fleitz's *Shoeless: The Life and Times of Shoeless Joe Jackson* (Jefferson, NC: McFarland, 2001), did not question Jackson's guilt or plead for his reinstatement in baseball but instead sought to separate truth from perception. In contrast to the sympathetic work on Jackson, the man behind the "Big Fix," gambler Arnold Rothstein, was harshly criticized in Leo Katcher's *The Big Bankroll: The Life and Times of Arnold Rothstein* (New York: Harper & Brothers, 1958). Katcher looked at Rothstein's entire criminal career and saw him assembling the same type of organization that business leaders were putting together in the twenties. Katcher argued that Rothstein created a crime machine that continued long after his death.

In *The Perils of Prosperity, 1914–1932* (Chicago: University of Chicago Press, 1958), William E. Leuchtenburg saw the twenties as a transitional period between traditional, rural America of the nineteenth century and the modern, urban America of the twentieth century. Edward J. Larson, in *Summer for the Gods: The Scopes Trial and America's Continuing Debate over Science and Religion* (New York: Basic Books, 1997), examined the tension between modernity and traditional America. James J. Flink, in *The Automobile Age* (Cambridge: MIT Press, 1988), looked at the impact of the automobile on American culture; while John D. Hicks, in *Republican Ascendancy, 1921–1933* (New York: Harper & Brothers, 1960), connected the business environment of the twenties with the political developments of the decade.

The life of Babe Ruth, who modernized the way baseball was played in the 1920s, was captured in three notable biographies—Ken Sobol's *Babe Ruth & the American Dream* (New York: Ballantine Books, 1974), Robert Creamer's *Babe: The Legend Comes to Life* (New York: Simon & Schuster, 1974), and Marshall Smelser's *The Life that Ruth Built* (New York: Quadrangle, 1975). Ray Robinson's *Iron Horse: Lou Gehrig in His Time* (New York: Norton, 1990) portrayed the life of Ruth's famous teammate.

Leon Litwack's *Trouble in Mind: Black Southerners in the Age of Jim Crow* (New York: Knopf, 1998) investigated how African Americans struggled to survive white supremacy in the South during segregation. Nathan Irvin Huggins, in *Harlem Renaissance* (New York: Oxford University Press, 1971), looked at the literature and art created by African Americans in the 1920s and the writers and artists who created it. Many biographies of the major civil rights leaders of the early twentieth century are also available. In *Up from History: The Life of Booker T. Washington* (Cambridge: Belknap Press, 2009) Robert J. Norrell presented a sympathetic biography of Washington that contextualized his accommodationist strategy within the racial hostility of the time. David Levering Lewis wrote a massive two-volume examination of W.E.B. Du Bois's life—*W.E.B. Du Bois, 1868–1919: Biography of a Race* (New York: Henry Holt, 1994) and *W.E.B. Du Bois, 1919–1963: The Fight for Equality and the American Century* (New York: Henry Holt, 2000). Colin Grant's *Negro with a Hat: The Rise and Fall of Marcus Garvey* (New York: Oxford University Press, 2010) looked at the leader of the Universal Negro Improvement Association.

As with the Black Sox Scandal, nonscholars pioneered the first significant examinations of the Negro leagues. The first major book on the Negro leagues, Robert Peterson's *Only the Ball Was White: A History of Legendary Black Players and All-Black Professional Teams* (New York: Oxford Univesity Press, 1970), attempted to document the achievements of Negro leaguers and argued for their inclusion in baseball's Hall of Fame. American studies professor Donn Rogosin, in *Invisible Men: Life in Baseball's Negro Leagues* (New York: Atheneum, 1987), not only offered a colorful account of the Negro leagues, but also argued that because Negro league teams won more than 60 percent of the games they played against white major leaguers, the Negro leagues undermined segregation by striking a blow against white superiority. SABR members Dick Clark and Larry Lester edited *The Negro League Book* (Cleveland: Society for American Baseball Research, 1984), an encyclopedic collection of Negro league stats, records, and biographies. John B. Holway's *The Complete Book of Baseball's Negro Leagues: The Other Half of Baseball History* (Fern Park, FL: Hastings House, 2001) is perhaps the most comprehensive source for Negro league standings, records, and rosters.

In recent years, the Negro leagues have become a major focus of scholars looking at race in twentieth-century America. David Wiggins and Patrick Miller assembled *The Unlevel Playing Field: A Documentary History of the African American Experience in Sport* (Urbana: University of Illinois Press, 2003), a collection of primary source documents on the Negro leagues. That same year, Leslie Heaphy, in *The Negro Leagues, 1869–1960* (Jefferson, NC: McFarland, 2003), explored the importance of Negro league players in American life. Heaphy found that after African Americans were forced out of white baseball and established their own teams in the nineteenth century, the Great Migration of African Americans from the rural South to the urban North in the first two decades of the twentieth century made it possible for black leaders to establish stable leagues in the 1920s. Neil Lanctot's *Negro League Baseball: The Rise and Ruin of a Black Institution* (Philadelphia: University of Pennsylvania Press, 2008) examined the economic impact the Great Depression and World War II had on the Negro leagues and integration. Thomas Aiello, in *The Kings of Casino Park: Black Baseball in the Lost Season of 1932* (Tuscaloosa: University of Alabama Press, 2011), looked at the Negro Southern League, which enjoyed major league status among the Negro leagues during the tumultuous season of 1932, the year after the original Negro National League folded and the year before the second Negro National League emerged.

Adrian Burgos Jr.'s *Cuban Star: How One Negro-League Owner Changed the Face of Baseball* (New York: Hill & Wang, 2011) documented the life of Alessandro Pompez, the owner of the New York Cubans. Newark Eagles owner Effa Manley was the subject of two biographies—James Overmyer's *Queen of the Negro Leagues: Effa Manley and the Newark Eagles* (Lanham, MD: Scarecrow Press, 1998) and Bob Luke's *The Most Famous Woman in Baseball: Effa Manley and the Negro Leagues* (Washington, DC: Potomac Books, 2011).

Michael Bernstein's *The Great Depression: Delayed Recovery and Economic Change in America, 1929–1939* (New York: Cambridge University Press, 1987) examined the economic factors of the Great Depression, while Morris Dickstein, in *Dancing in the Dark: A Cultural History of the Great Depression* (New York: Norton, 2009), looked at its cultural impact. *Franklin D, Roosevelt: A Rendezvous with Destiny* (Boston: Little, Brown, 1990), by Frank Freidel, is perhaps the best single-volume biography of FDR, while William E. Leuchtenburg's *Franklin D. Roosevelt and the New Deal, 1932–1940* (New York: Harper & Row, 1963) is the best single-volume on the New Deal.

Charles C. Alexander, in *Breaking the Slump: Baseball in the Depression Era* (New York: Columbia University Press, 2002), looked at baseball in the decade of the thirties, while *Wins, Losses, and Empty Seats: How Baseball Outlasted the Great Depression*, by David George Surdam (Lincoln: University of Nebraska Press, 2011), examined the operation of baseball during the Depression. Norman L. Macht's three-volume biography of Connie Mack—*Connie Mack and the Early Years of Baseball* (Lincoln: University of Nebraska Press, 2007), *The Turbulent and Triumphant Years, 1915–1931* (Lincoln: University of Nebraska Press, 2012), and *The Grand Old Man of Baseball: Connie Mack and His Final Years, 1932–1956* (Lincoln: University of Nebraska Press, 2012)—is the most thorough examination of the Philadelphia Athletics owner-manager.

Military historian John Keegan, in *The Second World War* (New York: Viking Press, 1990), offered a traditional history of World War II. *A Democracy at War: America's Fight at Home and Abroad in World War II*, by William L. O'Neill (New York: Free Press, 1993), looked at the diplomatic and political history of America's role in the war. John Morton Blum's *V Was for Victory: Politics and American Culture during World War II* (New York: Harcourt Brace Jovanovich, 1976) explored the intersection between culture and politics during the war, arguing that FDR abandoned the New Deal in exchange for conservative support for the war. Susan Hartmann, in *The Home Front and Beyond: American Women in the 1940s* (Boston: Twayne, 1982), examined the role of women during World War II.

Baseball during World War II has drawn the attention of a number of people. With *Even the Browns: The Zany True Story of Baseball in the Early 1940s* (Chicago: Contemporary Books, 1978), later republished as *Baseball Goes to War: Stars Don Khaki, 4-Fs Vie for Pennant* (Washington, DC: Farragut Classics, 1985), William R. Mead offered the first book to look at baseball during World War II. Two years after the appearance of *Even the Browns*, Richard Goldstein published *Spartan Seasons: How Baseball Survived the Second World War* (New York: MacMillan, 1980), a narrative of baseball during the war years. More recently, David Finoli offered an overview of baseball from 1942 through 1945 in *For the Good of the Country: World War II Baseball in the Major and Minor Leagues* (Jefferson, NC: McFarland, 2002). Tom E. Allen examined how the war affected 472 major leaguers in *If They Hadn't Gone: How World War II Affected Major League Baseball* (Springfield, MO: Moon City Press, 2004). John Klima's *The Game Must Go On: Hank Greenberg, Pete Gray, and the Great Days of Baseball on the Home Front in WWII* (New York: Thomas Dunne Books, 2015) is the latest overview of baseball during the war.

Other baseball historians have looked at specific aspects of the war's effect on the sport. Jeff Obermeyer studied the economic impact of the war in *Baseball and the Bottom Line in World War II: Gunning for Profits on the Home Front* (Jefferson, NC: McFarland, 2013). Bob Gilbert, in *They Also Served: Baseball and the Home Front* (New York: Crown, 1992), looked at how baseball helped boost morale during World War II, while Stephen R. Bullock explored the interaction between Major League Baseball and the military in *Playing for Their Nation: Baseball and the American Military during World War II* (Lincoln: University of Nebraska Press, 2004). With *Moe Berg: Athlete, Scholar, Spy* (Boston: Little, Brown, 1975), Louis Kaufman offered a biography of a major league player who became a spy during the war. Although more than

500 major league players served in the military during the war, only a handful of them saw combat, and only two major leaguers—Elmer Gedeon of the Senators and Harry O'Neill of the Athletics—were killed in the war. Minor leaguers, however, were not as lucky. Gary Bedingfield's *Baseball's Dead of World War II: Roster of Professional Players Who Died in Service* (Jefferson, NC: McFarland, 2009) examined the 127 minor league players who died in World War II. David R. Wells, in *Baseball's Western Front: The Pacific Coast League during World War II* (Jefferson, NC: McFarland, 2004), reviewed one of baseball's top minor leagues, the Pacific Coast League, during the war years. Merrie Fidler, in *The Origins and History of the All-American Girls Professional Baseball League* (Jefferson, NC: McFarland, 2010), looked at the operation of the AAGPBL, while Jim Sargent's *We Were the All-American Girls: Interviews with Players of the AAGPBL, 1943–1954* (Jefferson, NC: McFarland, 2013) contained interviews of forty-two women who played in the All-American League.

Robert W. Creamer chronicled the exciting 1941 season in *Baseball in '41: A Celebration of the "Best Baseball Season Ever"* (New York: Penguin Books, 1991). Red Sox slugger Ted Williams's life was examined in Leigh Montville's *Ted Williams: The Biography of an American Hero* (Norwell, MA: Anchor, 2005) and Ben Bradlee Jr.'s *The Kid: The Immortal Life of Ted Williams* (New York: Back Bay Books, 2014), while *Joe DiMaggio: The Hero's Life*, by Richard Ben Cramer (New York: Simon & Schuster, 2001), offered a brutally honest examination of the life of the Yankee Clipper.

After fighting against oppression during the war, many Americans reassessed racial attitudes after the war. Harvard Sitkoff offered a helpful overview of the civil rights movement in *The Struggle for Black Equality, 1954–1980* (New York: Hill & Wang, 1981). Noteworthy books on Martin Luther King Jr. and the Southern Christian Leadership Conference include *Parting the Waters: America in the King Years, 1954–1963*, by Taylor Branch (New York: Simon & Schuster, 1988); *To Redeem the Soul of America: The Southern Christian Leadership Conference and Martin Luther King*, by Adam Fairclough (Athens: University of Georgia Press, 1987); and David Garrow's Pulitzer Prize–winning biography *Bearing the Cross: Martin Luther King, Jr. and the Southern Christian Leadership Conference* (New York: William Morrow, 1986).

As one of the first American institutions to desegregate, baseball helped shape American society after the war. Brian Carroll looked at the impact of the African American press's coverage of baseball in *When to Stop the Cheering? The Black Press, the Black Community, and the Integration of Professional Baseball* (New York: Routledge, 2006). Lee Lowenfish's *Branch Rickey: Baseball's Ferocious Gentleman* (Lincoln: University of Nebraska Press, 2007) and Murray Polner's *Branch Rickey: A Biography* (Jefferson, NC: McFarland, 2007) are recent biographies of the general manager who signed Jackie Robinson to a major league contract. Bill Veeck's claim that he attempted to integrate the Philadelphia Phillies during World War II appeared in the autobiography he wrote with Edward Linn, *Veeck—As in Wreck: The Autobiography of Bill Veeck* (New York: Putnam, 1962).

Perhaps no baseball figure has received as much attention from scholars as Jackie Robinson. Arnold Rampersad, with *Jackie Robinson: A Biography* (New York: Ballantine Books, 1997), and Jules Tygiel, with *Baseball's Great Experiment: Jackie Robinson and His Legacy* (New York: Oxford University Press, 2000), both offered excellent biographies of Jackie Robinson. Robinson's first season in the major leagues is chronicled in Jonathan Eig's *Opening Day: The Story of Jackie Robinson's First Season* (New York: Simon & Schuster, 2007) and Scott Simon's *Jackie Robinson and the Integration of Baseball* (Hoboken, NJ: Wiley, 2007). Thomas W. Zeiler edited a primary source reader called *Jackie Robinson and Race in America: A Brief History with Documents* (Boston: Bedford/St. Martin's, 2014).

Other historians have looked at many of the factors that defined the fifties. Elaine Tyler May, in *Homeward Bound: American Families in the Cold War Era* (New York: Basic Books, 1988), investigated the link between white, middle-class American family life and the Cold War. Lynn Spigel's *Make Room for TV: Television and the Ideal Family in Postwar America* (Chicago: University of Chicago Press, 1992) looked at the impact television had on American culture in the postwar period. *Crabgrass Frontier: The Suburbanization of the United States*, by Kenneth T. Jackson (New York: Oxford University Press, 1985), examined American suburbs from the 1820s to the late twentieth century. Thomas C. Reeves's *The Life and Times of Joseph McCarthy* (Lanham, MD: Madison

Books, 1997) offered a recent biography of the US senator behind much of the anti-Communist hysteria of the early 1950s.

John P. Rossi, in *A Whole New Game: Off the Field Changes in Baseball, 1946–1960* (Jefferson, NC: McFarland, 1999), explored baseball between the end of World War II and the major league expansion of the early 1960s. Robert Weintraub's *The Victory Season: The End of World War II and the Birth of Baseball's Golden Age* (Boston: Little, Brown, 2013) reviewed the 1946 baseball season, the first season after the war ended. David Halberstam, in *The Summer of '49* (New York: Morrow, 1989), chronicled the 1949 pennant race between the Boston Red Sox and New York Yankees. Harvey Frommer's *New York City Baseball: The Last Golden Age, 1947–1957* (New York: Macmillan, 1980), republished as *New York City Baseball: The Golden Age, 1947–1957* (Boulder, CO: Taylor Trade Publishing, 2013), surveyed the era when New York City truly ruled the baseball world. In *The Last Good Season: Brooklyn, the Dodgers and Their Final Pennant Race Together* (New York: Doubleday, 2003), Michael Shapiro looked at Brooklyn's last pennant-winning season in 1956. Robert E. Murphy, in *After Many a Summer: The Passing of the Giants and the Dodgers and a Golden Age in New York Baseball* (Somerville, MA: Union Square Press, 2009), looked at the transfer of New York City's two National League teams to California, while Neil Sullivan's *The Dodgers Move West* (New York: Oxford University Press, 1989) examined the Dodgers' move from Brooklyn to Los Angeles. Steven Travers, in *A Tale of Three Cities: The 1962 Baseball Season in New York, Los Angeles, and San Francisco* (Sterling, VA: Potomac Books, 2009), looked at the 1962 National League season, which not only saw the creation of the New York Mets but also featured a tight pennant race between the Dodgers and Giants. In their respective autobiographies, Mickey Mantle and Billy Martin offered their own explanation for the 1956 incident at the Copacabana. While the conventional thought is Yankees right fielder Hank Bauer was responsible for the broken jaw suffered by the nightclub patron who was heckling the players, both Martin and Mantle claimed in their books—*Number 1*, by Billy Martin and Peter Golenbock (New York: Delacorte Press, 1980), and *The Mick: An American Hero: The Legend and the Glory*, by Mickey Mantle and Herb Gluck (New York: Doubleday, 1985)—that the nightclub's bouncer had punched the man.

Kim McQuaid's *The Anxious Years: America in the Vietnam-Watergate Era* (New York: Basic Books, 1989) offered an excellent overview of the period from 1968 to 1974. George C. Herring's *America's Longest War: The United States and Vietnam, 1950–1975* (New York: Wiley, 1979) was a groundbreaking examination of the Vietnam War. Tom Wells looked at the antiwar movement and its impact on government policy in *The War Within: America's Battle over Vietnam* (Berkeley: University of California Press, 1994). Despite the fact that she limited her book to middle-class white women, Betty Friedan's *The Feminine Mystique* (New York: Norton, 1963) played a key role in sparking the women's movement of the sixties and seventies. Sara Evans's *Personal Politics: The Roots of Women's Liberation in the Civil Rights Movement and the New Left* (New York: Knopf, 1979) looked at how the women's liberation movement grew out of the civil rights movement. Both Terry Anderson, in *The Movement and the Sixties* (New York: Oxford University Press, 1995), and Todd Gitlin, in *The Sixties: Years of Hope, Days of Rage* (New York: Bantam, 1987), examined the protest movements of the sixties, while James Miller's *"Democracy in the Streets": From Port Huron to the Siege of Chicago* (New York: Simon & Schuster, 1987) looked at the creation of the left-wing group Students for a Democratic Society. Allan Kozinn, in *The Beatles* (London: Phaidon, 1995), republished as *The Beatles: From Cavern to Rooftop* (London: Phaidon, 2010), explored both the music of the Beatles and the group's impact on society.

The protest movements of the sixties and seventies exerted an impact on baseball. Players' union president Marvin Miller's memoir, *A Whole Different Ball Game: The Sport and Business of Baseball* (New York: Birch Lane Press, 1991), looked back at his attempt to overturn the reserve clause. Robert F. Burk's *Marvin Miller, Baseball Revolutionary* (Urbana: University of Illinois Press, 2015) offered a biography of Miller. There are at least three biographies of Oakland's maverick owner Charles O. Finley—Bill Libby's *Charlie O. & the Angry A's: The Low and Inside Story of Charlie O. Finley and Baseball's Most Colorful Team* (New York: Doubleday, 1975), Herb Michelson's *Charlie O: Charles Oscar Finley vs. the Baseball Establishment* (Indianapolis, IN: Bobbs-Merrill, 1975), and *Charlie Finley: The Outrageous Story of Baseball's Super Showman*, by G. Michael Green and Roger D. Launius (New York: Walker, 2010). Brad Snyder wrote an excellent biography of Curt Flood, *A Well-Paid Slave:*

Curt Flood's Fight for Free Agency in Professional Sports (New York: Penguin, 2006). Robert M. Goldman's *One Man Out: Curt Flood vs. Baseball* (Lawrence: University of Kansas Press, 2008) examined Flood's legal case. Flood, with the help of Richard Carter, offered his own version of his dispute with baseball in his autobiography *The Way It Is* (New York: Trident Press, 1971).

Rick Perlstein, in *The Invisible Bridge: The Fall of Nixon and the Rise of Reagan* (New York: Simon & Schuster, 2014), examined America's turn to conservatism following the turmoil of Vietnam and Watergate. Political economists Barry Bluestone and Bennett Harrison, in *The Great U-Turn: Corporate Restructuring and the Polarizing of America* (New York: Basic Books, 1990), looked at the economic changes that have taken place in the United States since the mid-1970s.

Baseball also underwent significant economic changes during the period of the Great U-Turn. Ronald W. Cox and Daniel Skidmore-Hess, in *Free Agency and Competitive Balance in Baseball* (Jefferson, NC: McFarland, 2005), and Daniel Gilbert, in *Expanding the Strike Zone: Baseball in the Age of Free Agency* (Amherst: University of Massachusetts Press, 2013), examined baseball during the era of free agency. New York Yankees owner George Steinbrenner, the first baseball executive to take advantage of free agency, has been the subject of at least three biographies—Dick Schaap's *Steinbrenner!* (New York: Putnam, 1982), Peter Golenbock's *The Poor Little Rich Boy Who Built the Yankee Empire* (Malden, MA: Wiley, 2009), and Bill Madden's *Steinbrenner: The Last Lion of Baseball* (New York: Harper, 2010). *Moneyball: The Art of Winning an Unfair Game*, by Michael Lewis (New York: Norton, 2003), looked at how Oakland Athletics general manager Billy Beane used nontraditional methods to assemble a winning team despite being located in baseball's smallest market. Former player Jose Canseco admitted his own steroid use—and pointed the finger at other major leaguers—in *Juiced: Wild Times, Rampant 'Roids, Smash Hits, and How Baseball Got Big* (New York: Regan Books, 2005).

Rebecca T. Alpert's *Out of Left Field: Jews and Black Baseball* (New York: Oxford University Press, 2011) examined Jewish involvement in both the management of the Negro leagues and the movement to end segregation in baseball. Peter Levine, in *From Ellis Island to Ebbets Field: Sport and the American Jewish Experience* (New York: Oxford University

Press, 1992), and Jeffrey S. Gurock, in *Judaism's Encounter with American Sports* (Bloomington: Indiana University Press, 2005), looked at the role sports played in assimilation of Jewish immigrants into American society. *Playing America's Game: Baseball, Latinos, and the Color Line*, by Adrian Burgos Jr. (Berkeley: University of California Press, 2007), explored the relationship between black, white, and Hispanic players in both the Negro leagues before integration and the major leagues after integration. John Virtue's *South of the Color Barrier: How Jorge Pasquel and the Mexican League Pushed Baseball toward Racial Integration* (Jefferson, NC: McFarland, 1996) looked at the man who tried to convert the Mexican League into a full-fledged major league in the 1940s, and how the league demonstrated to Americans that white and black athletes could play baseball together. David Maraniss offered a biography of Pirates outfielder and Puerto Rican national hero Roberto Clemente in *Clemente: The Passion of Baseball's Last Hero* (New York: Simon & Schuster, 2006).

Other scholars have looked at baseball as an international game. Frank P. Jozsa Jr., in *Baseball, Inc.: The National Pastime as Big Business* (Jefferson, NC: McFarland, 2006), examined baseball as a global enterprise. George Gmelch edited a collection of essays on baseball in other countries in *Baseball without Borders: The International Pastime* (Lincoln: University of Nebraska Press, 2006). All-time home run leader Sadaharu Oh published an autobiography, *Sadaharu Oh: A Zen Way of Baseball* (New York: Vintage, 1985). Other books that examine baseball as an international game include Sayuri Guthrie-Shimizu's *Transpacific Field of Dreams: How Baseball Linked the United States and Japan in Peace and War* (Chapel Hill: University of North Carolina Press, 2012), Robert Whiting's *You Gotta Have Wa: When Two Cultures Collide on the Baseball Diamond* (New York: Macmillan, 1989), Robert Elias's *The Empire Strikes Out: How Baseball Sold US Foreign Policy and Promoted the American Way Abroad* (New York: New Press, 2010), and Joseph A. Reaves's *Taking in a Game: A History of Baseball in Asia* (Lincoln: University of Nebraska Press, 2002).

Doris Kearns Goodwin's fan memoir, *Wait Till Next Near: A Memoir* (New York: Simon & Schuster, 1997), demonstrated how baseball acted as a source of unity when she was growing up a Brooklyn Dodgers partisan on New York's Long Island in the 1950s. In *The Boys of Summer* (New

York: Harper & Row, 1972), former sportswriter Roger Kahn attempted to reconnect with the players he covered as a cub reporter assigned to the Brooklyn Dodgers in 1952. Peter Golenbock's *Bums: An Oral History of the Brooklyn Dodgers* (New York: Putnam, 1984) contains the recollections of dozens of people—players, coaches, sportswriters, and fans—associated with the Brooklyn Dodgers.

Glenngue Waggoner introduced the world to fantasy baseball with *Rotisserie League Baseball* (New York: Bantam Books, 1984), while statistician Bill James pioneered sabermetrics with the publication of *The 1977 Baseball Abstract: Featuring 18 Categories of Statistical Information That You Just Can't Find Anywhere Else* (Printed by author, 1977). *The Bill James Baseball Abstract* (Printed by author, 1978–1981; New York: Ballantine Books, 1982–1988) reappeared each of the next eleven years. James has also applied his analysis to players of the past with *The Bill James Historical Baseball Abstract* (New York: Villard, 1985; rev. ed., 1988) and *The New Bill James Historical Baseball Abstract* (New York: Free Press, 2001; rev. ed., 2003).

In addition to books written by scholars and sportswriters, readers may also find the Web site Baseball Reference (http://www.baseball-reference.com) of interest. Not only does this site contain league, team, and player stats from 1871 to the present, but it also includes box scores from every major league game since the middle of the 1910s. The Society for American Baseball Research, a baseball research and historical society, publishes several periodicals on baseball history, including two yearly publications, *The Baseball Research Journal* and *The National Pastime*. More information can be found on the SABR Web site (http://www.sabr.org).

Appendix 1

Major League Pennant Winners

Major League Pennant Winners

(*Won League Championship Series; teams in **bold** won World Series)

Year	National Association	W	L	Pct.
1871	Philadelphia Athletics	22	7	.759
1872	Boston Red Stockings	39	8	.830
1873	Boston Red Stockings	43	16	.729
1874	Boston Red Stockings	52	18	.783
1875	Boston Red Stockings	71	8	.899

Year	Div.	National League	W	L	Pct.	**American Association**	W	L	Pct.
1876	—	Chicago White Stockings	52	14	.788				
1877	—	Boston Red Stockings	42	18	.700				
1878	—	Boston Red Stockings	41	19	.683				
1879	—	Providence Grays	59	25	.702				
1880	—	Chicago White Stockings	67	17	.798				
1881	—	Chicago White Stockings	56	28	.667				
1882	—	Chicago White Stockings	55	29	.655	Cincinnati Reds	55	25	.688
1883	—	Boston Beaneaters	63	35	.643	Philadelphia Athletics	66	32	.673
1884	—	**Providence Grays**	84	28	.750	New York Metropolitans	75	32	.701
1885	—	Chicago White Stockings	87	25	.777	St. Louis Browns	79	33	.705
1886	—	Chicago White Stockings	90	34	.726	**St. Louis Browns**	93	46	.669
1887	—	**Detroit Wolverines**	79	45	.637	St. Louis Browns	95	40	.704
1888	—	**New York Giants**	84	47	.641	St. Louis Browns	92	43	.681
1889	—	**New York Giants**	83	43	.659	Brooklyn Bridegrooms	93	44	.679
1890	—	Brooklyn Bridegrooms	86	43	.667	Louisville Colonels	88	44	.667
1891	—	Boston Beaneaters	87	51	.630	Boston Red Stockings	93	42	.689

Year		Team	W	L	Pct.
1892	1st ½	Boston Beaneaters*	52	22	.703
		Overall: 1st place	102	48	.680
	2nd ½	Cleveland Spiders	53	23	.697
		Overall: 2nd place	93	56	.624
1893	—	Boston Beaneaters	86	43	.667
1894	—	Baltimore Orioles	89	39	.695
	2d place	New York Giants*	88	44	.667
1895	—	Baltimore Orioles	87	43	.669
	2d place	Cleveland Spiders*	84	46	.646
1896	—	Baltimore Orioles*	90	39	.698
	2d place	Cleveland Spiders	80	48	.625
1897	—	Boston Beaneaters	93	39	.705
	2d place	Baltimore Orioles*	90	40	.692
1898	—	Boston Beaneaters	102	47	.685
1899	—	Brooklyn Superbas	101	47	.682
1900	—	Brooklyn Superbas*	82	54	.603
	2d place	Pittsburgh Pirates	79	60	.568
1901	—	Pittsburgh Pirates	90	49	.647
1902	—	Pittsburgh Pirates	103	36	.741
1903	—	Pittsburgh Pirates	91	49	.650
1904	—	New York Giants	106	47	.693
1905	—	New York Giants	105	48	.686
1906	—	Chicago Cubs	116	36	.763
1907	—	Chicago Cubs	107	45	.704
1908	—	Chicago Cubs	99	55	.643
1909	—	Pittsburgh Pirates	110	42	.724
1910	—	Chicago Cubs	104	50	.675
1911	—	New York Giants	99	54	.647
1912	—	New York Giants	103	48	.682

American League	W	L	Pct.
Chicago White Sox	83	53	.610
Philadelphia Athletics	83	53	.610
Boston Americans	91	47	.659
Boston Americans	95	59	.617
Philadelphia Athletics	92	57	.622
Chicago White Sox	93	58	.616
Detroit Tigers	92	58	.613
Detroit Tigers	70	63	.588
Detroit Tigers	98	54	.645
Philadelphia Athletics	102	46	.680
Philadelphia Athletics	101	50	.669
Boston Red Sox	105	47	.691

(continued)

Year	National Association	W	L	Pct.		W	L	Pct.
1913	New York Giants	101	51	.664	**Philadelphia Athletics**	96	57	.627
1914	**Boston Braves**	94	59	.614	Philadelphia Athletics	99	53	.651
1915	Philadelphia Phillies	90	62	.592	**Boston Red Sox**	101	50	.669
1916	Brooklyn Robins	94	60	.610	**Boston Red Sox**	91	63	.591
1917	New York Giants	98	56	.636	**Chicago White Sox**	100	54	.649
1918	Chicago Cubs	84	45	.651	**Boston Red Sox**	75	51	.595
1919	**Cincinnati Reds**	96	44	.686	Chicago White Sox	88	52	.629
1920	Brooklyn Robins	93	61	.604	**Cleveland Indians**	98	56	.636
1921	**New York Giants**	94	59	.614	New York Yankees	98	55	.640
1922	**New York Giants**	93	61	.604	New York Yankees	94	60	.610
1923	New York Giants	95	58	.621	**New York Yankees**	98	54	.645
1924	New York Giants	93	60	.608	**Washington Senators**	92	62	.597
1925	**Pittsburgh Pirates**	95	58	.621	Washington Senators	96	53	.636
1926	**St. Louis Cardinals**	89	65	.578	New York Yankees	91	63	.591
1927	Pittsburgh Pirates	94	60	.610	**New York Yankees**	110	44	.714
1928	St. Louis Cardinals	95	59	.617	**New York Yankees**	101	53	.656
1929	Chicago Cubs	98	54	.645	**Philadelphia Athletics**	104	46	.693
1930	St. Louis Cardinals	92	62	.597	**Philadelphia Athletics**	102	52	.662
1931	**St. Louis Cardinals**	101	53	.656	Philadelphia Athletics	107	45	.704
1932	Chicago Cubs	90	64	.584	**New York Yankees**	107	47	.695
1933	**New York Giants**	91	61	.599	Washington Senators	99	53	.651
1934	**St. Louis Cardinals**	95	58	.621	Detroit Tigers	101	53	.656
1935	Chicago Cubs	100	54	.649	**Detroit Tigers**	93	58	.616
1936	New York Giants	92	62	.597	**New York Yankees**	102	51	.667
1937	New York Giants	95	57	.625	**New York Yankees**	102	52	.662
1938	Chicago Cubs	89	63	.586	**New York Yankees**	99	53	.651
1939	Cincinnati Reds	97	57	.630	**New York Yankees**	106	45	.702
1940	Cincinnati Reds	100	53	.654	**Detroit Tigers**	90	64	.584

Year		NL Team	W	L	Pct	AL Team	W	L	Pct
1941	—	Brooklyn Dodgers	100	54	.649	New York Yankees	101	53	.656
1942	—	St. Louis Cardinals	106	48	.688	New York Yankees	103	51	.699
1943	—	St. Louis Cardinals	105	49	.682	New York Yankees	98	56	.636
1944	—	St. Louis Cardinals	105	49	.682	St. Louis Browns	89	65	.578
1945	—	Chicago Cubs	98	56	.636	Detroit Tigers	88	65	.575
1946	—	St. Louis Cardinals	98	58	.628	Boston Red Sox	104	50	.675
1947	—	Brooklyn Dodgers	96	40	.610	New York Yankees	97	57	.630
1948	—	Boston Braves	91	62	.595	Cleveland Indians	97	58	.626
1949	—	Brooklyn Dodgers	97	57	.630	New York Yankees	97	57	.630
1950	—	Philadelphia Phillies	91	63	.591	New York Yankees	98	56	.636
1951	—	New York Giants	98	59	.624	New York Yankees	98	56	.636
1952	—	Brooklyn Dodgers	96	57	.627	New York Yankees	95	59	.617
1953	—	Brooklyn Dodgers	105	49	.682	New York Yankees	99	52	.656
1954	—	New York Giants	97	57	.630	Cleveland Indians	111	43	.721
1955	—	Brooklyn Dodgers	98	55	.641	New York Yankees	96	58	.623
1956	—	Brooklyn Dodgers	93	61	.604	New York Yankees	97	57	.630
1957	—	Milwaukee Braves	95	59	.617	New York Yankees	98	56	.636
1958	—	Milwaukee Braves	92	62	.598	New York Yankees	92	67	.597
1959	—	Los Angeles Dodgers	88	68	.564	Chicago White Sox	94	60	.610
1960	—	Pittsburgh Pirates	95	59	.617	New York Yankees	97	59	.630
1961	—	Cincinnati Reds	93	61	.604	New York Yankees	109	53	.673
1962	—	San Francisco Giants	103	62	.624	New York Yankees	96	66	.593
1963	—	Los Angeles Dodgers	99	63	.611	New York Yankees	104	57	.646
1964	—	St. Louis Cardinals	93	69	.574	New York Yankees	99	63	.611
1965	—	Los Angeles Dodgers	97	65	.599	Minnesota Twins	102	60	.630
1966	—	Los Angeles Dodgers	95	67	.586	Baltimore Orioles	97	63	.606
1967	—	St. Louis Cardinals	101	60	.627	Boston Red Sox	92	70	.568
1968	—	St. Louis Cardinals	97	65	.599	Detroit Tigers	103	59	.636
1969	East	New York Mets*	100	62	.617	Baltimore Orioles*	109	53	.673
1969	West	Atlanta Braves	93	69	.574	Minnesota Twins	97	65	.599

(continued)

Year		National Association	W	L	Pct.		W	L	Pct.
1970	East	Pittsburgh Pirates	89	72	.549	Baltimore Orioles*	108	54	.667
	West	Cincinnati Reds*	102	60	.630	Minnesota Twins	98	64	.605
1971	East	Pittsburgh Pirates*	97	65	.599	Baltimore Orioles*	101	57	.639
	West	San Francisco Giants	90	72	.556	Oakland A's	101	60	.627
1972	East	Pittsburgh Pirates	96	59	.619	Detroit Tigers	86	70	.551
	West	Cincinnati Reds*	95	59	.617	Oakland A's*	93	62	.600
1973	East	New York Mets*	82	79	.509	Baltimore Orioles	97	65	.599
	West	Cincinnati Reds	99	63	.611	Oakland A's*	94	68	.580
1974	East	Pittsburgh Pirates	88	74	.543	Baltimore Orioles	91	71	.562
	West	Los Angeles Dodgers*	102	60	.630	Oakland A's*	90	72	.556
1975	East	Pittsburgh Pirates	92	69	.571	Boston Red Sox*	95	65	.594
	West	Cincinnati Reds*	108	54	.667	Oakland A's	98	64	.605
1976	East	Philadelphia Phillies	101	61	.623	New York Yankees*	97	62	.610
	West	Cincinnati Reds*	102	60	.630	Kansas City Royals	90	72	.556
1977	East	Philadelphia Phillies	101	61	.623	New York Yankees*	100	62	.617
	West	Los Angeles Dodgers*	98	64	.605	Kansas City Royals	102	60	.630
1978	East	Philadelphia Phillies	90	72	.556	New York Yankees*	100	63	.613
	West	Los Angeles Dodgers*	95	67	.596	Kansas City Royals	92	70	.568
1979	East	Pittsburgh Pirates*	98	64	.605	Baltimore Orioles*	102	57	.642
	West	Cincinnati Reds	90	71	.559	California Angels	88	74	.543
1980	East	Philadelphia Phillies*	91	71	.562	New York Yankees	103	59	.636
	West	Houston Astros	93	70	.571	Kansas City Royals*	97	65	.599

Year	Division	National League	W	L	Pct	American League	W	L	Pct
1981		St. Louis Cardinals	59	43	.578	Milwaukee Brewers	62	47	.569
	East 1st ½	Philadelphia Phillies	34	21	.618	New York Yankees*	34	22	.607
		Overall: 3rd place	59	48	.551	Overall: 4th place	59	48	.551
	2nd ½	Montreal Expos	30	23	.566	Milwaukee Brewers	31	22	.585
		Overall: 2nd place	60	48	.551	Overall: 1st place	62	47	.569
		Cincinnati Reds	66	42	.611	Oakland A's	64	45	.587
	West 1st ½	Lost Angeles Dodgers*	36	21	.632	Oakland A's	37	23	.617
		Overall: 2nd place	63	47	.573	Overall: 1st place	64	45	.587
	2nd ½	Houston Astros	33	20	.623	Kansas City	30	23	.566
		Overall: 3rd place	61	49	.555	Overall: 4th place	50	53	.485
1982	East	St. Louis Cardinals*	95	67	.586	Milwaukee Brewers*	95	67	.586
	West	Atlanta Braves	89	73	.549	California Angels	93	69	.574
1983	East	Philadelphia Phillies*	90	72	.556	Baltimore Orioles*	98	64	.605
	West	Los Angeles Dodgers	91	71	.562	Chicago White Sox	99	63	.611
1984	East	Chicago Cubs	96	65	.596	Detroit Tigers*	104	58	.642
	West	San Diego Padres*	92	70	.568	Kansas City Royals	84	78	.519
1985	East	St. Louis Cardinals*	101	61	.623	Toronto Blue Jays	99	62	.615
	East West	Los Angeles Dodgers	95	67	.586	Kansas City Royals*	91	71	.562
1986	East	New York Mets*	108	54	.667	Boston Red Sox*	95	66	.590
	West	Houston Astros	96	66	.593	California Angels	92	70	.568
1987	East	St. Louis Cardinals	95	67	.586	Detroit Tigers	98	64	.605
	West	San Francisco Giants	90	72	.556	Minnesota Twins*	85	77	.525
1988	East	New York Mets	100	67	.625	Boston Red Sox	89	73	.549
	West	Los Angeles Dodgers*	94	72	.584	Oakland Athletics*	104	58	.642
1989	East	Chicago Cubs	93	69	.571	Toronto Blue Jays	89	73	.549
	West	San Francisco Giants*	92	70	.568	Oakland Athletics*	99	63	.611
1990	East	Pittsburgh Pirates	95	67	.586	Boston Red Sox	88	74	.543
	West	Cincinnati Reds*	91	71	.562	Oakland Athletics*	103	59	.636
1991	East	Pittsburgh Pirates	98	64	.605	Toronto Blue Jays	91	71	.562
	West	Atlanta Braves*	94	68	.580	Minnesota Twins*	95	67	.596

(continued)

Year		National Association	W	L	Pct.		W	L	Pct.
1992	East	Pittsburgh Pirates	96	66	.593	Toronto Blue Jays*	96	66	.593
	West	Atlanta Braves*	98	64	.605	Oakland Athletics	96	66	.593
1993	East	Philadelphia Phillies*	97	65	.599	Toronto Blue Jays*	95	67	.586
	West	Atlanta Braves	104	58	.642	Chicago White Sox	94	68	.580
1994	East	Montreal Expos	74	40	.649	New York Yankees	70	43	.619
	Central	Cincinnati Reds	66	48	.579	Chicago White Sox	67	46	.593
	West	Los Angeles Dodgers	58	56	.509	Texas Rangers	52	62	.456
1995	East	Atlanta Braves*	90	54	.625	Boston Red Sox	86	58	.597
	Central	Cincinnati Reds	85	59	.590	Cleveland Indians*	100	44	.694
	West	Los Angeles Dodgers	78	66	.542	Seattle Mariners	79	66	.545
	West Wildcard	Colorado Rockies	77	67	.585	New York Yankees	79	65	.549
1996	East	Atlanta Braves*	96	66	.593	New York Yankees*	92	70	.568
	Central	St. Louis Cardinals	88	74	.543	Cleveland Indians	99	62	.615
	West	San Diego Padres	91	71	.562	Texas Rangers	90	72	.556
	West Wildcard	Los Angeles Dodgers	90	72	.556	Baltimore Orioles	88	74	.543
1997	East	Atlanta Braves	101	61	.623	Baltimore Orioles	98	64	.605
	Central	Houston Astros	97	65	.599	Cleveland Indians*	86	75	.534
	West	San Francisco Giants	90	72	.556	Seattle Mariners	90	72	.556
	West Wildcard	Florida Marlins*	92	70	.568	New York Yankees	96	66	.593
1998	East	Atlanta Braves	106	56	.654	New York Yankees*	114	48	.704
	Central	Houston Astros	102	60	.630	Cleveland Indians	89	73	.549
	West	San Diego Padres*	98	64	.605	Texas Rangers	88	74	.543
	West Wildcard	Chicago Cubs	90	73	.552	Boston Red Sox	92	70	.586
1999	East	Atlanta Braves*	103	59	.636	New York Yankees*	98	64	.605
	Central	Houston Astros	97	65	.599	Cleveland Indians	97	65	.599
	West	Arizona Diamondbacks	100	62	.617	Texas Rangers	95	67	.586
	West Wildcard	New York Mets	97	66	.595	Boston Red Sox	94	68	.580

Year		Team	W	L	Pct	Team	W	L	Pct
2000	East	Atlanta Braves	95	67	.586	**New York Yankees***	87	74	.540
	Central	St. Louis Cardinals	95	67	.586	Chicago White Sox	95	67	.586
	West	San Francisco Giants	97	65	.599	Oakland Athletics	91	70	.565
	Wildcard	New York Mets*	94	68	.580	Seattle Mariners	91	71	.562
2001	East	Atlanta Braves	88	74	.543	New York Yankees*	95	65	.594
	Central	Houston Astros	93	69	.574	Cleveland Indians	91	71	.562
	West	**Arizona Diamondbacks***	92	70	.568	Seattle Mariners	116	46	.716
	Wildcard	St. Louis Cardinals	93	69	.574	Oakland Athletics	102	60	.630
2002	East	Atlanta Braves	101	59	.631	New York Yankees	103	58	.640
	Central	St. Louis Cardinals	97	65	.599	Minnesota Twins	94	67	.584
	West	Arizona Diamondbacks	98	64	.605	Oakland Athletics	103	59	.636
	Wildcard	San Francisco Giants*	95	66	.590	**Anaheim Angels***	99	63	.611
2003	East	Philadelphia Phillies	101	61	.623	New York Yankees*	101	61	.623
	Central	Chicago Cubs	88	74	.543	Minnesota Twins	90	72	.556
	West	San Francisco Giants	100	61	.621	Oakland Athletics	96	66	.593
	Wildcard	**Florida Marlins***	91	71	.562	Boston Red Sox	95	67	.586
2004	East	Atlanta Braves	96	66	.593	New York Yankees	101	61	.623
	Central	St. Louis Cardinals*	105	57	.648	Minnesota Twins	92	70	.568
	West	Los Angeles Dodgers	93	69	.574	Anaheim Angels	92	70	.568
	Wildcard	Houston Astros	92	70	.568	**Boston Red Sox***	98	64	.605
2005	East	Atlanta Braves	90	72	.556	New York Yankees	95	67	.586
	Central	St. Louis Cardinals	100	62	.617	**Chicago White Sox***	99	63	.611
	West	San Diego Padres	82	80	.506	LA Angels of Anaheim	95	67	.586
	Wildcard	Houston Astros*	89	73	.549	Boston Red Sox	95	68	.586
2006	East	New York Mets	97	65	.599	New York Yankees	97	65	.599
	Central	**St. Louis Cardinals***	83	78	.516	Minnesota Twins	96	66	.593
	West	San Diego Padres	88	74	.543	Oakland Athletics	93	69	.574
	Wildcard	Los Angeles Dodgers	88	74	.543	**Detroit Tigers***	95	67	.586

(continued)

Year		National Association	W	L	Pct.		W	L	Pct.
2007	East	Philadelphia Phillies	89	73	.549	Boston Red Sox*	96	66	.593
	Central	Chicago Cubs	85	77	.525	Cleveland Indians	96	66	.593
	West	Arizona Diamondbacks	90	72	.556	LA Angels of Anaheim	94	68	.580
	Wildcard	Colorado Rockies*	90	73	.552	New York Yankees	94	68	.580
2008	East	Philadelphia Phillies*	92	70	.568	Tampa Bay Rays*	97	65	.599
	Central	Chicago Cubs	97	64	.602	Chicago White Sox	89	74	.546
	West	Los Angeles Dodgers	84	79	.519	LA Angels of Anaheim	100	62	.617
	Wildcard	Milwaukee Brewers	90	72	.602	Boston Red Sox	95	67	.586
2009	East	Philadelphia Phillies*	93	69	.574	New York Yankees*	103	59	.636
	Central	St. Louis Cardinals	91	71	.562	Minnesota Twins	87	76	.534
	West	Los Angeles Dodgers	95	67	.586	LA Angels of Anaheim	97	65	.599
	Wildcard	Colorado Rockies	92	70	.568	Boston Red Sox	95	67	.586
2010	East	Philadelphia Phillies	97	65	.599	Tampa Bay Rays	96	66	.593
	Central	Cincinnati Reds	91	71	.562	Minnesota Twins	94	68	.580
	West	San Francisco Giants*	92	70	.568	Texas Rangers*	90	72	.556
	Wildcard	Atlanta Braves	91	71	.562	New York Yankees	95	67	.586
2011	East	Philadelphia Phillies	102	60	.630	New York Yankees	97	65	.599
	Central	Milwaukee Brewers	96	66	.593	Detroit Tigers	95	67	.586
	West	Arizona Diamondbacks	94	68	.580	Texas Rangers*	96	66	.593
	Wildcard	St. Louis Cardinals*	90	72	.556	Tampa Bay Rays	91	71	.562
2012	East	Washington Nationals	98	64	.605	New York Yankees	95	67	.586
	Central	Cincinnati Reds	97	65	.599	Detroit Tigers*	88	74	.543
	West	San Francisco Giants*	94	68	.580	Oakland Athletics	94	68	.580
	Wildcard	Atlanta Braves	94	68	.580	Texas Rangers	93	69	.574
	Wildcard	St. Louis Cardinals	88	74	.543	Baltimore Orioles	93	69	.574

Year	Division	NL Team	W	L	Pct	AL Team	W	L	Pct
2013	East	Atlanta Braves	96	66	.593	Boston Red Sox*	97	65	.599
	Central	St. Louis Cardinals*	97	65	.599	Detroit Tigers	93	69	.574
	West Wildcard	Los Angeles Dodgers	92	70	.568	Oakland Athletics	96	66	.593
	Wildcard	Pittsburgh Pirates	94	68	.580	Cleveland Indians	92	70	.568
		Cincinnati Reds	90	72	.556	Tampa Bay Rays	92	71	.564
2014	East	Washington Nationals	96	66	.593	Baltimore Orioles	96	66	.593
	Central	St. Louis Cardinals	90	72	.556	Detroit Tigers	90	72	.556
	West Wildcard	Los Angeles Dodgers	94	68	.580	LA Angels of Anaheim	98	64	.605
	Wildcard	Pittsburgh Pirates	88	74	.543	Kansas City Royals*	89	73	.549
		San Francisco Giants*	88	74	.543	Oakland Athletics	88	74	.543
2015	East	New York Mets*	90	72	.556	Toronto Blue Jays	93	69	.574
	Central	St. Louis Cardinals	100	62	.617	Kansas City Royals*	95	67	.586
	West Wildcard	Los Angeles Dodgers	92	70	.568	Texas Rangers	88	74	.543
	Wildcard	Pittsburgh Pirates	98	64	.605	New York Yankees	87	75	.537
		Chicago Cubs	97	65	.599	Houston Astros	86	76	.531
2016	East	Washington Nationals	95	67	.586	Boston Red Sox	93	69	.574
	Central	Chicago Cubs*	103	58	.640	Cleveland Indians*	94	67	.584
	West Wildcard	Los Angeles Dodgers	91	71	.562	Texas Rangers	95	67	.586
	Wildcard	New York Mets	87	75	.537	Baltimore Orioles	89	73	.549
		San Francisco Giants	87	75	.537	Toronto Blue Jays	89	73	.549

Pennant Winners of Other Major Leagues

Year	Union Association	W	L	Pct.
1884	St. Louis Maroons	94	19	.832
Year	Players' League	W	L	Pct.
1890	Boston Red Stockings	81	48	.628
Year	Federal League	W	L	Pct.
1914	Indianapolis Hoosiers	88	65	.575
1915	Chicago Whales	86	66	.566

Appendix 2

The World Series

Nineteenth-Century World Championship Series, 1882–1890
National League Champion vs. American Association Champion

Year	NL Champion	AA Champion	Winner	W–L(–T)
1882	Chicago White Stockings	Cincinnati Reds	Tie	1–1
1883	No series			
1884	Providence Grays	New York Metropolitans	Grays	3–0
1885	Chicago White Stockings	St. Louis Browns	Tie	3–3–1
1886	Chicago White Stockings	St. Louis Browns	Browns	4–2
1887	Detroit Wolverines	St. Louis Browns	Wolverines	10–5
1888	New York Giants	St. Louis Browns	Giants	6–5
1889	New York Giants	Brooklyn Bridegrooms	Giants	6–3
1890	Brooklyn Bridegrooms	Louisville Colonels	Tie	3–3–1

Note: In 1882 the league champion teams played two unsanctioned exhibition games.

Modern World Series, Since 1903
National League Champion vs. American League Champion

Year	NL Champion	AL Champion	Winner	W–L(–T)
1903	Pittsburgh Pirates	Boston Americans	Americans	5–3
1904	No World Series			
1905	New York Giants	Philadelphia Athletics	Giants	4–1
1906	Chicago Cubs	Chicago White Sox	White Sox	4–2
1907	Chicago Cubs	Detroit Tigers	Cubs	4–0–1
1908	Chicago Cubs	Detroit Tigers	Cubs	4–1
1909	Pittsburgh Pirates	Detroit Tigers	Pirates	4–3
1910	Chicago Cubs	Philadelphia Athletics	Athletics	4–1
1911	New York Giants	Philadelphia Athletics	Athletics	4–2
1912	New York Giants	Boston Red Sox	Red Sox	4–3–1
1913	New York Giants	Philadelphia Athletics	Athletics	4–1
1914	Boston Braves	Philadelphia Athletics	Braves	4–0
1915	Philadelphia Phillies	Boston Red Sox	Red Sox	4–1

(continued)

Year	NL Champion	AL Champion	Winner	W–L(–T)
1916	Brooklyn Robins	Boston Red Sox	Red Sox	4–1
1917	New York Giants	Chicago White Sox	White Sox	4–2
1918	Chicago Cubs	Boston Red Sox	Red Sox	4–2
1919	Cincinnati Reds	Chicago White Sox	Reds	5–3
1920	Brooklyn Robins	Cleveland Indians	Indians	5–2
1921	New York Giants	New York Yankees	Giants	5–3
1922	New York Giants	New York Yankees	Giants	4–0–1
1923	New York Giants	New York Yankees	Yankees	4–2
1924	New York Giants	Washington Senators	Senators	4–3
1925	Pittsburgh Pirates	Washington Senators	Pirates	4–3
1926	St. Louis Cardinals	New York Yankees	Cardinals	4–3
1927	Pittsburgh Pirates	New York Yankees	Yankees	4–0
1928	St. Louis Cardinals	New York Yankees	Yankees	4–0
1929	Chicago Cubs	Philadelphia Athletics	Athletics	4–1
1930	St. Louis Cardinals	Philadelphia Athletics	Athletics	4–2
1931	St. Louis Cardinals	Philadelphia Athletics	Cardinals	4–3
1932	Chicago Cubs	New York Yankees	Yankees	4–0
1933	New York Giants	Washington Senators	Giants	4–1
1934	St. Louis Cardinals	Detroit Tigers	Cardinals	4–3
1935	Chicago Cubs	Detroit Tigers	Tigers	4–2
1936	New York Giants	New York Yankees	Yankees	4–2
1937	New York Giants	New York Yankees	Yankees	4–1
1938	Chicago Cubs	New York Yankees	Yankees	4–0
1939	Cincinnati Reds	New York Yankees	Yankees	4–0
1940	Cincinnati Reds	Detroit Tigers	Reds	4–3
1941	Brooklyn Dodgers	New York Yankees	Yankees	4–1
1942	St. Louis Cardinals	New York Yankees	Cardinals	4–1
1943	St. Louis Cardinals	New York Yankees	Yankees	4–1
1944	St. Louis Cardinals	St. Louis Browns	Cardinals	4–2
1945	Chicago Cubs	Detroit Tigers	Tigers	4–3
1946	St. Louis Cardinals	Boston Red Sox	Cardinals	4–3
1947	Brooklyn Dodgers	New York Yankees	Yankees	4–3
1948	Boston Braves	Cleveland Indians	Indians	4–2
1949	Brooklyn Dodgers	New York Yankees	Yankees	4–1
1950	Philadelphia Phillies	New York Yankees	Yankees	4–0
1951	New York Giants	New York Yankees	Yankees	4–2
1952	Brooklyn Dodgers	New York Yankees	Yankees	4–3
1953	Brooklyn Dodgers	New York Yankees	Yankees	4–2
1954	New York Giants	Cleveland Indians	Giants	4–0
1955	Brooklyn Dodgers	New York Yankees	Dodgers	4–3
1956	Brooklyn Dodgers	New York Yankees	Yankees	4–3
1957	Milwaukee Braves	New York Yankees	Braves	4–3
1958	Milwaukee Braves	New York Yankees	Yankees	4–3
1959	Los Angeles Dodgers	Chicago White Sox	Dodgers	4–2
1960	Pittsburgh Pirates	New York Yankees	Pirates	4–3
1961	Cincinnati Reds	New York Yankees	Yankees	4–1

Year	NL Champion	AL Champion	Winner	W–L(–T)
1962	San Francisco Giants	New York Yankees	Giants	4–3
1963	Los Angeles Dodgers	New York Yankees	Dodgers	4–0
1964	St. Louis Cardinals	New York Yankees	Cardinals	4–3
1965	Los Angeles Dodgers	Minnesota Twins	Dodgers	4–3
1966	Los Angeles Dodgers	Baltimore Orioles	Orioles	4–0
1967	St. Louis Cardinals	Boston Red Sox	Cardinals	4–3
1968	St. Louis Cardinals	Detroit Tigers	Tigers	4–3
1969	New York Mets	Baltimore Orioles	Mets	4–1
1970	Cincinnati Reds	Baltimore Orioles	Orioles	4–1
1971	Pittsburgh Pirates	Baltimore Orioles	Pirates	4–3
1972	Cincinnati Reds	Oakland A's	A's	4–3
1973	New York Mets	Oakland A's	A's	4–3
1974	Los Angeles Dodgers	Oakland A's	A's	4–1
1975	Cincinnati Reds	Boston Red Sox	Reds	4–3
1976	Cincinnati Reds	New York Yankees	Reds	4–0
1977	Los Angeles Dodgers	New York Yankees	Yankees	4–2
1978	Los Angeles Dodgers	New York Yankees	Yankees	4–2
1979	Pittsburgh Pirates	Baltimore Orioles	Pirates	4–3
1980	Philadelphia Phillies	Kansas City Royals	Phillies	4–2
1981	Los Angeles Dodgers	New York Yankees	Dodgers	4–2
1982	St. Louis Cardinals	Milwaukee Brewers	Cardinals	4–3
1983	Philadelphia Phillies	Baltimore Orioles	Orioles	4–1
1984	San Diego Padres	Detroit Tigers	Tigers	4–1
1985	St. Louis Cardinals	Kansas City Royals	Royals	4–3
1986	New York Mets	Boston Red Sox	Mets	4–3
1987	St. Louis Cardinals	Minnesota Twins	Twins	4–3
1988	Los Angeles Dodgers	Oakland Athletics	Dodgers	4–1
1989	San Francisco Giants	Oakland Athletics	Athletics	4–0
1990	Cincinnati Reds	Oakland Athletics	Reds	4–0
1991	Atlanta Braves	Minnesota Twins	Twins	4–3
1992	Atlanta Braves	Toronto Blue Jays	Blue Jays	4–2
1993	Philadelphia Phillies	Toronto Blue Jays	Blue Jays	4–2
1994	*No World Series*			
1995	Atlanta Braves	Cleveland Indians	Braves	4–2
1996	Atlanta Braves	New York Yankees	Yankees	4–2
1997	Florida Marlins	Cleveland Indians	Marlins	4–3
1998	San Diego Padres	New York Yankees	Yankees	4–0
1999	Atlanta Braves	New York Yankees	Yankees	4–0
2000	New York Mets	New York Yankees	Yankees	4–1
2001	Arizona Diamondbacks	New York Yankees	Diamond-backs	4–3
2002	San Francisco Giants	Anahiem Angels	Angels	4–3
2003	Florida Marlins	New York Yankees	Marlins	4–2
2004	St. Louis Cardinals	Boston Red Sox	Red Sox	4–0
2005	Houston Astros	Chicago White Sox	White Sox	4–0
2006	St. Louis Cardinals	Detroit Tigers	Cardinals	4–1

(continued)

Year	NL Champion	AL Champion	Winner	W–L(–T)
2007	Colorado Rockies	Boston Red Sox	Red Sox	4–0
2008	Philadelphia Phillies	Tampa Bay Rays	Phillies	4–1
2009	Philadelphia Phillies	New York Yankees	Yankees	4–2
2010	San Francisco Giants	Texas Rangers	Giants	4–1
2011	St. Louis Cardinals	Texas Rangers	Cardinals	4–3
2012	San Francisco Giants	Detroit Tigers	Giants	4–0
2013	St. Louis Cardinals	Boston Red Sox	Red Sox	4–2
2014	San Francisco Giants	Kansas City Royals	Giants	4–3
2015	New York Mets	Kansas City Royals	Royals	4–1
2016	Chicago Cubs	Cleveland Indians	Cubs	4–3

Appendix 3

League Championship Series

American League Championship Series, Since 1969
(† = Qualified for playoffs as wildcard team)

Year	Winner	Division	Loser	Division	Result
1969	Baltimore Orioles	East	Minnesota Twins	West	3–0
1970	Baltimore Orioles	East	Minnesota Twins	West	3–0
1971	Baltimore Orioles	East	Oakland A's	West	3–0
1972	Oakland A's	West	Detroit Tigers	East	3–2
1973	Oakland A's	West	Baltimore Orioles	East	3–2
1974	Oakland A's	West	Baltimore Orioles	East	3–1
1975	Boston Red Sox	East	Oakland A's	West	3–0
1976	New York Yankees	East	Kansas City Royals	West	3–2
1977	New York Yankees	East	Kansas City Royals	West	3–2
1978	New York Yankees	East	Kansas City Royals	West	3–1
1979	Baltimore Orioles	East	California Angels	West	3–1
1980	Kansas City Royals	West	New York Yankees	East	3–0
1981	New York Yankees	East	Oakland A's	West	3–0
1982	Milwaukee Brewers	East	California Angels	West	3–2
1983	Baltimore Orioles	East	Chicago White Sox	West	3–1
1984	Detroit Tigers	East	Kansas City Royals	West	3–0
1985	Kansas City Royals	West	Toronto Blue Jays	East	4–3
1986	Boston Red Sox	East	California Angels	West	4–3
1987	Minnesota Twins	West	Detroit Tigers	East	4–1
1988	Oakland Athletics	West	Boston Red Sox	East	4–0
1989	Oakland Athletics	West	Toronto Blue Jays	East	4–1
1990	Oakland Athletics	West	Boston Red Sox	East	4–0
1991	Minnesota Twins	West	Toronto Blue Jays	East	4–1
1992	Toronto Blue Jays	East	Oakland Athletics	West	4–2
1993	Toronto Blue Jays	East	Chicago White Sox	West	4–2
1994	*No ALCS*				
1995	Cleveland Indians	Central	Seattle Mariners	West	4–2
1996	New York Yankees	East	Baltimore Orioles	East†	4–1
1997	Cleveland Indians	Central	Baltimore Orioles	East	4–2
1998	New York Yankees	East	Cleveland Indians	Central	4–2

(continued)

Year	Winner	Division	Loser	Division	Result
1999	New York Yankees	East	Boston Red Sox	East†	4–1
2000	New York Yankees	East	Seattle Mariners	West†	4–2
2001	New York Yankees	East	Seattle Mariners	West	4–1
2002	Anaheim Angels	West†	Minnesota Twins	Central	4–1
2003	New York Yankees	East	Boston Red Sox	East†	4–3
2004	Boston Red Sox	East†	New York Yankees	East	4–3
2005	Chicago White Sox	Central	LA Angels of Anaheim	West	4–1
2006	Detroit Tigers	Central†	Oakland Athletics	West	4–0
2007	Boston Red Sox	East	Cleveland Indians	Central	4–3
2008	Tampa Bay Rays	East	Boston Red Sox	East†	4–3
2009	New York Yankees	East	LA Angels of Anaheim	West	4–2
2010	Texas Rangers	West	New York Yankees	East†	4–2
2011	Texas Rangers	West	Detroit Tigers	Central	4–2
2012	Detroit Tigers	Central	New York Yankees	East	4–0
2013	Boston Red Sox	East	Detroit Tigers	Central	4–2
2014	Kansas City Royals	Central†	Baltimore Orioles	East	4–0
2015	Kansas City Royals	Central	Toronto Blue Jays	East	4–2
2016	Cleveland Indians	Central	Toronto Blue Jays	East†	4–1

National League Championship Series, Since 1969
(† = Qualified for playoffs as wildcard team)

Year	Winner	Division	Loser	Division	Result
1969	New York Mets	East	Atlanta Braves	West	3–0
1970	Cincinnati Reds	West	Pittsburgh Pirates	East	3–0
1971	Pittsburgh Pirates	East	San Francisco Giants	West	3–1
1972	Cincinnati Reds	West	Pittsburgh Pirates	East	3–2
1973	New York Mets	East	Cincinnati Reds	West	3–2
1974	Los Angeles Dodgers	West	Pittsburgh Pirates	East	3–1
1975	Cincinnati Reds	West	Pittsburgh Pirates	East	3–0
1976	Cincinnati Reds	West	Philadelphia Phillies	East	3–0
1977	Los Angeles Dodgers	West	Philadelphia Phillies	East	3–1
1978	Los Angeles Dodgers	West	Philadelphia Phillies	East	3–1
1979	Pittsburgh Pirates	East	Cincinnati Reds	West	3–0
1980	Philadelphia Phillies	East	Houston Astros	West	3–2
1981	Los Angeles Dodgers	West	Montreal Expos	East	3–2
1982	St. Louis Cardinals	East	Atlanta Braves	West	3–0
1983	Philadelphia Phillies	East	Los Angeles Dodgers	West	3–1
1984	San Diego Padres	West	Chicago Cubs	East	3–2

Year	Winner	Division	Loser	Division	Result
1985	St. Louis Cardinals	East	Los Angeles Dodgers	West	4–2
1986	New York Mets	East	Houston Astros	West	4–2
1987	St. Louis Cardinals	East	San Francisco Giants	West	4–3
1988	Los Angeles Dodgers	West	New York Mets	East	4–3
1989	San Francsico Giants	West	Chicago Cubs	East	4–1
1990	Cincinnati Reds	West	Pittsburgh Pirates	East	4–2
1991	Atlanta Braves	West	Pittsburgh Pirates	East	4–3
1992	Atlanta Braves	West	Pittsburgh Pirates	East	4–3
1993	Philadelphia Phillies	East	Atlanta Braves	West	4–2
1994	*No ACLS*				
1995	Atlanta Braves	East	Cincinnati Reds	Central	4–0
1996	Atlanta Braves	East	St. Louis Cardinals	Central	4–3
1997	Florida Marlins	East[+]	Atlanta Braves	East	4–2
1998	San Diego Padres	West	Atlanta Braves	East	4–2
1999	Atlanta Braves	East	New York Mets	East[+]	4–2
2000	New York Mets	East[+]	St. Louis Cardinals	Central	4–1
2001	Arizona Diamondbacks	West	Atlanta Braves	East	4–1
2002	San Francisco Giants	West[+]	St. Louis Cardinals	Central	4–1
2003	Florida Marlins	East[+]	Chicago Cubs	Central	4–3
2004	St. Louis Cardinals	Central	Houston Astros	Central[+]	4–3
2005	Houston Astros	Central[+]	St. Louis Cardinals	Central	4–2
2006	St. Louis Cardinals	Central	New York Mets	East	4–3
2007	Colorado Rockies	West[+]	Arizona Diamondbacks	West	4–0
2008	Philadelphia Phillies	East	Los Angeles Dodgers	West	4–1
2009	Philadelphia Phillies	East	Los Angeles Dodgers	West	4–1
2010	San Francisco Giants	West	Philadelphia Phillies	East	4–2
2011	St. Louis Cardinals	Central[+]	Milwaukee Brewers	Central	4–2
2012	San Francisco Giants	West	St. Louis Cardinals	Central[+]	4–3
2013	St. Louis Cardinals	Central	Los Angeles Dodgers	West	4–2
2014	San Francisco Giants	West[+]	St. Louis Cardinals	Central	4–1
2015	New York Mets	East	Chicago Cubs	Central[+]	4–0
2016	Chicago Cubs	East	Los Angeles Dodgers	West	4–0

National League Split-Season Series, 1892
Winner of First Half vs. Winner of Second Half

Year	Winner	Half	Loser	Half	Result
1892	Boston Beaneaters	1st	Cleveland Spiders	2nd	3–0

Temple Cup Series, 1894–1897, and
Chronicle-Telegraph Cup Series, 1900
First-Place National League Team vs. Second-Place
National League Team

Year	Winner	Position	Loser	Position	Result
1894	New York Giants	1st place	Baltimore Orioles	2nd place	4–0
1895	Cleveland Spiders	2nd place	Baltimore Orioles	1st place	4–1
1896	Baltimore Orioles	1st place	Cleveland Spiders	2nd place	4–0
1897	Baltimore Orioles	2nd place	Boston Beaneaters	1st place	4–1
1900	Brooklyn Superbas	1st place	Pittsburgh Pirates	2nd place	3–1

Appendix 4

Division Series

American League Division Series, 1981 and Since 1995
(† = Qualified for playoffs as wildcard team)

Year	Winner	Division	Loser	Division	Result
1981	New York Yankees	East (1st ½)	Milwaukee Brewers	East (2nd ½)	3–2
					3–0
	Oakland A's	West (1st ½)	Kansas City Royals	West (2nd ½)	
1995	Cleveland Indians	Central	Boston Red Sox	East	3–0
	Seattle Mariners	West	New York Yankees	East†	3–2
1996	New York Yankees	East	Texas Rangers	West	3–1
	Baltimore Orioles	East†	Cleveland Indians	Central	3–1
1997	Baltimore Orioles	East	Seattle Mariners	West	3–1
	Cleveland Indians	Central	New York Yankees	East†	3–2
1998	New York Yankees	East	Texas Rangers	West	3–0
	Cleveland Indians	Central	Boston Red Sox	East†	3–1
1999	New York Yankees	East	Texas Rangers	West	3–0
	Boston Red Sox	East†	Cleveland Indians	Central	3–2
2000	Seattle Mariners	West†	Chicago White Sox	Central	3–0
	New York Yankees	East	Oakland Athletics	West	3–2
2001	New York Yankees	East	Oakland Athletics	West†	3–2
	Seattle Mariners	West	Cleveland Indians	Central	3–2
2002	Minnesota Twins	Central	Oakland Athletics	West	3–2
	Anaheim Angels	West†	New York Yankees	East	3–1
2003	New York Yankees	East	Minnesota Twins	Central	3–1
	Boston Red Sox	East†	Oakland Athletics	West	3–2
2004	New York Yankees	East	Minnesota Twins	Central	3–1
	Boston Red Sox	East†	Oakland Athletics	West	3–0
2005	Chicago White Sox	Central	Boston Red Sox	East†	3–0
	LA Angels of Anaheim	West	New York Yankees	East	3–2
2006	Detroit Tigers	Central†	New York Yankees	East	3–1
	Oakland Athletics	West	Minnesota Twins	Central	3–0

(continued)

Year	Winner	Division	Loser	Division	Result
2007	Boston Red Sox	East	LA Angels of Anaheim	West	3–0
	Cleveland Indians	Central	New York Yankees	East†	3–1
2008	Boston Red Sox	East†	LA Angels of Anaheim	West	3–1
	Tampa Bay Rays	East	Chicago White Sox	Central	3–1
2009	New York Yankees	East	Minnesota Twins	Central	3–0
	LA Angels of Anaheim	West	Boston Red Sox	East†	3–0
2010	Texas Rangers	West	Tampa Bay Rays	East	3–2
	New York Yankees	East†	Minnesota Twins	Central	3–0
2011	Texas Rangers	West	Tampa Bay Rays	East†	3–1
	Detroit Tigers	Central	New York Yankees	East	3–2
2012	Detroit Tigers	Central	Oakland Athletics	West	3–2
	New York Yankees	East	Baltimore Orioles	East†	3–2
2013	Detroit Tigers	Central	Oakland Athletics	West	3–2
	Boston Red Sox	East	Baltimore Orioles	East†	3–2
2014	Baltimore Orioles	East	Detroit Tigers	Central	3–0
	Kansas City Royals	Central†	LA Angels of Anaheim	West	3–0
2015	Toronto Blue Jays	East	Texas Rangers	West	3–2
	Kansas City Royals	Central	Houston Astros	West†	3–2
2016	Cleveland Indians	Central	Boston Red Sox	East	3–0
	Toronto Blue Jays	East†	Texas Rangers	West	3–0

National League Division Series, 1981 and Since 1995
(† = Qualified for playoffs as wildcard team)

Year	Winner	Division	Loser	Division	Result
1981	Montreal Expos	East (2nd ½)	Philadelphia Phillies	East (1st ½)	3–2
	Los Angeles Dodgers	West (1st ½)	Houston Astros	West (2nd ½)	3–2
1995	Atlanta Braves	East	Colorado Rockies	West†	3–1
	Cincinnati Reds	Central	Los Angeles Dodgers	West	3–0
1996	Atlanta Braves	East	Los Angeles Dodgers	West†	3–0
	St. Louis Cardinals	Central	San Diego Padres	West	3–0
1997	Atlanta Braves	East	Houston Astros	Central	3–0
	Florida Marlins	East†	San Francisco Giants	West	3–0
1998	Atlanta Braves	East	Chicago Cubs	Central†	3–0
	San Diego Padres	West	Houston Astros	Central	3–1

Year	Winner	Division	Loser	Division	Result
1999	Atlanta Braves	East	Houston Astros	Central	3–1
	New York Mets	East[†]	Arizona Diamondbacks	West	3–1
2000	St. Louis Cardinals	Central	Atlanta Braves	East	3–0
	New York Mets	East[†]	San Francisco Giants	West	3–1
2001	Atlanta Braves	East	Houston Astros	Central	3–0
	Arizona Diamondbacks	West	St. Louis Cardinals	Central[†]	3–2
2002	St. Louis Cardinals	Central	Arizona Diamondbacks	West	3–0
	San Francisco Giants	West[†]	Atlanta Braves	East	3–2
2003	Chicago Cubs	Central	Atlanta Braves	East	3–2
	Florida Marlins	East[†]	San Francisco Giants	West	3–1
2004	St. Louis Cardinals	Central	Los Angeles Dodgers	West	3–1
	Houston Astros	Central[†]	Atlanta Braves	East	3–2
2005	St. Louis Cardinals	Central	San Diego Padres	West	3–0
	Houston Astros	Central[†]	Atlanta Braves	East	3–1
2006	New York Mets	East	Los Angeles Dodgers	West[†]	3–0
	St. Louis Cardinals	Central	San Diego Padres	West	3–1
2007	Colorado Rockies	West[†]	Philadelphia Phillies	East	3–0
	Arizona Diamondbacks	West	Chicago Cubs	Central	3–0
2008	Los Angeles Dodgers	West	St. Louis Cardinals	Central	3–0
	Philadelphia Phillies	East	Milawaukee Brewers	Central[†]	3–1
2009	Los Angeles Dodgers	West	St. Louis Cardinals	Central	3–0
	Philadelphia Phillies	East	Colorado Rockies	West[†]	3–1
2010	Philadelphia Phillies	East	Cincinnati Reds	Central	3–0
	San Francisco Giants	West	Atlanta Braves	East[†]	3–1
2011	St. Louis Cardinals	Central[†]	Philadelphia Phillies	East	3–2
	Milwaukee Brewers	Central	Arizona Diamondbacks	West	3–2
2012	San Francisco Giants	West	Cincinnati Reds	Central	3–2
	St. Louis Cardinals	Central[†]	Washington Nationals	East	3–2

(continued)

Year	Winner	Division	Loser	Division	Result
2013	St. Louis Cardinals	Central	Pittsburgh Pirates	Central[†]	3–2
	Los Angeles Dodgers	West	Atlanta Braves	East	3–1
2014	St. Louis Cardinals	Central	Los Angeles Dodgers	West	3–1
	San Francisco Giants	West[†]	Washington Nationals	East	3–1
2015	New York Mets	East	Los Angeles Dodgers	West	3–2
	Chicago Cubs	Central[†]	St. Louis Cardinals	Central	3–1
2016	Los Angeles Dodgers	West	Washington Nationals	East	3–2
	Chicago Cubs	East	San Francisco Giants	West[†]	3–1

Appendix 5

Wild Card Games

American League Wild Card Games, Since 2012

Year	Visiting Team	Division	Home Team	Division	Winner	Score
2012	Baltimore Orioles	East	Texas Rangers	West	Orioles	6–1
2013	Tampa Bay Rays	East	Cleveland Indians	West	Rays	4–0
2014	Oakland Athletics	West	Kansas City Royals	Central	Royals	9–8 (12)
2015	Houston Astros	West	New York Yankees	East	Astros	3–0
2016	Baltimore Orioles	East	Toronto Blue Jays	East	Blue Jays	2–5 (11)

National League Wild Card Games, Since 2012

Year	Visiting Team	Division	Home Team	Division	Winner	Score
2012	St. Louis Cardinals	Central	Atlanta Braves	East	Cardinals	6–3
2013	Cincinnati Reds	Central	Pittsburgh Pirates	Central	Pirates	6–2
2014	San Francisco Giants	West	Pittsburgh Pirates	Central	Giants	8–0
2015	Chicago Cubs	Central	Pittsburgh Pirates	Central	Cubs	4–0
2016	San Francisco Giants	West	New York Mets	East	Giants	3–0

Appendix 6

Major League Baseball Clubs

EXCEPT IN A FEW RARE CASES, baseball team nicknames, which were usually assigned by sportswriters, were not official in the nineteenth and early twentieth centuries. In the first two decades of the twentieth century, American League teams were often called the "Americans," National League teams were often called the "Nationals," and Federal League teams were often called the "Feds" or "Federals."

CURRENT MAJOR LEAGUE BASEBALL FRANCHISES

Arizona Diamondbacks (Phoenix): NL Expansion Team, 1998. Arizona Diamondbacks, 1989–present.

Atlanta Braves: Originally a National Association Team (1871–1875); Charter NL Team, 1876. Boston Red Stockings, 1876–1882; Boston Beaneaters, 1883–1906; Boston Doves, 1907–1910; Boston Rustlers, 1911; Boston Braves, 1912–1935; Boston Bees, 1936–1940; Boston Braves, 1941–1952; Milwaukee Braves, 1953–1965; Atlanta Braves, 1966–present.

Baltimore Orioles: Charter AL Team, 1901. Milwaukee Brewers, 1901; St. Louis Browns, 1902–1953; Baltimore Orioles, 1954–present.

Boston Red Sox: Charter AL Team, 1901. Boston Americans, 1901–1907 (although Americans was the most frequently used nickname for the Boston club in the early twentieth century, the team was also referred to as the Boston Invaders, Boston Somersets, Boston Pilgrims, Boston Puritans, and Boston Plymouth Rocks before 1908); Boston Red Sox, 1908–present.

Chicago Cubs: Originally a National Association Team (1871, 1874–1875); Charter NL Team, 1876. Chicago White Stockings, 1876–1889; Chicago Colts, 1890–1897; Chicago Orphans, 1898–1902; Chicago Cubs, 1903–present.

Chicago White Sox: Charter AL Team, 1901. Chicago White Sox, 1901–present.

Cincinnati Reds: Originally an American Association Team (1882–1889), transferred to the NL, 1890. Cincinnati Reds, 1890–1953; Cincinnati Redlegs, 1954–1960; Cincinnati Reds, 1961–present.

Cleveland Indians: Charter AL Team, 1901. Cleveland Blues, 1901; Cleveland Bronchos, 1902; Cleveland Naps, 1903–1914 (also called the Cleveland Molly McGuires from 1909 to 1911); Cleveland Indians, 1915–present.

Colorado Rockies (Denver): NL Expansion Team, 1993. Colorado Rockies, 1993–present.

Detroit Tigers: Charter AL Team, 1901. Detroit Tigers, 1901–present.

Houston Astros: NL Expansion Team, 1962, transferred to the AL, 2013. Houston Colt .45s, 1962–1964; Houston Astros, 1965–present.

Kansas City Royals: AL Expansion Team, 1969. Kansas City Royals, 1969–present.

Los Angeles Angels of Anaheim (Los Angeles area): AL Expansion Team, 1961. Los Angeles Angels, 1961–September 1, 1965; California Angels, September 2, 1965–1996; Anaheim Angels, 1997–2004; Los Angeles Angels of Anaheim, 2005–present.

Los Angeles Dodgers: Originally an American Association Team (1884–1889), transferred to the NL, 1890. Brooklyn Bridegrooms, 1890–1898; Brooklyn Superbas, 1899–1910; Brooklyn Dodgers, 1911–1913; Brooklyn Robins, 1914–1931; Brooklyn Dodgers, 1932–1957; Los Angeles Dodgers, 1958–present.

Miami Marlins: NL Expansion Team, 1993. Florida Marlins, 1993–2011; Miami Marlins, 2012–present.

Milwaukee Brewers: AL Expansion Team, 1969, transferred to NL, 1998. Seattle Pilots, 1969; Milwaukee Brewers, 1970–present.

Minnesota Twins (Minneapolis–St. Paul): Charter AL Team, 1901. Washington Senators, 1901–1904; Washington Nationals, 1905–1956 (when the team was officially the Nationals, it was still popularly called the Senators); Washington Senators, 1957–1960; Minnesota Twins, 1961–present.

New York Mets: NL Expansion Team, 1962. New York Mets, 1962–present.

New York Yankees: Charter AL Team, 1901. Baltimore Orioles, 1901–1902; New York Highlanders, 1903–1912; New York Yankees, 1913–present.

Oakland Athletics: Charter AL Team, 1901. Philadelphia Athletics, 1901–1954; Kansas City Athletics, 1955–1967; Oakland Athletics, 1968–1970; Oakland A's, 1971–1982; Oakland Athletics, 1983–present.

Philadelphia Phillies: Added to the NL, 1880. Worcester Ruby Legs, 1880–1882; Philadelphia Quakers, 1883; Philadelphia Phillies, 1884–present (also called the Philadelphia Blue Jays, 1944–1950).

Pittsburgh Pirates: Originally an American Association Team (1882–1886), transferred to the NL, 1887. Pittsburgh Alleghenys, 1887–1890; Pittsburgh Pirates, 1891–present.

St. Louis Cardinals: Originally an American Association Team (1882–1891), transferred to the NL, 1892. St. Louis Browns, 1892–1898; St. Louis Perfectos, 1899; St. Louis Cardinals, 1900–present.

San Diego Padres: NL Expansion Team, 1969. San Diego Padres, 1969–present.

San Francisco Giants: Added to the NL in 1879. Troy Trojans, 1879–1882; New York Gothams, 1883–1884; New York Giants, 1885–1957 (also called the New York Mules, 1890); San Francisco Giants, 1958–present.

Seattle Mariners: AL Expansion Team, 1977. Seattle Mariners, 1977–present.

Tampa Bay Rays (Tampa–St. Petersburg): AL Expansion Team, 1998. Tampa Bay Devil Rays, 1998–2007; Tampa Bay Rays, 2008–present.

Texas Rangers (Dallas–Fort Worth): AL Expansion Team, 1961. Washington Senators, 1961–1971; Texas Rangers, 1972–present.

Toronto Blue Jays: AL Expansion Team, 1977. Toronto Blue Jays, 1977–present.

Washington Nationals: NL Expansion Team, 1969. Montreal Expos, 1969–2004; Washington Nationals, 2005–present.

NINETEENTH-CENTURY NATIONAL LEAGUE TEAMS

Baltimore Orioles: Transferred from AA to the NL, 1892. Baltimore Orioles, 1892–1899. Contracted from NL following 1892 season.

Boston Red Stockings/Beaneaters: Charter NL Team, 1876. Boston Red Stockings, 1876–1882; Boston Beaneaters, 1883–1906. Currently the Atlanta Braves.

Brooklyn Bridegrooms/Superbas: Transferred from AA to the NL, 1890. Brooklyn Bridegrooms, 1890–1898; Brooklyn Superbas, 1899–1910. Currently the Los Angeles Dodgers.

Buffalo Bisons: Buffalo Bisons, 1879–1885.

Chicago White Stockings/Colts: Originally a National Association Team; Charter NL Team, 1876. Chicago White Stockings, 1876–1889;

Chicago Colts, 1890–1897; Chicago Orphans, 1898–1902. Currently the Chicago Cubs.

Cincinnati Reds: Charter NL Team, Cincinnati Reds, 1876–1880. Expelled from NL following 1880 season.

Cincinnati Reds: Transferred from AA to the NL, 1890. Cincinnati Reds, since 1890.

Cleveland Blues: Cleveland Blues, 1881–1884.

Cleveland Spiders: Transferred from AA to NL, 1889. Cleveland Spiders, 1889–1899. Contracted from NL following 1899 season.

Detroit Wolverines: Detroit Wolverines, 1881–1888.

Hartford Dark Blues: Originally a National Association Team; Charter NL Team, 1876. Hartford Dark Blues, 1876–1877. (Team played most of its 1877 home games in Brooklyn.)

Indianapolis Blues: Indianapolis Blues, 1878.

Indianapolis Hoosiers: Indianapolis Hoosiers, 1887–1889.

Kansas City Cowboys: Kansas City Cowboys, 1886.

Louisville Colonels: Transferred from AA to NL, 1892. Louisville Colonels, 1892–1899. Contracted from NL following 1899 season.

Louisville Grays: Charter NL Team, 1876. Louisville Grays, 1876–1877. Expelled from NL following 1877 season.

Milwaukee Cream Citys: Milwaukee Cream Citys, 1878.

New York Mutuals: Originally a National Association Team; Charter NL Team, 1876. New York Mutuals, 1876. Expelled from NL following 1876 season.

New York Giants: Moved from Troy, 1883. New York Gothams, 1883–1884; New York Giants, 1885–1889; New York Mules, 1890; New York Giants, 1891–1957. Currently the San Francisco Giants.

Philadelphia Athletics: Originally a National Association Team; Charter NL Team, 1876. Philadelphia Athletics, 1876. Expelled from NL following 1876 season.

Philadelphia Phillies: Moved from Worcester, 1883. Philadelphia Quakers, 1883; Philadelphia Phillies, since 1884.

Pittsburgh Alleghenys/Pirates: Transferred from AA to NL, 1887. Pittsburgh Alleghenys, 1887–1892. Pittsburgh Pirates, since 1891.

Providence Grays: Providence Grays, 1878–1885.

St. Louis Brown Stockings: Originally a National Association Team; Charter NL Team, 1876. St. Louis Brown Stockings, 1876–1877.

St. Louis Browns/Perfectos: Transferred from AA to NL, 1892. St. Louis Browns, 1892–1898; St. Louis Perfectos, 1899; St. Louis Cardinals, since 1900.

St. Louis Maroons: Originally a Union Association Team; transferred to NL, 1885. St. Louis Maroons, 1885–1886.

Syracuse Stars: Syracuse Stars, 1879.

Troy Trojans (Troy, NY): Troy Trojans, 1879–1882. Moved to New York, 1883.

Washington Senators: Washington Senators, 1886–1889.

Washington Senators: Transferred from AA to NL, 1892. Washington Senators, 1892–1899. Contracted from NL following 1899 season.

Worcester Ruby Legs: Worcester Ruby Legs, 1880–1882. Moved to Philadelphia, 1883.

NATIONAL ASSOCIATION TEAMS, 1871–1875

Baltimore Canaries: 1872–1874.

Baltimore Marylands: 1873.

Boston Red Stockings: 1871–1875. Charter NL Team, 1876. Currently the Atlanta Braves.

Brooklyn Atlantics: 1872–1875.

Brooklyn Eckfords: 1872.

Chicago White Stockings: 1871, 1874–1875. Charter NL Team, 1876. Currently the Chicago Cubs.

Cleveland Forest Citys: 1871–1872.

Elizabeth Resolutes (Elizabeth, NJ): 1873.

Fort Wayne Kekiongas: 1871.

Hartford Dark Blues: 1874–1875. Charter NL Team, 1876.

Keokuk Westerns (Keokuk, IA): 1875.

Middletown Mansfields (Middletown, CT): 1872.

New Haven Elm Citys: 1875.

New York Mutuals: 1871–1875. Charter NL Team, 1876.

Philadelphia Athletics: 1871–1875. Charter NL Team, 1876.

Philadelphia Centennials: 1875.

Philadelphia White Stockings: 1873–1875.

Rockford Forest Citys (Rockford, IL): 1871.

St. Louis Brown Stockings: 1875. Charter NL Team, 1876.

St. Louis Red Stockings: 1875.

Troy Haymakers (Troy, NY): 1871–1872.

Washington Blue Legs: 1873.

Washington Nationals: 1872, 1875.

Washington Olympics: 1871–1872.

AMERICAN ASSOCIATION TEAMS, 1882–1891

Baltimore Orioles: 1882–1889. Charter AA Team, 1882.

Baltimore Orioles: 1890–1891. Moved from Brooklyn, midseason 1890. Transferred to NL, 1892.

Boston Red Stockings: 1891.

Brooklyn Trolley Dodgers: Brooklyn Atlantics, 1884; Brooklyn Grays, 1885–1887; Brooklyn Bridegrooms, 1888–1889. Transferred to NL, 1890.

Brooklyn Gladiators: 1890. Moved to Baltimore, midseason 1890.

Cincinnati Killers: 1891. Transferred to Milwaukee, midseason 1891.

Cincinnati Reds: 1882–1889. Charter AA Team, 1889. Transferred to NL, 1890.

Cleveland Blues: 1887–1888. Transferred to NL, 1889.

Columbus Buckeyes: 1883–1884.

Columbus Solons: 1889–1891.

Indianapolis Hoosiers: 1884.

Kansas City Cowboys: 1888–1889.

Louisville Eclipse/Colonels: Louisville Eclipse, 1882–1884; Louisville Colonels, 1885–1891. Charter AA Team, 1882. Transferred to NL, 1892.

Milwaukee Brewers: 1891. Moved from Cincinnati, midseason 1891.

New York Metropolitans: 1883–1887.

Philadelphia Athletics: 1882–1891. Charter AA Team, 1882.

Pittsburgh Alleghenys: 1882–1886. Charter AA Team, 1882. Transferred to NL, 1887.

Richmond Virginians: 1884. Replaced Washington Statesmen, midseason 1884.

Rochester Hop Bitters: 1890.

St. Louis Browns: 1882–1891. Charter AA Team, 1882. Transferred to NL, 1892.

Syracuse Stars: 1890.

Toledo Blue Stockings: 1884.

Toledo Maumees: 1890.

Washington Statesmen: 1884. Dropped out of AA, midseason 1884.

Washington Senators: 1891. Transferred to NL, 1892.

UNION ASSOCIATION TEAMS, 1884

Altoona Mountain Citys (Altoona, PA): 1884. Dropped out of UA, midseason 1884.

Baltimore Monumentals: 1884.

Boston Red Stockings: 1884.

Chicago Browns: 1884. Moved to Pittsburgh, midseason 1884.

Cincinnati Outlaw Reds: 1884

Kansas City Cowboys: 1884. Replaced Altoona Mountain Citys, midseason 1884.

Milwaukee Brewers: 1884. Replaced Wilmington Quicksteps, midseason 1884.

Philadelphia Keystones: 1884. Dropped out of UA, midseason 1884.

Pittsburgh Stogies: 1884. Moved from Chicago, midseason 1884. Dropped out of UA, midseason 1884.

St. Louis Maroons: 1884.

St. Paul Saints: 1884. Replaced Pittsburgh Stogies, midseason 1884.

Washington Nationals: 1884.

Wilmington Quicksteps (Wilmington, DE): Replaced Philadelphia Keystones, midseason 1884. Dropped out of UA, midseason 1884.

PLAYERS' LEAGUE TEAMS, 1890

Boston Red Stockings: 1890.

Brooklyn Wonders: 1890.

Buffalo Bisons: 1890.

Chicago Pirates: 1890.

Cleveland Infants: 1890.

New York Giants: 1890.

Philadelphia Quakers: 1890.

Pittsburgh Burghers: 1890.

FEDERAL LEAGUE TEAMS, 1914–1915

Baltimore Terrapins: 1914–1915. (Also called the "Balt-Feds.")

Brooklyn Tip-Tops: 1914–1915. (Also called the "Brook-Feds.")

Buffalo Blues: 1914–1915. (Also called the "Buf-Feds.")

Chicago Whales: 1914–1915. (Also called the "Chi-Feds.")

Indianapolis Hoosiers: 1914. (Also called the "Hoosier-Feds.") Moved to Newark, 1915.

Kansas City Packers: 1914–1915. (Also called the Kaw-Feds.")

Newark Peppers: 1915. (Also called the "Newk-Feds.") Moved from Indianapolis, 1915.

Pittsburgh Rebels: 1914–1915. (Also called the "Pitt-Feds.")

St. Louis Terriers: 1914–1915. (Also called the "Slou-Feds.")

Appendix 7

Baseball Executives

Commissioners of Baseball, Since 1920

Commissioner	Term
Kenesaw Mountain Landis	1920–1944
Albert B. "Happy" Chandler	1944–1951
Ford Frick	1951–1965
William Eckert	1965–1968
Bowie Kuhn	1969–1984
Peter Ueberroth	1984–1989
A. Bartlett Giamatti	1989
Francis Thomas "Fay" Vincent	1989–1992
Allan Huber "Bud" Selig (Acting Commissioner)	1992–1998
Allan Huber "Bud" Selig (Commissioner)	1998–2015
Robert D. "Rob" Manfred, Jr.	2015–present

Presidents of the National Association of Professional Base Ball Players, 1871–1875

President	Term
James W. Kearns	1871
Robert V. Ferguson	1872–1875

Presidents of the National League, 1876–1999

President	Term
Morgan G. Bulkeley	1876
William Hulbert	1877–1882
Arthur Soden	1882
Abraham G. Mills	1883–1884
Nicholas Young	1885–1902
Harry Pulliam	1903–1909
John Heydler	1909

(continued)

President	Term
Thomas Lynch	1910–1913
John K. Tener	1913–1918
John Heydler	1918–1934
Ford Frick	1934–1951
Warren Giles	1951–1969
Charles Stoneham "Chub" Feeney	1970–1986
A. Bartlett Giamatti	1986–1989
Bill White	1989–1994
Leonard S. Coleman Jr.	1994–1999

Presidents of the American Association of Professional Base Ball Players, 1882–1891

President	Term
Harmar Denny "H.D." McKnight	1882–1885
Wheeler C. Wyckoff	1886–1889
Zach Phelps	1890
Allan W. Thurman	1890–1891
Louis Kramer	1891
Ed Renau	1891
Zach Phelps	1891

Presidents of the American League, 1900–1999

President	Term
Byron Bancroft "Ban" Johnson	1900–1927
Ernest Barnard	1927–1931
William "Will" Harridge	1931–1959
Joseph Edward "Joe" Cronin	1959–1973
Leland Stanford "Lee" MacPhail, Jr,	1973–1984
Robert William "Bobby" Brown	1984–1994
Gene Budig	1994–1999

President of the Union Association, 1883–1884

President	Term
Henry Victor Lucas	1883–1884

President of the Players' League, 1890

President	Term
John Montgomery Ward	1890

Presidents of the Federal League, 1914–1915

President	Term
John T. Powers	1913
James A. Gilmore	1913–1915

President of the Continental League, 1959–1960

President	Term
Branch Rickey	1959–1960

Executive Directors of the Major League Baseball Players Association, Since 1956

Executive Director	Term
Bob Feller (President)	1956–1959
Frank Scott	1959–1966
Marvin Miller	1966–1982
Ken Moffett	1982–1983
Marvin Miller (Interim Executive Director)	1983
Donald Fehr (Acting Executive Director)	1983–1985
Donald Fehr	1985–2009
Michael Weiner	2009–2013
Tony Clark	2013–present

Notes

CHAPTER 3

1. David Brock in *Baseball before We Knew It: A Search for the Roots of the Game* (Lincoln: University of Nebraska Press, 2005, 58–61) suggests that Graves may have named the wrong Doubleday. Abner Doubleday's cousin, Abner Demas Doubleday, lived in Cooperstown in 1839, and Brock notes that he may have been the Doubleday who taught the youth of Cooperstown a game that was already popular in the New York City area.

CHAPTER 11

1. There is a popular legend that when Robinson was jeered in Cincinnati, shortstop Pee Wee Reese, a southerner from across the Ohio River in Kentucky, silenced the crowd by putting his arm around the Brooklyn first baseman. Unfortunately, there are no contemporary accounts describing that gesture in any of the Cincinnati or New York City newspapers covering the game. Three witnesses later came forward to verify the event, but all of their accounts are questionable. If the hug occurred, it was more likely to have happened in 1948. Nonetheless, in 2005 a statue of Reese and Robinson, with their arms on each other's shoulder, was erected outside KeySpan Park in Brooklyn.

Index

About the Authors

Martin C. Babicz teaches history at the University of Colorado Boulder for the Sewall Hall History & Culture Residential Academic Program, the Communications & Society Residential Academic Program, and the History Department. Babicz teaches several courses on American history, including "America through Baseball." He is the author of a chapter exploring the historiography of sports and pastimes of the 1920s in *A Companion to Warren G. Harding, Calvin Coolidge, and Herbert Hoover* (2014).

Thomas W. Zeiler is professor of history at the University of Colorado at Boulder, where he directs the Program in International Affairs. He teaches and researches on U.S. foreign policy, diplomatic history, globalization, World War II, and sports history. Among the courses he teaches is "America through Baseball." His books include *Ambassadors in Pinstripes: The Spalding World Baseball Tour and the Birth of the American Empire* (2006).